Accountants' Truth

Accountants' Truth

Knowledge and Ethics in the Financial World

Matthew Gill

OXFORD
UNIVERSITY PRESS

OXFORD
UNIVERSITY PRESS

Great Clarendon Street, Oxford OX2 6DP

Oxford University Press is a department of the University of Oxford.
It furthers the University's objective of excellence in research, scholarship,
and education by publishing worldwide in

Oxford New York

Auckland Cape Town Dar es Salaam Hong Kong Karachi
Kuala Lumpur Madrid Melbourne Mexico City Nairobi
New Delhi Shanghai Taipei Toronto

With offices in

Argentina Austria Brazil Chile Czech Republic France Greece
Guatemala Hungary Italy Japan Poland Portugal Singapore
South Korea Switzerland Thailand Turkey Ukraine Vietnam

Oxford is a registered trade mark of Oxford University Press
in the United Kingdom and in certain other countries

Published in the United States
by Oxford University Press Inc., New York

British Library Cataloguing in Publication Data
Data available

Library of Congress Cataloging in Publication Data
Data available

Typeset by SPI Publisher Services, Pondicherry, India
Printed in Great Britain
on acid-free paper by the
MPG Books Group, Bodmin and King's Lynn

ISBN 978-0-19-954714-2

1 3 5 7 9 10 8 6 4 2

Acknowledgements

I gratefully acknowledge the financial support of the Arts and Humanities Research Council (doctoral award 2003/104923), and the Andrew W. Mellon Foundation (postdoctoral fellowship 2006–8), without either of which this project could not have been completed in its current form. I would also like to thank PricewaterhouseCoopers' Business Recovery Services practice for enabling me to work in the context of an extended career break. The material that first appeared in Gill (2007), published by Routledge, and in Gill (2008), published by Oxford University Press and the Society for the Advancement of Socio-Economics, is used here with the kind agreement of the original publishers. The book is based on anonymous interviews with twenty people, and I am very grateful to all of them for sharing their thoughts and experiences with me.

As a doctoral student in Sociology at the London School of Economics, I was privileged to be supervised by Richard Sennett. He was, and continues to be, an inspiration, and I will always be indebted to him for his support, guidance, and example. Don Slater assisted with supervision, and I am grateful to him for the rigour with which he challenged my thinking, and for kindling my interest in economic sociology. Nikolas Rose helped me to focus the project, and Nigel Dodd helped me to work through its underpinnings in social theory. Craig Calhoun at New York University not only made important comments on my work at various stages, but also created, with Richard Sennett, a vibrant peer group of graduate students on both sides of the Atlantic. I am grateful to the members of both groups for their input and collegiality.

At Washington University in Saint Louis, Steven Zwicker created a productive environment in which to do postdoctoral work at the intersection between the humanities and social sciences. I thank him, my postdoctoral colleagues, and everyone associated with the Modeling Interdisciplinary Inquiry program. I was very fortunate to be mentored by Larry May, who made incisive and wide-ranging comments on the manuscript, and encouraged me to participate in the intellectual life of the Philosophy department. Joe Loewenstein in the Interdisciplinary Project in the Humanities, Andrew Rehfeld in Political Science, and David Rudner in Anthropology also created stimulating intellectual communities.

Acknowledgements

Special thanks are due to friends and colleagues other than my institutional mentors who have, at different stages, read and commented on full drafts of the text: Georgina Born, Jonathan Clarke, Lena Royant, Victor Seidler, and Andrew Smith. Their suggestions and criticisms have been invaluable. I would also like to thank Thomas Ahrens, Lara Bovilsky, Howard Brick, William Davies, David Gilchrist, Nathaniel Goldberg, Bob Hancké, Gwynneth Hawkins, Anthony Hopwood, Monika Krause, Patrick McGovern, Ian MacMullen, Andrea Mennicken, Jesse Potter, Saskia Sassen, Jeffrey Seidman, Matthew Wisnioski, Marion Wrenn, and Stephen Zeff for helpful comments and discussions. I am indebted to many other teachers, colleagues, students, and friends, who are too numerous to mention here. David Musson and Matthew Derbyshire at Oxford University Press have been supportive and efficient, and I am grateful to them, to the anonymous reviewers, and to everyone involved in production.

My brother, Nicholas Gill, not only made extensive comments on the manuscript, but has been a valued interlocutor and friend throughout. My parents, Thomas and Elaine Gill, have supported me in countless ways. I dedicate this book to them, with love and thanks.

M.J.G.

London
January 2009

Contents

Contents

List of Figures

List of Abbreviations

ACA	Associate Chartered Accountant
ACCA	Association of Chartered Certified Accountants
BCCI	Bank of Credit and Commerce International
CIPFA	Chartered Institute of Public Finance and Accountancy
FRS	Financial Reporting Standard
FTSE 100	Financial Times Stock Exchange 100 share index
IASB	International Accounting Standards Board
IASC	International Accounting Standards Committee
ICAEW	Institute of Chartered Accountants in England and Wales
ICAS	Institute of Chartered Accountants of Scotland
IFRS	International Financial Reporting Standard
KPMG	Klynveld Peat Marwick Goerdeler
P&L	Profit and loss account
SAS	Statement of Auditing Standards
SSAP	Statement of Standard Accounting Practice
VAT	Value added tax

1
Introduction

Accountancy tends to capture the public imagination only when something goes spectacularly wrong. The latest banking fiasco or corporate disgrace[1] appears as an isolated scandal, different in kind from the everyday process of doing business and accounting for it. In some cases, this appearance of isolation is correct: blatant fraud is exceptional. In others, however, accounting scandals can seem like intensifications of the everyday, the logical conclusions, perhaps, of how things are routinely done across the business and financial community. It does not make sense, in such cases, to try to understand them in isolation. This book therefore focuses on the day-to-day of financial work which is cumulatively more important than the scandals that hit the headlines. Through doing so, nonetheless, it also helps to show how things can go strikingly wrong.

People often think of financial scandals as presenting a problem of trust. Can those who run the financial world (accountants and auditors, bankers and analysts, underwriters and actuaries) be trusted? Yet when the issue at stake is not one of blatant fraud, answering this question requires us to explore what exactly it is that we trust these individuals to do. We trust accountants, in particular, to construct the knowledge on which financial decisions are based. This book will therefore show that underlying the manifest problem of trust in the financial world is a more fundamental problem of knowledge. It will demonstrate that the way in which accountants construct knowledge is multifaceted and ethically demanding, and that understanding it is crucial to evaluating their actions, either individually or as a profession.

My findings are based on interviews with chartered accountants working in the largest accountancy practices in London. The interviews reveal that although accounting knowledge can seem indisputably factual after it has been constructed, the process of constructing it is contested and opaque. Accountants nonetheless tend to describe their work as if it were straightforward and technical, creating a discrepancy between their discourse and their practice. The discrepancy matters, because accountants' technical discourse obscures the ways in which they must resolve accounting questions in practice, and so

undermines their ethical reasoning. Insofar as increasingly technical accounting rules perpetuate this discrepancy, therefore, such rules can be counterproductive. Instead, I will conclude that our best approach to avoiding future
scandals is to redefine and reinvigorate professional ethics in the financial
world.

Of course, this is easier said than done. Actually achieving it requires that
the tacit norms according to which accountants construct knowledge on a
day-to-day basis, as distinct from their technical discourse, be brought into
full view. The substantive aim of this book is to do just that, and, in
the process, to develop a vocabulary in which the ethics of accounting practice
can be articulated, evaluated, developed, and reinforced. Before embarking
on this empirical project, however, it will help to clarify the stakes involved
if we pause a little longer on the question of public trust, first with respect
to the financial world in general, and then with respect to one illustrative
example – that of Enron – in particular.

Trust, crime, and conformity

When financial decisions are made badly, the direct consequences can be
catastrophic, destroying jobs, wiping out pension funds, or weakening the
wider economy. Yet financial scandals also have the indirect consequence of
undermining trust both in the financial system and in those who work within
it. This is significant because advanced global capitalism relies very heavily
on that kind of trust. When small investors buy shares in a portfolio of
companies, governments tax profits, traders buy and sell commodities and
derivatives, or insurers underwrite financial risks, it is impossible for them
to develop relationships of personal trust with all the individuals involved.
Instead, they must place trust in numbers (Porter 1995). 'Trust in numbers,
however, works only if those who produce the numbers can be trusted: it
displaces, rather than solves, modernity's problem with trust' (MacKenzie
2003, 8). In practice, trust in numbers not only displaces, but also concentrates
the need for trust. Trust must now be concentrated in those individuals
who claim the expertise and authority to produce and to interpret numbers.
With respect to financial matters, that claim is the preserve of professional
accountants.

The need to place trust in accountants does not only arise from considerations of time and distance that limit direct personal contact in the global
economy, but also from the increasing complexity of modern commercial life.
Financial decisions can be complex and abstract beyond the cognitive capacities of individuals. We trust accountants not only to represent decisions in
financial terms, therefore, but also to simplify them. Simplification, however,
embodies some decisions in advance of making further decisions possible;

it facilitates the recognition of some options and perspectives at the expense of others. Simplification is not always oversimplification, and it can be a mistake to criticize it as such.[i] Yet although there is a pragmatic need for the simplification accounting offers, as that simplification becomes more extensive the decisions accountants make in achieving it become more consequential. In this respect, accounting offers an important case study of the more general challenge we face concerning the role of experts in an increasingly specialized society.

Trust in accountants, then, is unavoidable. However, since it is impractical to build up relationships of trust with them all as individuals, this means in practice that they must be trusted as a coherent group, who are assumed to approach specific situations with a common competence and ethos. The claim to worthiness of such trust is the claim traditionally made by the professions. Yet accountants are not only professionals, but are also businesspeople and, often, employees of large organizations. An assessment of their trustworthiness as professionals therefore needs to be informed by a more general understanding of crime and deviance in commercial and organizational life.[2]

Edwin Sutherland, who coined the term 'white collar crime' to describe 'crime committed by a person of respectability and high social status in the course of his occupation', found that such crime was less studied, less stigmatized, and less severely punished than more straightforward but less consequential crimes such as robbery and burglary. His reasons for this included the complexity and abstraction of these crimes, the dispersal of harm across many individuals and across time, and the social status of the perpetrators (Sutherland 1949, 9, 47–50). These remain significant reasons why fraud and embezzlement, the paradigmatic breaches of trust in the financial world, can tend to be approached leniently. Such crimes are straightforward, however, in that there is at least an individual criminal who can be held clearly responsible.

The picture is more complicated when we consider crimes perpetrated by individuals on behalf of their employers, or by organizations within which no individual criminal can be clearly identified. Classic examples include the heavy electrical equipment antitrust cases, where major companies were found to have colluded illegally in order to fix prices; and the case of Goodrich, where an aircraft brake that engineers knew would be unsafe was manufactured anyway, risking the life of a test pilot and potentially of many other people had the test flights not failed. These are contrasting examples, and

---

[i] By simplification I mean the representation of a matter in a way that makes decision-making with respect to it more straightforward, either through reduction of complexity or through alignment with familiar conventions. I will use the term standardization to refer to explicit attempts to develop such conventions.

teach different lessons: in the antitrust cases, that external requirements such as obedience to the law can be outweighed in the minds of corporate managers by the financial interests of their companies (Geis 1987; see also Bakan 2005, 61–84),[3] and in the case of Goodrich, that the diffusion of responsibility within organizations can lead to outcomes no individual would have wanted (Vandivier 1972). Common to both of these examples, however, is the fact that they arose from people doing what they and at least some of their colleagues thought they were supposed to do, rather than deviating from those expectations.

Both of the above examples might be characterized as ultimately deviant outcomes, precipitated by incentives such as profit and job security that should never have been taken to such extremes. Yet socially deviant behaviour can become normalized within organizations in ways that make it seem less a question of crime than of organizational management. Diane Vaughan (1997), for instance, in her study of the mistaken decision to launch the *Challenger* space shuttle that then exploded, emphasizes the banality of the mistake itself. She argues that the existence of rules that demanded to be followed blindly contributed to causing the disaster, so that the failing was not one of deviance, but of conformity. We might respond to such disasters by designing better systems or writing better rules, and much can be gained by doing this, particularly when learning from large mistakes.[4] Yet the *Challenger* example suggests that such a response has limits. No system of rules can predict every eventuality in the real world, so any such system needs to build in both enough flexibility for individuals to respond sensibly to unforeseen situations, and the expectation that they will do so. Insofar as this is done, it both displaces the problem of trust back onto individuals and raises the bar: not only must individuals be trusted not to behave criminally, but they must be trusted to behave responsibly and far-sightedly.

Individuals' behaviour, then, can be significantly influenced by the structure and rules of the organizations in which they work, and yet if those organizations micromanage them to the point that they cease to think for themselves, mistakes and disasters become more likely. Crime itself may also become more likely, because over-regulation undermines individuals' commitment to the regulatory framework. This problem exists much more generally, but is particularly relevant to accounting, because of the centrality of rules to defining accounting knowledge and governing accounting work. Individuals who think of themselves simply as working within the rules may not accept the burden of trust that society places on them, or they may not even recognize or understand it. Breaches of that trust, therefore, cannot be readily dismissed as deviance, but instead seem like the consequences of normal and accepted behaviour. The case of Enron provides a graphic illustration of how easily this situation can get out of hand.

Enron

Enron's bankruptcy in December 2001 offers an important example of these issues, not only because of its sheer magnitude,[5] but also because it proved so difficult to attribute blame. Enron was, after all, the quintessential late-twentieth-century corporate success story. It prided itself on its innovation and cleverness in the deregulated energy market, having transformed itself from a conventional operator of natural gas pipelines into an energy-trading company to rival the Wall Street banks. Even the company's finance department, which managed the now notorious debt structure underlying the business, was transformed into a profit centre (Fusaro and Miller 2002, 130–1; McLean and Elkind 2003b, 138; Swartz and Watkins 2003, 151–2). Enron executives saw themselves not as crooks, but as visionary leaders driving the liberating ethos of entrepreneurial, flexible capitalism on into a new century.

In accounting terms, certainly, Enron pushed that ethos to its limits and beyond. It did not provide sufficient information about its business units' performance or about its transactions with related parties to give a clear view of its activities. It set up special purpose entities which kept the full extent of its debt off its balance sheet. It recognized the gross value of trades, rather than the spread between their sale and purchase price, as revenue. It sold and revalued assets to create profit at strategic times (Benston et al. 2003, 24; Fusaro and Miller 2002, 13, 79, 113). Yet such a strategy was not merely the work of Andrew Fastow, Enron's chief financial officer. It made good sense to a group of self-consciously clever people in a hyper-competitive environment who were trying to persuade each other that they were winners. Even Enron's auditors, in a 1996 exchange with Enron employee and future whistle-blower Sherron Watkins, apparently saw asset valuation as a matter of strategy: if Enron chose to account for a rise in an asset's value in a strong market, it would simply have to account for a corresponding fall in a weak one (Swartz and Watkins 2003, 97). The bankers, lawyers, auditors, and management team implicated in the Enron scandal made no secret of how they thought. They were the cream of their institutions, which had spent years appraising them, selecting them, and grooming them as such. If the cream were not who they should have been, then a much broader explanation is needed than merely to criticize their personal standards of behaviour. In their institutional contexts, those standards were consistently recognized as being very high.

For the Enron scandal to be possible, a whole range of professionals (auditors, bankers, analysts, company directors, corporate lawyers) had to collectively fail to question the legitimacy of certain actions. We can begin to understand such a failure by exploring how the protagonists tried to limit their responsibility after the event. The following exchange took place between a director of Citigroup (David Bushnell) and a congressional investigator (Senator Carl

Levin) after Enron's bankruptcy. Levin was interrogating Bushnell about Citigroup's dealings with the company:

LEVIN: Would you agree that you have a responsibility not to participate in a deception?
BUSHNELL: We have a responsibility to our clients, both investors and to the customers who need capital, to do things in accordance with the rules as they're established.
LEVIN: I'm really surprised that you can't answer that question with a yes, that you have an obligation not to participate in a deception; it seems to me that's an easy one.
BUSHNELL: It depends on what the definition of a deception is.
LEVIN: You can define it any way you want; don't you think that the bank has an obligation not to participate in a deception? You define deception.
BUSHNELL: Yes. (*The Banks that Robbed the World* 2003)

This exchange could be read in at least three ways, all of which tell us something important. Firstly, and most clearly, it could be read as Bushnell's attempts to equivocate eventually being thwarted by Levin. Bushnell begins by using his industry's jargon to restate an unfavourable formulation of his firm's responsibilities. When this fails, he appeals to the ambiguity of language. Only when pressed still further is he forced to answer the question as put.

In a second reading, Citigroup rightly operates at the very limits of the rules in order to optimally fulfil its primary 'responsibility to our clients'. Bushnell's equivocation is the logical conclusion of finance conceived as an amoral game in which stretching the rules constitutes excellence on the part of the player. Bushnell's firm is a bad player because it was caught. Bushnell, in this view, is a precocious youngster from the world of city boys and whiz-kids being ticked off by the older Levin for playing too hard.

Finally, in a third reading, Bushnell gradually realizes that he is now in an unfamiliar context where his language does not make sense. In his familiar environment, an appeal to the 'needs' of the 'client' carries enormous weight, as demonstrated by the fact that for Bushnell even the duty to obey the rules is owed not to state, society, or law but to the client. Here, the appeal is surprisingly ineffective. He is being asked instead to talk in terms of 'deception', a word he does not ordinarily use and of which he is therefore suspicious. It is too simplistic to say that a discussion about 'the rules as they're established' would have been non-evaluative and therefore straightforward, whereas a discussion of deception is normative and therefore more difficult. Bushnell is happy to talk about responsibility and need in relation to clients, but appears to lack the language to do so more generally.[6]

This third reading might, from Levin's perspective, seem too kind to Bushnell, but it is actually harsher, from that perspective, than Levin's own view. Because Levin assumes that deception in general means something to Bushnell, he finds Bushnell's responses in this specific exchange disappointing. However, if Levin had actually believed that Bushnell had no concept of social responsibility beyond his duty to his client, then he could have accepted the banker's responses as both predictable and honest. It would be a mistake, therefore, to think that Levin triumphs in the above exchange. Bushnell's acceptance that he has a responsibility not to participate in a deception is a mere platitude, because Bushnell considers deception to be a vacuous term. He eventually utters the platitude precisely in order to avoid having to define deception in a meaningful way. Yet Levin seems not to have understood that, for Bushnell, his victory is hollow, because he has not taken Bushnell's initial rules-bound response seriously enough.

To interpret such exchanges is an urgent task: pension funds across the United States lost billions of dollars in value following Enron's collapse. The first reading above would blame an individual. The second reading would blame either competitive human nature or a competitive economic system. Whilst recognizing the validity of these readings (and I do not deny that Bushnell is being evasive), the third reading would highlight a specific form of apparently factual discourse that is poorly adapted to conceptualizing certain moral and ethical issues, and therefore poorly adapted to evaluating certain types of action. We will see in later chapters that, as the number and variety of protagonists involved in Enron's collapse suggest, the limitations of Bushnell's language are endemic in the financial world.

Prosecutors have found it difficult to convict banks such as Citigroup over the Enron affair because such convictions must take place in technical terms. 'How do you prosecute individual bankers when accountants and lawyers gave their consent?' (McLean and Elkind 2003a). Enron's chief executive officer, Jeff Skilling, used the same defence: ' "Show me one fucking transaction that the accountants and the attorneys didn't sign off on ... if they concoct some bull-shit, they're going to have a fight on their hands, because it – is – not – there!" ' (McLean and Elkind 2003b, 414). Yet Andersen, Enron's auditors, 'would later admit to errors of a technical nature ... but nothing more' (Fusaro and Miller 2002, 135). For them, restricting their responsibility to the 'technical' made their conduct an issue not of wrongdoing, but of human error. Even the Enron board claimed that it did what it should have done based on the information it was given (McLean and Elkind 2003b, 408–9). The demarcation of a sphere of work as technical, then, seems to cut both ways: for the technician, it legalistically limits their responsibility; and for the non-technician, it means that the technician can be assumed to have covered all of the moral angles. The broader issue is the reduction of the ethical to the technical or, as I shall explain below, of values to facts, with the rules-bound rationalism that this entails.

Rules, discourse, and everyday practice

In order to understand how scandals such as Enron are possible in the financial world, we must recognize that protagonists like Bushnell do not behave as they do out of deviance, but in accordance with a collective ethos. The rules lack purchase over that ethos, because the ethos encompasses the way in which rules are to be approached. We might condemn such an ethos as dysfunctional, but it is nonetheless real and credible to those involved. It forms a basis for mutual trust between insiders, the demands of which can be felt more keenly than those of public trust when the two conflict. The collective ethos that forms the basis for accountants' mutual trust, therefore, needs to be developed in a way that makes it more worthy of public trust: we cannot simply demand worthiness of public trust in terms that lack credibility with practitioners. It is thus a mistake for reformers to think that problems can be solved simply by writing a solution into the rules. Rule changes can be effective, but only if they catalyse a change in accountants' attitudes towards their work. If they do not do so, then as the example of Bushnell illustrates, those accountants will simply work around the new rules in order to proceed as before. Too great an emphasis on rules, moreover, can make things worse. Accounting scandals in which people either manipulate rules or fail to think about the wider implications of their actions both exemplify tendencies that are exacerbated by a rules-based conception of legitimate behaviour. Consequently, although a normal practice founded on rules might seem like a solution when things go well, it can contribute to the problem when things go badly.

Our inquiry into how accountants construct knowledge therefore needs to begin from the underlying norms according to which accountants approach the rules, rather than from the rules themselves. Yet the rules-based self-understanding that prevails in accounting leaves even accountants unable to articulate the messy and pragmatic reality of accounting work. This means that just as we cannot look to the rules for a description of practice, neither can we look to accountants to describe their practice to us. Nonetheless, at a tacit level, accountants understand the ways in which they construct knowledge very well. Our first task, therefore, is to make their tacit knowledge explicit.

Since accountants construct knowledge in numbers and words, our exploration of how they do so will need to pay particular attention to their collective discourse.[ii] A focus on discourse makes it possible to analyse what is common to the interpretative practices of accountants working in different organizations, rather than what is deviant about those practices as applied by particular individuals in particular contexts. Discourses, such as that of client service appealed to by Bushnell, transcend organizational boundaries. They affect

---

[ii] A 'discourse' is often taken to mean the verbal equivalent of a text, but I am not using it in that sense here. I am instead following Michel Foucault, who uses 'discourse' to refer to sustained patterns of written or spoken language use. Foucault's usage makes it possible to emphasize the way a discourse (such as accounting discourse) changes over time or reinforces a regime of truth (e.g. see Foucault 1998, 17–35, 100–2). By accounting discourse, I refer broadly to accountants' use of language in a way that encompasses client service discourse and other sub-discourses.

what can credibly be said by peers in a particular line of work, and what can be understood by them. More broadly, the gradual global standardization of accountants' discourse, and its dominance as a means of representing commercial life, render it increasingly influential over the nature and limits of understanding and communication in the financial world.

In order to hear a discourse in which homogenization, not diversity, is the salient characteristic, I interviewed the most archetypal representatives of the British accounting profession: young, male chartered accountants working in the largest accountancy firms in London (PricewaterhouseCoopers, Ernst & Young, KPMG, and Deloitte). The discourse used by accountants working at the 'big four' firms is particularly significant because these firms constitute a gold standard against which the rest of the profession benchmarks itself. The firms are training grounds for future leaders of the financial world. When accountants leave these firms, they take the discourse with them, and so its influence not only becomes widespread, but widespread amongst those occupying senior positions.[7] I spoke to my interviewees about instances in which they made accounting judgements and interpretations, about the technical and practical constraints they confronted, about how they negotiated those constraints, and about their experience of living within them. I conducted twenty interviews in total between June 2003 and October 2004, and interpreted them in the light of my own experience of training and working as a chartered accountant with PricewaterhouseCoopers in London for four years. Full details of my methodology, including selection of interviewees, interview technique, and interpretative strategies, together with a discussion of the advantages and limitations of interview-based insider research, are given in the appendix at the end of this book.

The social world of the chartered accountant

In order to understand how accountants construct knowledge, we first need some sense of the environment in which they work, and the nature of their involvement in it. This section therefore describes the training and everyday experience of accountants such as those I interviewed, together with their reasons for embarking on and continuing their careers with the big four firms. It draws on my own experience and on the existing ethnographies of chartered accountants' training in England,[8] as well as on my conversations with interviewees.

Trainee chartered accountants generally start directly from university, or perhaps after a gap year, and very few are older than their mid-twenties.[9] They enter large, prestigious firms in which they occupy the lowest level in an elaborate hierarchy. The vast majority join the audit departments of these firms, where they work on teams responsible for providing independent opinions on clients' financial statements. There is a competitive market for audits, and since their output (a clean audit opinion) is difficult to differentiate in the market, auditors seek to retain clients by building relationships with them based on high standards of service. Much of the work is carried out at clients' premises, and auditors adapt their working hours to those of the client. Clients are required by law to obtain audit opinions, however, and so tend to see at least the more junior auditors as a necessary evil. As one interviewee put it: 'The clients that I worked for... had a general attitude which was "we're tolerating you because you have to be here and do your work and get out of here".'

Audits are carried out in small teams, from two or three people for the smallest clients up to twenty plus for the largest. For trainees, the work is often of a routine nature, involving a lot of basic checking that is colloquially referred to as 'ticking and bashing' (Coffey 1993, 368ff.). Nonetheless, because of the extreme youth of the workforce, auditors may be supervising colleagues' work within a year or two of joining, and can be responsible for the day-to-day management of audit teams within three years. Audits are tightly budgeted in terms of the staff time allocated to each area of work. Teams may work together for anything from a week to several months, at which point they will be disbanded and put into new teams with different colleagues for the next audit. Several hundred trainees can be referred to colloquially as the 'audit pool', from which they are plucked as and when someone of their level in the hierarchy is needed. When not at clients' premises, they work in a quiet and studious atmosphere in their firms' large open-plan offices. There is considerable competitiveness between individuals, and a degree of bravado about working long hours to meet clients' tight reporting deadlines (see Coffey 1993, 231). The culture also exhibits a pervasive masculinity which can be unfavourable towards female accountants (see Anderson-Gough, Grey, and Robson 2005; 1998a, 75–6; Grey 1994, 493).

Clearly there are routine and impersonal aspects to this work, with corresponding impacts on accountants' subjective experience of it: few junior auditors love what they do.[10] Yet audit training in the United Kingdom is widely regarded, and certainly marketed, as an entry point into the business elite.[11] As the next section will show, a consequence of this is that many of the most ambitious accountants approach their time as auditors instrumentally, gaining a qualification and experience that they can then apply in a different setting. The elite to which young accountants seek entry is sometimes a social one, as accounting can be a route into the middle class. It is certainly financial, since the profession is known for being extremely well paid, particularly at more senior levels. However this is not simply avarice: although my interviewees may have been uncomfortable articulating it to me as an explicit motivation, there is an ethos to working with and accumulating money that was emboldened by the enterprise culture of the 1980s and sees commercial success as a moral achievement.[12] As Chapter 6 will show, my interviewees commonly expressed a desire to 'add value' through their financial work. This ethos is reflected in Andrew Fastow's view that Enron's finance function ought to make money in its own right.

Chartered accountants' training is a demanding rite of passage that remains a bond between them throughout their careers. A training contract lasts for three years, which is the time necessary to accumulate the work experience and exam passes required to become a member of the Institute of Chartered Accountants in England and Wales (ICAEW).[13] Few people voluntarily leave their firms before qualifying, but failure in the professional exams can be grounds for automatic dismissal, and such failures are common. The firms' policies in this regard are therefore writ large in accountants' early experience, and can put them under considerable pressure. The figure current amongst my own colleagues was that around 90 of our peer group of 200 or so people were dismissed for failing exams within six months of joining (a figure that was, however, unusually high).[14] Many of those of us who passed found ourselves at clients' premises on the Monday after the exam results were published in Saturday's edition of *The Times* newspaper, to discover that our colleagues who had failed had been told not to join us there, and that we would not be seeing them again (see also Coffey 1993, 441–96).

Teaching in preparation for the exams is contracted out to independent companies, and trainees are taught classroom style, full time, at these companies' premises, for continuous periods of between six weeks and three months depending on the set of exams to be taken. Michael Power describes the approach to knowledge that is encouraged:

At the induction stage students are informed that training for professional examinations bears little relation to the experience of studying at university or college. This observation is often made with barely disguised disdain for the latter. Progress can now be made towards a more 'mature' stage of knowledge acquisition and learning beyond the undeveloped outlook of a university. This attitude is visible in parallel with an explicit claim that rote learning, akin to the studying methods of the middle school years, will be required at least until the intermediate stage.... Learning double-entry bookkeeping is described to students as similar to learning to ride a bike, i.e. not an intellectual process. (Power 1991, 339–40; see also Coffey 1993, 345–54)

There is a substantial and detailed body of accounting and auditing standards (Accounting Standards Board 2001, 1,671 pages; Auditing Standards Board 2001, 1,313 pages).[15] Trainees must learn and internalize much of this huge volume of material, and use it accurately and at speed in the exams. Teaching therefore focuses on exam technique, and the results of frequent mock exams are posted on the classroom wall in rank order to encourage competitiveness. Because time is short, it is allocated to the numerical rather than discursive aspects of the syllabus, where improvements are most measurable. Where written answers are required, trainees are encouraged to treat them as similarly to the rest of the material as possible, for instance by memorizing lists. Pressure on time means that broader questions raised in the classroom often go unanswered: 'you don't need to know that' is a familiar refrain to any chartered accountant. Power, again, states the consequences strongly:

Far from contributing to the ethical education of individuals, for whom professional service for the sake of some notion of public interest is a guiding theme, the reality of examination training involves the cultivation of strategic attitudes in which the very possibility of critically questioning the relation of the profession to a wider polity is entirely eroded. (Power 1991, 348–9)

Recent syllabus changes have tried to increase the proportion of critical thinking as compared to rote learning assessed in the exams, although in the overall context described here the effect of such changes must be limited. The 'strategic attitudes' to which Power refers are reinforced by the need to juggle work and study, as accountants become accustomed to the divided loyalties between firm, profession, client, and career that will characterize their working lives. These divided loyalties will be discussed further in Chapter 6.

Who completes this process of training and socialization, and then remains working at the big four firms? Aside from money, the two most common reasons my interviewees gave for joining their firms were gaining the qualification and drifting. There were some other motivators, such as the variety of tasks and clients, but for most it was just a very sensible thing to do in the absence of a strong desire to do anything else. Accountancy is an easy choice, perhaps, for bright graduates wanting to meet the expectations placed on them. One interviewee, whom I shall call Graham,[iii] had studied accounting and law at university, but did not seem to know why. Most of the people on his course went into accountancy, and the firms' marketing to university students was good. He commented vaguely that 'I don't know, it's a good sort of general field that you can just go into and once you've done your three years there are lots more opportunities, so, yeah'. Sebastian lacked any positive motivation: 'I could have done other things, but I can't actually to this day think of anything that I would have really wanted to do.' Terry explained that it was a principle of his career planning 'not to get into too much depth or detail', implying that the flexibility gained by lack of commitment to any particular line of work was itself an asset. Several interviewees cited variety as a motivator, and this enabled them to defer pinning down what was satisfying or otherwise about their work whilst treating it as a learning opportunity in the meantime.[16]

[iii] I have protected the identities of interviewees, employers, and any clients they referred to by changing their names and altering those features of the situations discussed which might easily identify them (including places). I have minimally adapted the interview transcriptions in order to improve their flow as text rather than speech.

Accounting tends to attract those already strongly motivated by money, and this motivation is reinforced by their socialization into accounting work. Some interviewees even talked of themselves as if they were companies or commodities. Simon, for instance, said of his current job that 'I'm going to stick with it for the short term until I've worked out what my career options are, but I'll probably eventually move out and diversify, just for the sake of my own marketability'. 'Short term', 'options', 'diversify', and 'marketability' are terms more readily associated with commercial strategy than life planning. Similarly, Daljit's curriculum vitae (CV) has come to be the most direct means he has of narrating his working life: 'You can see the last two years, my CV's just, it's a different story completely to being an auditor.'

For those interviewees who had left the audit practice for different parts of their firms, the most common reason was boredom or frustration with auditing, rather than an active desire to work in their new department. Joe assumes this narrative to be so well established that no explanation of his transition to his new role is necessary other than that 'I fell into it desperately trying to get out of audit'. Tom, one of those who stayed in audit after qualifying, said his main reason for not moving on was 'laziness'. As a result of this general attitude towards auditing, most of those who had moved within their firms found their new roles more interesting, more commercially relevant, or more highly valued by clients. In only a minority of cases, though, were these positive motivators clearly independent of a comparison with auditing.

The vast majority of interviewees, then, said that their motivation to do accounting work was instrumental, enabling them to gain a qualification, money, status, and so on. Perhaps as a result of this, Daljit expressed 'fear of not achieving...satisfaction in what you've done...because you are hell bent on the next promotion and making more money'. Simon also seemed to feel that he was losing his grip on his values as a result of his work. When we spoke after his interview, he said his long-term aspiration was to do something charitable, but he had no idea what form this might take or how to make sense of the impulse in relation to what he currently did day to day. Greg gave the following reasons why he found it difficult to discuss his values with colleagues:

A lot of people who go into accountancy are people who didn't know what they wanted to do, who felt a bit lost after they graduated, they didn't have that direction...and they joined an organization and did work for three years which is very objective and there's very set rules, and so first of all they didn't have much direction and then they're having what other creativity or direction or values in inverted commas, kind of beaten out of them by these big chunky textbooks and study books.

Greg despaired of the majority of his colleagues: 'In this organization people are pretty compliant, they're good graduates who didn't know what they wanted to do.' 'Good graduates' here is patronizing, as if the accountants were still children, able in the abstract but in need of reassurance, approval, and direction from someone else. Accountants thus characterized resemble the 'insecure overachievers' that Laura Empson reports one large firm, at least, deliberately seeking to recruit. According to that firm's head of human resources, such recruits were desirable because they were more likely to believe the firm's claim 'that they had been chosen by the best firm in the business and that they were, therefore, the best of their generation of recruits'. They were then more likely to develop commitment to the firm as a result (Empson 2004, 766–7). Underlying all this, perhaps, is a sense that accountants lack confidence, drifting into a well-paid but stereotypically uninspiring profession without any particular sense of purpose, and yet clinging to it.[17] Nonetheless, most must move on from the firm that trains them: the large accounting firms are pyramid organizations, with very few partners compared to the number of trainees. This fuels the competitiveness of the working environment amongst those who aspire to move up rather than out.

Facts, ethics, and truth in accounting

Having described the work done by accountants in the large firms, their reasons for doing it, and the social context in which they find themselves, we can now identify how they are most likely to breach public trust. Unlike the rogue executives who account for many of the headlines, they are not in a position to create complex financial structures in order to conceal a company's losses, for instance. However they are in a position to overlook, facilitate, or approve doing so. Even if they do none of these things explicitly, they might not notice, understand, care about, or have time to investigate dubious actions by clients. Moreover, they may feel pressured to accept such actions in order to retain the perpetrators as clients of their firms. All these forms of complicity have ill-defined boundaries, which are difficult to regulate. Accountants must therefore be trusted to work at these boundaries. Several aspects of their general motivations and early career experience as described above seem likely, on the face of it, to foster an instrumental and disengaged approach to their work, rather than to foster a collective ethos in which public trust would be well placed. To see how far this is actually the case, however, we will need to look closely at what kind of knowledge accountants construct, and how.

I have refined the concepts in terms of which I will describe the construction of accounting knowledge in the light of my findings whilst studying accountants. To have fixed such concepts in advance would have foreclosed my exploration before it even began. That would have been particularly problematic with respect to the study of truth in accounting, given the notorious philosophical difficulty of defining truth in any case. Bernard Williams, indeed, argues against doing so:

In particular, we should resist any demand for a definition of truth, principally because truth belongs to a ramifying set of connected notions, such as meaning, reference, belief, and so on, and we are better employed in exploring the relations between these notions than in trying to treat one or some of them as the basis of the others. It is also true that if any of these notions has a claim to be more basic and perspicuous than the others, it is likely to be truth itself. (2002, 63)

Our focus here is on how accountants negotiate the field of meaning described by these 'connected notions'. Only after studying how truth is negotiated by accountants in their own language is it possible to evaluate how they do so and how they might do so differently. Nonetheless, the vocabulary through which I have come to understand accountants' construction of knowledge at the end of my exploration will be essential to my description of it in these pages. In this section, therefore, I ask the reader to adopt a conceptual toolkit in advance, with the promise that future chapters will flesh out its empirical foundations. The central concept in this toolkit is the accounting fact.

We began from the premise that underlying the problem of trust in the financial world is a deeper problem of knowledge. Knowledge in accounting is increasingly reduced to facts constructed technically by experts. Yet to construct facts is an irreducibly ethical activity, as a close analysis of the discourse in which accountants do so will demonstrate. Although accounting facts are necessary to the functioning of the modern economy, we will see that when they are constructed unthinkingly or when too large a sphere of meaning is condensed into factual form, the effect is to obscure the judgement involved. This may be done as a rhetorical technique or by accident, but in either case the truthfulness of accounting knowledge is impaired.

Do we, then, place too much trust in facts? This question might be asked, for instance, about a company's profit figure. As a summation of the relevant debits and credits over a period, profit includes all of the assumptions made when preparing a company's profit and loss account. Such assumptions are inevitable. As Paul Montagna puts it:

No two auditors will agree exactly on the monetary value of most items listed on the financial statements of a client. The latitude given to them in their work is allowed because it has to be allowed. Even if a fixed and unvarying value would be placed on physical goods, it would be impossible to know the exact status of these goods at most stages of their processing in an organization. (1974, 129)

Moreover, many of the items represented in financial statements do not even have physical substance, and accountants may differ not only over the precise measurement of an item but over the accounting technique most appropriate to its valuation. The idea that figures such as profit can be trusted as facts, therefore, needs to be thought of not as self-evident, but as a historical phenomenon in itself.

It has not always been possible to think of accounting facts in abstraction from any normative perspective on the world they describe. The earliest known champion of double-entry bookkeeping, Luca Pacioli, positioned it within the field of rhetoric when he published his manual of the technique, *De Computis et Scripturis*, in 1494.[18] Double-entry bookkeeping gradually became a powerful way in which merchants tried to demonstrate the moral legitimacy of their activities in a Christian context suspicious of usury. For every debit, there was also a credit, and this double entry demonstrated that a merchant's dealings were balanced, rather than excessive or extortionate. Beyond this, 'the conventions of double-entry writing simply excluded allusions to what no rules of writing could control: shipwrecks, storms at sea, and the wild fluctuations in currency rates that characterized the early modern economy' (Poovey 1998, 36). In these ways, accounting served to enhance merchants' reputations, and therefore their creditworthiness (Aho 1985, 23; Carruthers and Espeland 1991; Poovey 1998; Thompson 1994).

Modern accounting, however, soon outgrew its dependence on formal rhetoric and religion. It spread due to the mobility, interconnectedness, and education of merchants (Carruthers and Espeland 1991, 52). Over subsequent centuries, together with descriptive statistics and quantitative knowledge more broadly, it became increasingly useful to government and to entrepreneurs, because it offered a systematic and apparently neutral way of configuring information that was seemingly immune from interpretative challenge (McKendrick 1970; Poovey 1998; Porter 1995). Accounting facts took hold, then, because of an intersection of religious, commercial, and political forces, which enabled them to proliferate in spheres where they would previously have seemed out of place.[19] Modern accounting did not originate as an uncontroversial advance in the quality of knowledge, but as a rhetorical means of claiming to be trustworthy, and subsequent chapters will demonstrate that it remains a product of that heritage.

What defines a fact for our purposes, therefore, is its social status as such, rather than its validity according to an objective standard.[20] A fact, in this sociological sense, can be thought of as a statement that commands the general agreement of a given community, and seems indisputable to them. In this case, the relevant community is the accounting profession as a whole, rather than humanity at large: facts can evolve within accountancy which might not be accepted as such outside of it. This definition of fact implies the contrasting concept of the value statement, being a statement that does not command general adherence, but instead seems value-laden to the community in question. Facts cannot be considered as entirely distinct from value statements, because in accounting at least their status as such is rarely absolute. The acceptance of particular statements as facts, by excluding argument from the sphere of meaning encompassed by those facts, displaces any residual disagreement, and also structures other arguments to which the facts might be relevant. The construction of facts is therefore a value-laden practice, and is salient to questions of value in fields of meaning surrounding that of a given fact itself.[21] When its consensual origin is forgotten, however, a fact can seem irreducible and therefore immune to being broken down and reconfigured in a different way.

I do not assume anything substantive about what should be considered a fact. Instead, I will explore how the socially constructed category of fact is used by accountants, and in particular how the scope and authority of facts in accountancy enable value statements to be defined as such and consequently excluded from accountants' frame of reference. In accountancy, with its aspirations towards transparency and simplification, we will see that there is a particularly strong tendency for facts to develop in areas of meaning that would not be seen as factual in other discourses. Accounting facts therefore come to encompass what other discourses might classify as value statements. The normative presumptions that then seem to be embodied in accounting facts are not actively concealed, but rather they are taken for granted, and come to seem indisputable as a result of their apparently factual status.

Looking at accounting facts will offer an entry point to understanding both the kind of truth accountants produce and the conception of truthfulness that results in such truth. However the sphere of meaning Bernard Williams describes as being referred to by truth is more profound than that of fact. It includes not just connections between agreed facts, but the significance of specific facts and connections, and the level and type of commitment they command from their adherents. In other words, truth describes a connection between knowledge and ethics, the particular character of which needs to be explored empirically. Accountants with particular ethical perspectives more readily understand and construct particular types of knowledge, so the two issues of knowledge and of ethics are inseparable. Accountants' discourse, as we will see, both reflects and influences the ethical perspective they adopt towards accounting decisions. Exploring accountants' discourse will help to shed light on the issues of ethics and interpretation that infuse even accountancy's most sanitized statements of fact. It will be a constructively critical project, not because it will attempt to specify what accountants' ethics should be, but because it will demonstrate that they currently take a particular form which should be subject to more rigorous debate than a purely factual discourse admits.

By ethics, here, I do not mean what my interviewees would mean. As Chapter 7 will demonstrate 'ethics', ironically, has become a technical term in accountancy. It tends to refer to accepted behaviour in some fairly narrowly prescribed areas, for instance with respect to money laundering, conflicts of interest, and whistle-blowing. Instead, I use it to demarcate a broader field of empirical inquiry, which is well described by Michel Foucault's definition of ethics as 'the kind of relationship you ought to have with yourself... which determines how the individual is supposed to constitute himself as a moral subject of his own actions' (1983, 238). This relationship to self is not only a subjective orientation, but also a social construct.[22] Ethics in this sense concerns how a person should be changed by his or her actions, and by extension what actions he or she should pursue in order to flourish. Yet although Foucault emphasizes that ethics are a shared imperative of social life, he nonetheless distinguishes ethics from morals, by which he refers to the prevalent behavioural code that individuals in a society are expected to observe.

Undoubtedly some facts need to be constructed, at least provisionally, if thought and communication are to be made manageable. Accounting facts perform a valuable function in narrowing the debates that must be engaged in during everyday economic life. As Theodore Porter puts it regarding quantification more generally, the accounting fact 'has the virtues of its vices' (1995, 86). It facilitates simplification and standardization, but at the expense of complexity, specificity, and depth. My aim is to make the particular factual basis of contemporary financial decisions more readily debatable, which is a pressing task because the discourse of factuality itself tends to resist such debate. Yet doing so should catalyse efforts to achieve simplification more sensitively in the public interest, rather than undermining any basis on which simplification might be achieved at all. This distinction must be clearly drawn if we are to encourage the kind of empathy that can connect abstract financial knowledge to its specific human implications, at the same time as maintaining the capacity to make decisions based on such knowledge. We will see that accountants themselves find this proposition challenging, being both keen to construct and use facts, and concerned that doing so sometimes seems to draw them onto questionable ethical terrain. In order to appraise the form of knowledge that facilitates the administration of global capitalism, therefore, this book will also need to engage in an ethical sociology that illuminates the challenges individuals confront when working in the financial world. Those individuals, as we shall see, negotiate the ethics and politics of factuality every day.

Although the issues outlined here are particularly pressing with respect to accounting knowledge, they are also relevant to the construction of knowledge in other spheres. There are two implications of this. Firstly, insofar as accountancy's emphasis on facts created by experts is symptomatic of modern society's more general approach to the construction and evaluation of knowledge, this study should resonate well beyond the financial world. Secondly, however, the more general context of the problem suggests caution in simply criticizing the accounting profession. The profession is in a weak position given the contested nature of financial matters, and appealing to a factual discourse could be seen as its reluctant last resort when other sources of authority fail. In a world where factuality is expected, it is difficult not to conform to that expectation. We will see in Chapter 6 that although professionalism does offer a basis for public trust that is less dependent on accounting facts, accountants doubt that it can lend sufficient authority to their work.

Plan of the book

Taking my conversations with practising accountants as its starting point, this book will explore the day-to-day construction of accounting knowledge in a way that addresses important questions about trust, truthfulness, professionalism, and ethics. Chapter 2 will show how accounting work can be interpreted as performance, and will expose the inadequacy of imperatives such as honesty and transparency as a means of capturing the performative requirements of truthfulness. Once established, this performative perspective will be implicit throughout the rest of the book. Chapter 3 will take an empirical overview of the themes that will be covered in more depth in subsequent chapters, by reviewing interviewees' responses to a fictional scenario that I gave to them. Chapter 4 will analyse those practices that accountants call technical and that are used to shape multifarious commercial experience into a convenient factual form. Chapter 5 will look at how accountants exploit their technical frame, and how they cope with its fragility, by examining how considerations which cannot be rendered technical are dealt with, particularly through extended metaphors of strategy and sport. Chapter 6 will discuss accountants' professionalism, and will explore the influence it has over the construction of accounting knowledge in the context of the competing imperatives of commercialism and client service. Chapter 7 will look more broadly at how the practice of constructing accounting facts engages, shapes, and relies upon the ethical characters of the people who do so, and will explore the proposition that accounting's apparently factual basis, reinforced by its rules-based ethical and technical standards, limits its receptiveness to alternative forms of information and inhibits the ethical maturation of accountants. Chapter 8 will conclude by suggesting that increasingly technical accounting rules can be counterproductive, and that our focus, instead, should be on redefining and reinvigorating professional ethics in the financial world. It will draw together the findings of the previous chapters in order to discuss how this might best be achieved.

Clearly, this is an interdisciplinary study, to which a wide range of previous work is relevant. My primary aim, however, is not to contribute to a particular literature, but to describe a social problem in a way that makes it more

tractable. I have therefore introduced the book by outlining that social problem and formulating a means of understanding it, and have deferred engagement with the relevant intellectual debates until they arise in the chapters that
follow. The general reader will, I hope, find this approach intuitive. Specialists
in accounting will also find the whole to be of greater interest than the sum
of its parts, since the book relates accounting knowledge, ethics, and practice
in new ways. Specialists in the sociology of work and the professions will be
particularly interested in Chapters 2 and 6, economic sociologists in Chapters 4
and 5, and business ethicists in Chapter 7. The overall focus of the book,
however, is necessarily more general. This is both because accounting practice
itself does not respect intellectual boundaries, and because solutions to the
problems I explore must ultimately be found through the development of
accountants' own existing discourse, even if that process is catalysed from
without. Only when practitioners can recognize, articulate and grapple
with these problems in their own terms, will solutions that were previously
unimaginable gradually become possible.

2
Performance and Truthfulness

Accounting, as we saw in Chapter 1, is a practice oriented towards the construction of facts. It is therefore consequential in ways that other practices are not. An accounting fact, once constructed, becomes transferable beyond the context of its construction. Users in different contexts accept accounting facts on the assumption that they would have constructed them in the same way, had they been involved in doing so. The construction of such facts must therefore be held to generally accepted standards. In the important sphere of accounting practice that falls beyond the scope of rules, I want to suggest that those standards are best conceived as ethical standards of truthfulness, rather than as either objective standards of factual correctness on the one hand, or conventional standards of social behaviour on the other.

This is a fine line to tread, but the importance of treading it can be illustrated by looking at the two extremes on either side. Asking that accountants 'tell the truth', as a dismayed media and public tends to do after the latest accounting scandal, wrongly assumes that the salient facts are readily discernible and need only be impartially represented. This chapter will call into question both the value and the attainability of such impartial representation. Accountants' function is to edit and simplify information, and there is a trade-off between simplicity and transparency, because simplification entails removing complexity from view. Conversely, describing accounting as a social practice tends to offer too shallow an impression of accountants' involvement in the construction of knowledge. We will see that accounting is a psychologically and even emotionally involving activity, and that shared standards appropriate to the construction of accounting knowledge must take this into account.[23] An ethical standard of truthfulness, I will argue, can be more meaningful than an agreement to adhere to common practices that might just as well be different, but without implying that accountants' responsibilities can or should be reduced to the transparent reporting of pre-existing facts.[24]

Empirically, this chapter will focus on the ways in which accountants present themselves in the process of giving an account, and on the reciprocal effect that self-presentation has on the accounts they give.[25] Accountants themselves partially articulate this relation through the concept of performance, and so I will begin by looking closely at what they take performance to mean, both in its literal sense of carrying out a task, and in what is here its metaphorical sense of dramatic acting. I will then explore the consequences of accountants being performers in this dual sense with respect to the truthfulness of the knowledge they construct. Lastly, I will show how accountants find themselves obliged to manage their emotions in order to perform as is required to construct credible accounting knowledge. We will see that the two meanings of performance, describing quality of work and quality of self-presentation, can be indistinguishable in practice, with important consequences for the ethics of accounting work. The performative perspective developed here will underpin subsequent chapters, informing their exploration of how accountants play a variety of roles, including those of technocrats, bureaucrats, experts, strategists, professionals, pragmatists, sportspeople, and more.

Performance and role-play

Accountants sometimes talk of themselves metaphorically as dramatic actors. Jason used a common cliché when he referred to what he could 'bring to the show'. Oliver recalled being engaged to 'play the good cop' on a bank's behalf. Yet the word 'performance' in accounting, as in many other working environments, refers most directly to the quality of a person's work. Evaluations of individuals' work may be specific to particular tasks, but are often generalizations about how well a person does his or her job. My interviewees were acutely aware of their own and others' performance in this sense, and many were quick to make negative judgements. Tom, for instance, recalled the incompetence of an insurance client's debt collectors: 'I'm astonished with how many completely useless people they employ... absolutely extraordinary.' He went on to illustrate the point:

[The debtors' ledger entries] had some monthly commentaries against them which were just hilarious to read. I mean they were just hilarious.... The commentary would be like, 'I phoned to so and so at XY bank and asked him when he was going to pay this amount of money. He said "What?"' And that would be the monthly commentary!

Tom enjoyed telling such colourful war stories. In this case, he took pleasure in the rough justice that 'the banks seemed to know that they were Muppets, and were just taking the piss, were just refusing to pay, you know'.

The severity of my interviewees' criticism of others' performance, and the enjoyment they found in such criticism, would seem to go beyond mere description. It might reflect resentment at having to resolve the problems created by others, or envy of their lack of perfectionist scruples, or simply the obviousness of errors and failings in an occupation construed as technical. Such criticisms do, however, perform an important additional function. In an environment where performance depends on peer review, peers must pass judgement readily, and those who perform better than others must ensure that they are seen to do so. Tom criticizes his client's staff at least in part to make himself look better than them.

Although there are various audiences for an accountant's performance, including clients, colleagues, and the wider public, the audience which claims to objectively grade accountants' performances consists of their seniors within their firms. Such gradings might be discussed, for instance, in what Barry referred to as a 'performance review', which is a formal appraisal meeting between an accountant and his or her line manager. Alistair trotted out the official line:

We're judged within a set of core competencies... you've got to excel in all those five or six competencies to rise to the top because there is a defined appraisal process that occurs every six months. There's a main one that's annual, and you're judged on three sixty degree appraisal on those criteria. And provided you get the right feedback, then obviously you go on to the next grade.

Three-hundred-and-sixty-degree appraisal means that the views of everyone accountants have worked with, whether above, below, or alongside them in the hierarchy, are taken into account when evaluating their performance. Everyone reviews everyone else, resulting in a kind of diffused panopticon made coherent and credible by the objectification of the technical sounding 'core competencies'. Needless to say, however, reviewing one's seniors is perceived as a hazardous activity. Kumar said that giving 'constructive feedback' to a manager was one of the occasions when he had had to tread most carefully in his working life.

Daljit, having done a lot of work for a senior partner who then left his firm, commented after his interview that without that partner as a 'champion' the work he had done 'didn't count' because it was not visible to anyone currently in a position of power. Both Barry and Daljit said after their interviews that it was important to do highly visible work, and that less competent people who worked in the office might be more likely to be promoted than more competent people who were always out at clients' premises. My interviewees' intense concern with how others perceive them, therefore, reflects the extent to which their career prospects depend on those perceptions.

For at least some of my interviewees, however, performing was more than a necessary evil, and they enjoyed playing to an audience. Oliver found it 'exciting' to work on jobs that were 'publicly sensitive'. Graham also conceptualized his motivation in terms of visibility to a wider public:

I'm just more interested in the external, factual reporting side of things rather than the internal workings of a company.

Is that because it's more concrete and tangible, or...

It's more visible.

Right.

You know, you pick up the papers and you're more likely to read about XYZ company has just released results of, you know, massive loss or whatever, and, you're more likely to have some sort of role in that rather than, you know, another company has reorganized its IT function and spent a billion pounds, I mean, whatever, it's not very exciting to me.

Graham's motivation resembles that of a fame-hungry youth, valuing himself and others according to the recognition they achieve in the media. He does make a distinction between the 'concrete and tangible' and the 'visible', but in order to focus on the latter rather than the former. His emphasis on the 'factual' is not an emphasis on the 'concrete and tangible', but explicitly on its representation which is for him more 'exciting'. This is a peculiar orientation for an auditor whose 'role', one might have thought, is to ensure that 'the external, factual reporting' does actually reflect 'the internal workings of a company'.

Daljit said it was accepted in his firm that successful accountants were those who excelled at perception management:

The biggest single thing is that they manage people's perceptions well. And there are so many cases you can think of. The person I was just speaking to in fact, he does it very well.... You cover weaknesses by managing people's perceptions. People perceive you as being very good even though in a lot of instances, the substance simply isn't there, but you've got someone else who can fill that gap for you. But there's a perception that this person is very good. And that's, in professional services, the partners have explained this to me many times, that professional service firms are all about managing perceptions, internally and externally.

Perception management is not discussed here as a regrettable aberration, or even as a necessary evil, but applauded as a desirable skill. The two senses of the word 'performance' in accounting, relating to quality of work and to quality of self-presentation, have become inextricable. Even those interviewees who were troubled by this felt obliged to play along. As Adrian succinctly put it: 'I would like to be a better bullshitter.'[26]

Greg discovered the importance of perceptions the hard way. He emailed a partner in his firm's tax practice to question an action by that partner on ethical grounds, and the partner consequently complained about him to the head of Greg's practice area. After being admonished by his line manager for causing this complaint, Greg realized that 'the head of the practice, the only thing he's ever heard about me is that I got him an irate phone call from one of his colleagues, so in his eyes I'm a bit annoying really'. Whether the partner Greg criticized was right to be irate is simply irrelevant, because Greg did not have sufficient access to the head of the practice to argue his case. Immediate perception, though, is more than a level at which Greg is forced to act. It sets the terms in which others judge him, and in which he therefore judges himself: 'You've got to be a positive role model to yourself almost, and other people, because your boss who saw you do that will say "aw, shouldn't have done that, what a stupid guy", then he will tell other people, and no one will do stuff like that any more.' Greg knows that if he took anything too far the consequences would be so severe that he himself would 'say "fuck that, I don't want to do that again"'. In order to sustain his own character, Greg needs to come across as acceptable to others. He therefore translates perception management into a pragmatic ethical imperative, and finds himself arguing against whistle-blowing: 'Kicking things up in the air is the right way to go... very, very rarely, very rarely. You want to create good vibes out of challenging things, I think.'

Surrounded by performers, my interviewees were sometimes unsure what to believe, and left feeling considerable anxiety because they had no way of knowing whether appearances were meaningful. For instance, when I asked Simon when he had had to behave cautiously at work, he told me about a time when he realized he had forgotten to put a value added tax (VAT)[27] return in with its covering letter to a client. Simon was afraid: 'Those few moments were terrible.' Although Simon wanted to conceal his mistake, he needed reassurance from someone else that he was behaving appropriately. 'I spoke to someone on my left, that's what I did. I guess it's a kind of personality trait that I'll try and confide in someone, I'm very trusting.' This vocabulary seems over the top with respect to an administrative error, but what was really at stake was Simon's more general self-presentation as competent, which he feared that even this small error might undermine. Simon's colleague, however, told him that 'it doesn't matter too much', which gave Simon the confidence to take the VAT return to a partner to be signed and re-sent. He recalled that on meeting the partner 'she was very nice about it. I was very impressed about how nice she was because I didn't really know her. She was very professional about it.' Simon was relieved by the partner's response, but he nonetheless interpreted her niceness as a 'professional' achievement by which he was 'impressed': he felt well managed as much as reassured. Despite everyone involved being nice to him, Simon was still worried after the event that people might remember that he was 'unreliable' in this instance, and talk badly of him behind his back. The world of appearance is an uncertain one, in which no one can really tell where they stand, and within that world neither the partner nor the colleague sitting next to him could have set Simon at ease, however hard they had tried.

Simon interprets the partner as playing a role. Her performance, in other words, adopts a pre-existing form that is not original to her, and behind which her deepest feelings remain inscrutable. Yet the problem here may not be that inscrutability itself, but Simon's discomfort with it. Richard Sennett's analysis of theatricality in public life explains why:

Convention is itself the single most expressive tool of public life. But in an age wherein intimate relations determine what shall be believable, conventions, artifices, and rules appear only to get in the way of revealing oneself to another; they are obstructions to intimate expression.... With an emphasis on psychological authenticity, people become inartistic in daily life because they are unable to tap the fundamental creative strength of the actor, the ability to play with and invest feeling in external images of self. Thus we arrive at the hypothesis that theatricality has a special, hostile relation to intimacy; theatricality has an equally special, friendly relation to a strong public life. (Sennett 2002, 37)

Simon's desire to know what people really think, and his anxiety in the absence of such knowledge, might therefore be misguided. Instead, he should perhaps take his colleagues' professionalism at face value, without trying to delve behind it in a way that would overburden professional life with intimacy. The artificiality of accountants' professional relationships might, on this view, be applauded for maintaining a distinction between public and intimate life. Yet insofar as we live 'in an age wherein intimate relations determine what shall be believable' that artificiality seems like pretence.

As a tax adviser, Simon's job involves selling tax advice to clients, and his pride in his highly polished sales patter was clear during his interview. When Simon applies his skill at selling tax products to the task of selling himself, however, he experiences his salesmanship as a kind of role-play that goes beyond conscious performance to become a subconscious psychological orientation. He described such a deep experience of role-play during the following exchange:

Do you think you've always told the truth at work?

I don't like lying, not outright lying. I certainly think a facet of being in a consultancy business... is that you need to sell yourself in the best light possible. So that would often involve, not consciously but subconsciously trying to draw attention to things you've done. Maybe glossing what you've done, or making it seem like a more clever thing that you've done than what you've actually done.

How can that be subconscious?

Because you get yourself into the frame of mind of someone who wants to be recognized for what they're doing... and that will be a conscious selling effort but it'll only be conscious to step into the shoes of the person who's selling, it's not conscious once I'm in the shoes of the salesman. Does that make sense?

Okay, so there's a selling to yourself process to be done.

Yeah, I think it's actually, well it's probably worse than that, I'm probably so used to it I just literally switch mindsets.

Simon's subtle substitution of 'sell' for 'set' in the common cliché 'to set something in its best light' indicates how pervasive the selling impulse is for him. He himself argues that his salesmanship is subconscious, in order to explain how it is honest. What is conscious is the adoption of a 'frame of mind'. Having adopted that 'frame of mind', Simon simply plays the role of 'someone who wants to be recognized for what they're doing'. In Constantin Stanislavsky's terms, he is playing an objective: the details of behaviour need not be thought about, because they will follow subconsciously from pursuit of the objective (1980, 114–17, 281).

During our interview, I misunderstood the experience Simon was describing. I thought that in order to 'step into . . . the shoes of the salesman' he would need to persuade himself of the appropriateness of that action, or in other words to persuade himself that, given his performance, selling himself was appropriate and honest. But Simon corrected me: 'It's probably worse than that, I'm probably so used to it I just literally switch mindsets.' He adopts a persona whose assumptions are given, and need not be evaluated. To use Arlie Hochschild's convenient shorthand for Stanislavsky's distinction between a great performance and a mediocre one, Simon is deep acting rather than surface acting, adopting a mindset and drawing directly on his psychological resources at the moment of performance, rather than superficially adapting his behaviour in order to pretend (Hochschild 1983, 35–42; Stanislavsky 1980, 281–313). This enables him to behave convincingly as a salesman, regardless of whether he is himself convinced, or whether he would be convinced if he thought in terms of his own conviction. Simon manages the potential contradiction between behaviour and belief by preventing it from arising, switching between mindsets rather than trying to integrate all of his behaviours into a unified world view or practical orientation. As a consequence he was able to argue, when I pressed him after the above exchange, that 'it's not really a lie, it's just I suppose changing the presentation'.

Daljit gave an example of how an act of self-salesmanship might seem to change the salesman. In order to make himself credible to a shipping client, he would try to 'speak in the client's language', imitating their terminology of TUs (ten metre equivalent units). 'I mean it's a self-fulfilling prophecy because by virtue of the fact you do try and understand what these little hooks are, you actually do develop a certain amount of specialism.' However Daljit considers the tendency for pretence to become reality problematic, and comments that 'the danger is you become something you're not or try to and in fact, you're probably better off staying the way you are, warts and all'. Becoming something you are not, rather than becoming something you were not, suggests a paradoxical tension at a moment in time rather than a smooth transition through time; Daljit sees himself as having a core self that is not changeable. On this assumption, 'staying the way you are' might seem advisable from the points of view both of credibility with the client and of one's own psychology.

Yet accountants clearly do attempt such self-transformations, as we saw when Greg sought to be a positive role model to himself in choosing whether to challenge his superiors or bite his tongue. Consequently, accountants come to occupy an uncomfortable hinterland between self-conscious performance and unconscious socialization that resembles deep acting, but outside the theatre and extended over time.

My interviewees, then, appear to lack what Sennett calls 'the ability to play with and invest feeling in external images of self'. Given their attention to performance, this lack seems surprising until it is interpreted in the light of Denis Diderot's eighteenth-century dialogue on the paradox of acting. Diderot argues that the best actors are paradoxically those who do *not* actually feel what they pretend to feel, because actual feeling causes actors to lose control over their performances. 'What, then, is a great actor? A man who, having learnt the words set down for him by the author, fools you thoroughly, whether in tragedy or comedy' (Diderot 1957, 33). In Sennett's terms, such an actor plays with external images of self *without* investing feeling in them. This description of surface acting might equally have been written to describe the least sincere kind of salesman.

William Archer's nineteenth-century response to Diderot suggests, however, that the double-edged ability Sennett describes is not as paradoxical as Diderot argues. Archer claims that there is no paradox because actors are capable of a 'dual consciousness' and therefore their emotion on stage can be genuinely experienced, or deep acted, at the same time as it is consciously monitored (Archer 1957, 184). Simon's capacity to 'switch mindsets' might seem to imply that Archer's view of acting is applicable in the context of accounting work. Yet at the level of their more ongoing performance, rather than with respect to particular sales calls or meetings, my interviewees were not able to maintain a dual consciousness. Their performance, unlike the theatre actor's, lasts for months and years, not just for an evening. Without dual consciousness, Diderot's paradox becomes a paradox again, and over an extended time the possibility of surpassing it through sheer talent at pretending seems even more remote. For the accountant, then, the paradox raises the following question: If you cannot maintain a convincing performance without adopting your role as yourself, do you pretend badly like an insincere salesman, or do you invest your whole self and become a sincere one? As the remainder of this chapter will show, my interviewees found no easy answer to this question. Their difficulty is symptomatic of what Sennett would see as a collective inability to demarcate an impersonal sphere of work, the practical implications of which are the personal demands made by work which I will discuss towards the end of the chapter. In order to understand these demands fully, however, it is first necessary to discuss how my interviewees' performance and role-play affects how they work with accounting information, and particularly how it affects the standards of honesty and transparency they apply when doing so.

Honesty and transparency

Daljit categorically denied lying. 'I can't say I've ever lied at a client or internally. I wouldn't lie, and I think that's very important. I certainly haven't lied, and I'd go out of my way not to.' Yet honesty understood as not lying only precludes the most extreme distortions of the facts. Many interviewees found my question as to whether they told the truth at work simplistic, given that the assessment of accounting information, in Sam's words, 'is both a matter of fact and a matter of judgement'. In a situation where the valuation of a company was subject to commercial dispute, Sebastian said it was an accepted part of the bargaining process that both sides would try to prepare numbers which suited their case. In this context, he mocked the idea of 'the truth as it were shining through'.

Liam argued that the requirements of honesty vary according to context, depending circularly on the assumptions of others as to how honest an accountant is being:

It's not unprofessional to represent part of the truth in order to, or a slightly slanted presentation of the truth in order to get a specific end, provided that no one is under the impression that you are providing anything other than that slightly directed form of the truth.... I don't think there's anything unprofessional in giving views of facts directed by whoever it should be.

It might be tempting to respond to the distorting effect of commercial interest on accounting information by demanding transparency, or in other words by demanding that accountants' decisions be open to full scrutiny by interested parties. Accountants might achieve transparency by, for instance, disclosing the details relating to a controversial accounting treatment alongside that treatment itself. Yet the more disclosure is made in support of an accounting decision, the more responsibility for evaluating that decision is delegated to the reader of the information. Sometimes, as I will illustrate with respect to the disclosure of provisions in Chapter 4, making the readers of financial statements aware of exactly what has been done can even substitute for an auditor requiring a client to account for an item differently. Insofar as accountants have responsibilities of authorship or even editorship with respect to the accounts they give, therefore, these must take precedence over the pursuit of transparency.

Daljit recommended being 'honest' about a company's financial difficulties as the best means of managing the expectations of stakeholders (which is a clichéd accounting soft skill) in order to try and maintain their support for the company. Whichever takes precedence in his own mind, he at least feels that in his professional discourse managing expectations, rather than honesty, is the practice that has more intrinsic credibility. Yet could managing expectations actually be what honesty means in accounting? The manager of expectations goes beyond transparency to proactively inform people of what he thinks they need to know, and must inevitably be selective in doing so. However, managing expectations also implies a willingness to manipulate those whose expectations are being managed, as I discovered when Barry criticized a client's finance director for failing to manage the expectations of his company's bankers:

I found a significant hole in the forecast. To be fair to the finance director, it was quite obvious, because it was called 'The Difference' [laughs] and he had the audacity to put in front of his board . . . on the face of the forecast that was in the board pack they had a line on there saying 'Difference' . . . with no explanation on it at all . . . thirty million quid!

Barry only credits the finance director with transparency here by way of qualification to his broader criticism. The reason for the difference was that the company was now underperforming relative to a previous forecast given to the bank. The finance director had not updated the bank by way of a profit warning and revised forecast that this was the case. Hence his 'audacity'. He should have resolved this situation as a matter of priority before coming to the board meeting. Failing that, the finance director should at least have tried to offer some excuse or 'explanation'. Failing even that, he should have had some shame: Barry was astonished by the brazen prominence of the difference 'on the face of the forecast that was in the board pack'.[28] The finance director's blunt transparency here is a marker of incompetence. He should have known how important this matter was, and should have resolved it, or at least proposed a resolution to it, or explained it. Since he had done none of these, some attempt to conceal the matter, or to disclose it more discreetly, would actually have inspired more confidence. At least Barry would have felt that the finance director understood the gravity of the situation his company was in. Perceived competence is more important than transparency, in this situation where the two are in contradiction; but the contradiction itself is caused by the finance director's ineptitude at managing the bank's expectations.

The way in which the finance director should have glossed his forecast in this scenario is often referred to by accountants as 'managing information'. Managing information could seem quite a complex exercise, but Greg found it easier than lying. 'I would say I sometimes manage information. I wouldn't, lying is a very complicated thing, and too much effort, I think.' If Greg lies, he has to cover his tracks, whereas if he merely manages information, being caught out is less consequential because he can simply make more information available without embarrassment. Greg justified 'managing information' on the grounds that it saves time. Effectively, he argued that if he did not make choices about how to simplify a situation, his listeners would do so anyway, but without the benefit of his knowledge of that situation:

Especially in London . . . time is money. The revenue we get in is completely based on chargeable time, everyone's very conscious of the time they spend on everything, so people don't have time to hear the context of everything. They've got very little time to know the context of anything really.

The consequences of this approach to time became clear when Daljit and I discussed how consultation within his firm ensured that the right accounting decisions were made. If you are unsure and consult someone, that person is likely to be 'risk averse' and 'will just want it never ever to come back and haunt them'. They will therefore advise colleagues to be cautious, 'and that's why it works'. However, I suggested to Daljit that there is then an expectation that you prioritize, and do not tell people about things unless there is a real need to consult. Daljit agreed strongly: 'Yeah, absolutely right.' Consultation creates more work, and so must be used sparingly because time is short. Good accountants get a lot done in a short time, and their conception of truthfulness needs to be consistent with that way of working.[29]

Adrian found himself in a quandary with respect to time-pressured audit work. On the one hand, he could not imagine a world without deadlines for the reporting of financial information. Yet with deadlines 'people perceive that it's a risk management game, you've got a certain amount of time to do as much as you can and then bugger off, which is the wrong way round'. Simon, not being an auditor himself, put the problem more bluntly:

It's a joke the way it's organized. You know, it goes to the lowest bidder and so people don't allocate enough time such that if problems do arise, they can't fit it into the budget they've agreed. And the whole idea of a fixed fee audit is flawed. You're supposed to be trying to find potential problems. How can you fix your time?

When I asked Graham whether he and his colleagues always told the truth at work, he responded negatively and put his answer down to time pressure. However he went on to talk about prioritization, illustrating a related but distinct reason why accountants' truthfulness can slide:

No, I definitely think that people aren't necessarily, always, giving the full picture of what's going on, whether that's through an effort to appear in control or a conscious decision not to tell something. You know most of the time it's trying, it's prioritizing what you're doing, and it's by default that there is actually something that you've missed or omitted to tell.

The second sentence here reveals that the 'effort to appear in control' and the 'conscious decision not to tell something' are not mutually exclusive as Graham tries to imply. A decision not to tell something is part and parcel of the effort to appear in control. That transparency can fall into 'default' as a result of 'prioritizing' demonstrates that the latter takes precedence over the former. The appearance of control is what matters, because it sustains trust in accountants, without which their simplifications would cease to be accepted as authoritative. Graham later justifies his 'effort to appear in control' on the grounds that a lot of adjustments of accounts, due to people constantly re-evaluating their judgements and interpretations of accounting information, would damage 'market confidence'. It can therefore, in his words, be 'right' not to make too many adjustments, and it can be 'right' to fudge this year's accounts to fit in with last year's.

My interviewees did not talk about transparency, as we have seen, because it is for them an impossible dream which, in any case, would defeat the object of their work. They did talk about honesty, but it had a confused meaning, shifting between not lying and managing expectations. Neither term was adequate to the challenge they faced, which was not to be honest or transparent in any static way, but rather to practise the construction of accounting information ethically. To do so entails, amongst other things, diligence, competence, not lying, prioritization, and the management of expectations and relationships. These are both performative and ethical imperatives, and to explore the interrelation of performance and ethics further it will be helpful to revisit my exchange with Simon, discussed in the previous section.

It is important to take Simon's initial reaction to my question about truth-telling seriously. He said 'I don't *like* lying' (my emphasis) rather than 'I don't lie'. The distinction is important, because it suggests that Simon does not merely know when he lies, but experiences displeasure when doing so. It might be said that Simon is ethically disposed against lying, but towards salesmanship. Yet if we look at the other explicitly evaluative phrase in the quotation, the picture becomes more complicated. Simon comments that to 'literally switch mindsets' in order to sell himself is 'probably worse than' doing so as a result of having successfully sold himself to himself. His dislike of lying is not matched by a dislike of selling per se, although he does dislike it, but it is matched by a dislike of the particular psychology of selling he feels obliged to adopt. It is not enough, therefore, to say that Simon can become the kind of salesman required in the accounting field at will. He can step into and out of that role, and is critical of it, and is unhappy when practising it. Yet this does not mean that he acts freely, but rather that he feels the constraints over when he must and must not act as a salesman more acutely. He is fully socialized into his work, yet still he cannot make a virtue of necessity.

If my interviewees' self-awareness undermines their investment in their performance, they nonetheless keep performing anyway, perhaps because they have no alternative. People who do jobs they dislike often do not invest in those jobs, but go through the motions. Yet for accountants, going through the motions convincingly entails *pretending* to invest in their work. Accountants therefore find themselves both wanting to invest in their work, and needing to make that investment in order to function convincingly, at the same time as being disillusioned with it. Unable to lose themselves entirely in their accounting work, my interviewees find themselves distanced from the information they produce. They have learnt not to take it too seriously, but at the cost of making it less compelling. The accountant's performance demands a more fundamental and lasting suspension of disbelief than does the dramatic actor's, yet for accountants whose project is to construct facts not fictions the suspension feels fragile, artificial and forced. The adaptability required of accountants' performances exacerbates this difficulty: there is no straightforward leap of faith that accountants seeking to really believe in what they did might make.

When I asked Tom what his aspirations were with respect to his work, he replied: 'I suppose ultimately it's to get out without having any Enrons or Parmalats happening.' He wants to keep his distance, seeing his involvement in the profession negatively in terms of personal risk rather than as an opportunity to engage in a meaningful collective endeavour. In what might seem to be a contrasting example, Jason resigned from a previous job in industry, because a fraud was being perpetrated by the finance director to whom he reported. This was clearly a difficult decision for him to make, of which he was proud. Yet even after resigning, he did not communicate the problem to anyone in higher authority. Jason's own explanation of this, that he thought complaining internally was pointless and that complaining externally did not cross his mind, is believable. Yet he also felt embarrassed in his work environment by the strength of his ethical feelings. He was very aware that 'the expedient thing' would have been to 'get off your high horse about this', and could only defend not doing so in non-professional terms: 'Personally instinctively I couldn't do that.' His rejection of the role of whistle-blower, even after resigning on principle, suggests that he perceived its potential repercussions as extending well beyond his current job. Perhaps he feared receiving bad references, or gaining a damaging reputation as a troublemaker. In any case, Jason's actions offer an example of what Jonathan Cobb more generally calls a drawback of the permeability of a social system:

[T]he person does not come to exercise control over his situation, transforming the conditions of his or her life, but instead simply moves from one set of circumstances to another. Circumstances, the structure of society, remains and you move; and as a result, you leave situations, classes, structures, as they are. (Sennett and Cobb 1977, 271)

Largely because of the prestige of his professional qualification, Jason could just move. In an environment where emotional engagement can be fraught with the risk of ridicule and psychological distress, his decision is understandable. While Jason's situation was unique amongst my interviewees, his general approach was not. Many planned to move around for variety and interest, rather than making a deep commitment to any one area or organization. If my interviewees have an abstract desire to engage with their work, therefore, they nonetheless find themselves maintaining a strategic distance from it in practice. Yet they cannot maintain this distance straightforwardly because, as the next section will show, emotional labour constitutes a significant part of the work itself.

Emotional labour

Emotional labour means the use of one's emotions as tools of one's trade. The concept originates in Hochschild's study of modern service work, based largely on interviews with, and observations of, flight attendants at Delta Airlines in the late 1970s and early 1980s. In the service economy Hochschild describes, '[s]eeming to "love the job" becomes part of the job; and actually trying to love it, and to enjoy the customers, helps the worker in this effort'.[30] Emotional labour is thus a way of trying to make a performance seem truthful in a situation where performance, and not truthfulness, is the ultimate objective. Hochschild describes the consequences of trying to love one's work in order to perfect its performance in terms of alienation. 'Beneath the difference between physical and emotional labour there lies a similarity in the possible cost of doing the work: the worker can become estranged or alienated from an aspect of self – either the body or the margins of the soul – that is *used* to do the work' (1983, 6, 7). Although I will question Hochschild's theoretical assumptions, emotional labour accurately describes some important aspects of my interviewees' performative experience.

Accountants must manage their own and others' emotions in order to maintain a stable aura of professionalism during their work. This is not the same as repressing emotion in order to avoid frustration with a task to which emotions are irrelevant. Because accounting work is interpersonal, the adoption of an unemotional attitude is actually part of the work, and of course 'unemotional' is a misnomer for a particular emotional orientation, that of a professional-seeming coolness consistent with technocracy. If emotion, as Hochschild suggests, 'is our experience of the body ready for an imaginary action', then emotional coolness in an accounting context would suggest a bodily readiness for clear-headed calculation or rational argument (1983, 220). When a partner became 'upset' and 'very annoyed' during a discussion with Greg, for instance, Greg interpreted the partner's display of emotion as a poor reflection on himself, despite still believing the partner to be wrong about the point at issue. Greg had failed in his role as subordinate to absorb tension and thus keep things cool and professional.

Barry, perhaps because he was one of the more senior people I spoke to, was unusual amongst my interviewees in explicitly discussing his emotion management. At first, he connected professionalism, lack of emotion, and performative blandness. 'I've always tried to retain a relatively professional demeanour and not bring emotion into arguments at work...I very much have tried to keep it fairly monotone.' Barry went on, however, to complicate his position, recalling being criticized during a performance review for 'not varying energy levels enough, because people interpreted my energy levels as if you like an outward sign of how seriously I was taking the situation'. Barry speculated that this feedback had originated from a 'very very excitable partner' who had asked for a piece of work to be done by a deadline. 'I calmly said "fine, it'll happen", and made it happen, but didn't do it in a fluster of activity and get very very excited about it.' Consequently the partner did not feel confident, whilst Barry was working, that Barry would complete the work on time, as he was unsure of Barry's commitment to doing so.

The question of energy levels resurfaced in Barry's next performance review. 'What then happened a year later was that somebody criticized me for what they called leakage because they felt that in certain situations I could leak too much energy and betray too much emotion.' Barry had overcompensated in response to the previous year's appraisal. Now, his feedback was that 'you give quite a lot away, you're leaking when you do that, because people can see emotionally where you're going with it'. This feedback related particularly to Barry's negotiating style: his reviewers were concerned that Barry's display of emotion might expose his underlying agenda and so weaken his bargaining position. Failure to conceal that agenda invoked the emotive language not only of gifting, which in an economy of exchange is a criticism, but of self-betrayal.

As a result of all this feedback, Barry gradually gained performative mastery over his energy levels. He demonstrated this mastery in a subsequent dispute with a client:

I tried to absorb his energy levels by staying fairly quiet in that situation but then at the end I did raise my energy levels, arm movements, firmer tone, sit forwards, make a point, 'this this this this and this is what's going to happen for all the reasons I've outlined already'.

Barry recalls his actions as a series of imperatives in the present tense, reliving them as an embodied experience. As much as changing his energy levels in order to alter his performance here, he deliberately performs particular actions in order to change his energy levels. He experiences and manipulates his energy levels as an integral part of his physicality. Indeed, the very terminology of 'energy levels' is drawn from the domain of physical theatre, and underlines the embodied, performative nature of Barry's work.

Barry went on to describe a situation in which he had very consciously used his energy levels strategically. Another firm alongside which his firm was working had made a major mistake in some forecast numbers. Barry, having spotted this and then received a 'humble, incredibly humble' phone call from the partner in the other firm, felt jubilant: 'I said to myself "I knew I was fucking right".' Yet he made a very conscious decision not to respond angrily 'and in many respects that made it more difficult for [the partner], because I didn't bollock him and allow him to release his, if you like perhaps for him to get defensive'. In other words, Barry did not give the other firm's partner the opportunity to clear the air through emotional labour, but instead left him grateful and in Barry's debt for the rest of the project. Barry received concrete rewards for this approach in terms of extra work being done by the other firm, staff from the other firm cancelling holiday to work for him, and overruns of time not being charged to him.

Barry concluded our discussion of energy levels by commenting that he had learnt over time that different energy levels affect the way people perceive him in different situations and 'to the extent that you can I think you need to try and attune yourself to that. I think different people respond differently to emotional reaction and now I know that and again it's just this question I think of political antennae if that's the right phraseology.' He has learnt, in other words, to embody his strategic thinking, so that strategy is no longer merely rational, but a matter of corporeal attunement. Barry no longer thinks that all situations require the same response, or that his emotions should or could be excluded from his work. Moreover, he has learnt these things not by going outside an emotionless accounting profession, but rather by engaging in emotionally sophisticated accounting practice as encouraged by the appraisal process of his accounting firm.

Barry's performance of emotional labour illustrates just how far the two meanings of performance, as quality of work and quality of self-presentation, can overlap in accounting practice. More generally, emotional labour is surely inevitable to some degree in a service economy, so simply lamenting its necessity is of limited consequence. What matters is how it is managed, how it is recompensed, and what implications it has for the broader emotional life of those who carry it out. Yet Hochschild's fairly straightforward extension of Marx's humanism, and in particular his theory of alienation, makes it difficult to get beyond lamentation. The problematic assumption is that each person has a core human potential which alienation thwarts.

The alternative to such idealistic humanism, however, seems to be a vicious circle in which the only remedy for alienation is the ever more subtle alignment of a worker's psychology to the demands of work. Proponents of this alternative might argue with Nikolas Rose that the intrusion of management into psychology has the potential to overcome even corporeal resistance to it. If 'working hard produces psychological rewards and psychological rewards produce hard work' then perhaps '[t]he government of work now passes through the psychological strivings of each and every one of us for what we want' (1999, 119). Yet if this is happening, it is by no means happening universally. Even corporate managers, whose role in governing work such a development would presumably assist, appear to need what Robert Jackall calls 'a psychic asceticism of a high degree' in order to deflect the emotional strain their own roles would otherwise place upon them (1988, 203–4). Amongst managers, Jackall observed emotional withdrawal rather than emotional adaptation.

In any case, Rose criticizes our contemporary 'ethics of individual autonomy and personal authenticity' which creates a 'psy shaped space . . . at the heart of each modern individual'. In place of this, he asks, by way of a thought experiment:

> Could one not imagine another kind of freedom, whose ethics were resolutely 'superficial'? An ethics whose vectors did not run from outer to inner, and did not question appearances in the name of their hidden truth, but which ran across the outsides, between, among persons, where subjectivities were distributed, collective and oriented to action? An ethic, that is to say, that did not seek to problematize, to celebrate or to govern the soul? (1999, 272)

Clearly if one could imagine such a superficial ethic, the psychological intrusion of work might either be avoidable insofar as the depths of the psyche were irrelevant to it, or might be inconsequential insofar as that psyche was merely a construct derived from a flawed conception of ethics in the first place.

Rose's proposal for a superficial ethic is ultimately a proposal for a different kind of human self. It is not unimaginable, but the question is whether it is desirable. My interviewees were not engaged by superficiality, and experienced it, moreover, not merely as an absence but as a lack. They wanted to be able to invest emotionally in their work. One might argue that even that desire was derived from an oppressive psychological obligation to pursue personal authenticity. If the 'psy shaped space' could truly be purged from existence, then perhaps behaving with indifference to our own activity would not be emotionally strenuous. Yet such a purge seems distant indeed, and the collective illusion of a purge, or the ethical exhortation to cultivate a superficial self in which individuals do not believe, might be the least sufferable of all the ethical options.

Conclusion

The rules, conventions, and practices of the accounting profession are largely given for most accountants. However the facts of the matter, with respect to specific accounting problems they encounter in their day-to-day work, often are not. Those have to be constructed in ways that are acceptable to others within the field. Therefore despite the technocratic ideal and the desire for simplicity which will be discussed in Chapters 4 and 5, the fundamental benchmark for accountants is not transparency with respect to a truth which is out there, but performance with respect to the conventions of its production accepted within their profession. Such performance is not merely the passive fulfilment of a prescribed role, although it can sometimes feel like that, but it is also an ethically inflected practice through which accountants negotiate the relationships between themselves, their colleagues, and their work. A good performance is not, therefore, mere theatrical artifice, but may as we have seen entail suspension of disbelief, deep acting, emotional labour, switching mindsets, or adapting one's energy levels to the situation at hand.

The ethical dilemmas of accountancy, therefore, go beyond the simple opposition of truth and lies, and concern what Foucault would call the exercise of power through the production of truth (1980b, 93). Such power is by no means freely vested in the accountants I interviewed, but their performances are nonetheless powerful for an audience which understands how they are constrained, and can read more into them than a futile attempt at transparency. We have seen that the credibility and usefulness of the information accountants produce depends on how well they are seen to perform with respect to a variety of related standards, including competence, managing information, managing expectations, simplifying, and negotiating. Truthfulness in accounting therefore relies on an accountant's performance in both of that word's intimately related senses, concerning quality of work and concerning quality of presentation.

We have already seen that accountants' performances offer an example of what Sennett calls the expressiveness of convention in public life. Sennett's more general hypothesis is that the quest for intimacy undermines the expressiveness of convention and renders the modern individual an actor deprived of an art (Sennett 2002, 264). At this level, accountants are perhaps the exception that proves the rule. At least in their working lives, they practise a highly developed art every day. Their difficulty is that, as illustrated by Simon's anxiety over what his apparently supportive colleagues *really* think, they only seem able to validate that practice by conceiving of it in intimate as well as in performative terms. What accountants need, perhaps, rather than a superficial ethic, is an ethos which engages them deeply without demanding the intimate revelation of their psychological depths in order for that engagement to be believed in a given situation.

From the point of view of maximizing the truthfulness of accounts, the cultivation of such an ethos is a central challenge facing the accounting profession at the present time. Yet it is beyond the purview of simplistic demands that accountants 'tell the truth'. This kind of ethos, moreover, cannot simply be imposed by regulators from above: they can do little in this regard beyond supporting and encouraging practitioners as they gradually develop their ethos themselves. Both practitioners and regulators, therefore, need to start from a subtle understanding of accountants' current ethical relationship to their practice and of the future potential that relationship contains. For this reason, the next three chapters look closely at how account-ants presently construct facts. Chapter 3 uses a hypothetical scenario to give an overview of the process, and Chapters 4 and 5 look in more detail at its technical and its non-technical aspects respectively. Only after this closely focused exploration will we be in a position to consider the place of profes-sionalism and professional ethics, and the prospects for increasing the truth-fulness of accounting knowledge.

3

Champion Chicken

This chapter will examine my interviewees' responses to a brief scenario I asked them to read before we met.[31] The scenario presents a fictional company – Champion Chicken – which is discussing an accounting problem with its auditors. The problem is straightforward in technical terms. Interviewees might well have come across something similar themselves, and the relevant accounting standards are covered early in accountants' professional training. Nonetheless, the problem is what an accountant might call 'judgemental': something more than a competent application of the accounting standards is needed in order to resolve it. The scenario therefore offers a direct insight into how accountants construct facts in situations that are too ambiguous to be predetermined by rules.

The Champion Chicken scenario enabled me to explore how different interviewees responded to the same accounting problem, and to challenge them to explain their reasoning and defend it against possible alternatives. The results prefigure many of the issues addressed later in the book. We will see that, despite appearing to be technically definitive, accountants' strategies of simplification depend heavily on pragmatic and normative considerations. Failure to fully acknowledge these considerations, however, leaves accountants without an adequate language in which to debate their impact.

The text of the Champion Chicken scenario is reprinted below:

Champion Chicken scenario

Paul is an assistant manager in the audit division of Staines & Slough, an accounting practice in the United Kingdom. His most important client is Champion Chicken, a London-based supplier of ready-cooked rotisserie chickens to British supermarkets (turnover £200 million, profit before tax £0.2 million).

Champion Chicken has recently experienced financial difficulties. An economic downturn has meant that consumers have economized by buying uncooked or frozen chicken instead of ready-cooked products. Champion is forecast to breach its bank covenants next year, and has begun to negotiate new credit terms.

Champion Chicken's bankers, London Money, are insisting that it cut costs, and to enable it to do so they have financed the construction of a new centralized roasting facility on a brownfield site near Birmingham. The facility became fully operational shortly before the year end, after a series of teething troubles. The most serious of these involved setting the correct temperature for the ovens. Difficulties in doing this initially resulted in chicken worth £0.4 million being overcooked and therefore unusable.

Angela, the management accountant responsible for the new roasting facility, had submitted a budget to Steve, the finance director in London, for the cost of the project. Apart from the £0.4 million worth of overcooked chicken, costs have been in line with Angela's budget. She does not want to add the cost of the chicken to the asset value of the facility, as this would appear to be an overspend on her part. Similarly, she does not view the item as an operating expense, because it distorts the normal cost of roasting, which she is keen to demonstrate is lower at the new facility than before. She has reported the cost to Steve as an exceptional item.

Steve has informed his contacts in the City that Champion has rationalized its operations and is well placed to achieve revenue and earnings growth next year. A £0.4 million expense against profit would undermine his credibility and jeopardize his negotiations with London Money. He wants to capitalize the overcooked chicken along with the rest of the commissioning costs of the new roasting facility.

The audit partner, Geoff, is a new partner at Staines & Slough, and won the audit of Champion Chicken from a competitor two years ago. This was seen as a major coup at the time, and he is keen to maintain a strong client relationship. He has carried out several special projects for Champion recently, including helping them prepare information to support negotiations with London Money. Paul works on a few of Geoff's clients, and has a good reputation in the office. He hopes to be made a manager in a few months' time.

Paul has come across the overcooked chicken as a capital item whilst reviewing the audit of fixed assets. Champion Chicken's business is capital-intensive, with fixed assets totalling £300 million, and no mention of the overcooked chicken is made in the draft accounts. The accounts are due to be published in three days' time, so Paul is very busy finalizing the audit.

Three accounting options

Before looking at what my interviewees made of this scenario, I will outline the three accounting options suggested in it, indicating briefly what the accounting standards have to say about each one, and what the consequences of each would be for Champion Chicken's accounts. A suspension of disbelief is needed during this exposition, while I lay the groundwork for the rest of the chapter: it is important to understand the scenario from a technical accounting perspective before engaging in a critique of that perspective and its limitations.

The relevant parts of Champion Chicken's financial statements are its balance sheet and its profit and loss account (P&L). The balance sheet lists the assets and liabilities of the company at the end of its accounting year. The P&L summarizes its performance during that year, beginning with revenue (or turnover) and subtracting various expenses to leave the retained profit for the year, which reflects a corresponding increase in the company's assets shown on its balance sheet. Sample profit and loss accounts and balance sheets for Champion Chicken are given in Figures 3.1 and 3.2 (on pages 44–5), illustrating the effects of the possible accounting treatments. The numbers in bold are those referred to in the scenario or directly affected by a particular treatment. The other numbers do not affect the scenario, but have been added to complete the illustration.

Capitalizing the overcooked chicken, or from Paul's point of view making no change to the financial statements as he finds them (option A in Figures 3.1 and 3.2), means, in this case, accounting for the chicken as a fixed asset on the balance sheet. A fixed asset is an asset from which a return is generated through continuing use within the business, rather than through sale of the asset: Champion's new roasting facility, for instance, would be a fixed asset. If capitalized, the overcooked chicken would not feature as an expense in the P&L, and would not reduce the year's profit before tax figure of £0.2 million. Clearly, overcooked chicken is not a fixed asset in its own right, so the debate turns on whether its cost can be considered part of the cost of establishing the new roasting facility. Financial Reporting Standard (FRS) 15 states that '[t]he costs associated with a start-up or commissioning period should be included in the cost of the tangible fixed asset only where the asset is available for use but incapable of operating at normal levels without such a start-up or commissioning period' (paragraph 14).[32] Interviewees therefore discussed the precise nature of the teething troubles that gave rise to the overcooked chicken. If the amount were capitalized, it would be depreciated over the 'useful economic life' (FRS 15, paragraph 2) of the roasting facility, meaning that its cost would be transferred from the balance sheet to the P&L gradually over, say, sixteen years. Its impact on Champion Chicken's profit figure would then be £0.4 million/16 = £25,000 per year for each of the next sixteen years, rather than £0.4 million for this year only.

If the chicken were not capitalized, it would have to be treated as an expense. Two questions would remain, however: firstly, whether the chicken is an exceptional item or not (option B or C in Figure 3.1), and secondly, if it is, how it should be disclosed in the P&L (option B1 or B2). FRS 3 defines exceptional items as '[m]aterial items which derive from events or transactions that fall within the ordinary activities of the reporting entity and which... need to be disclosed by virtue of their size or incidence if the financial statements are to give a true and fair view' (paragraph 5). Exceptional items appear on their own line in a P&L account, rather than being subsumed into a larger number. They should be included in a P&L above operating profit (above the line), unless they fall into one of three categories of exceptional costs which should appear below it. The only one of these categories that might include Champion's overcooked chicken is 'costs of a fundamental reorganization or restructuring having a material effect on the nature and focus of the reporting entity's operations' (paragraph 20b).

Operating profit is often taken as a measure of the trading performance of a company, because it excludes the costs of financing, taxation, etc. that do not directly reflect trading. Therefore, if Champion's overcooked chicken was exceptional and could be disclosed below operating profit (below the line), then the company would appear to be performing better (option B1 in Figure 3.1, where a reader can more clearly see that, were it not for the exceptional item, Champion would be profitable). However most interviewees did not think that the company's restructuring constituted a change in the nature or focus of Champion's operations, because it was still in the rotisserie chicken business. Whatever the conclusion to this question, though, it is at the lower line of profit before tax that the overcooked chicken would cause Champion to report a loss. This is unavoidable if the item appears anywhere in the P&L, as a straightforward trading expense or as any form of exceptional item.

If the overcooked chicken was not disclosed below the operating profit line, it would need to go above the line, and the question as to whether it was exceptional or not would then concern whether to draw attention to it on a line of its own (option B2) rather than including it in the same line as the cost of successfully processed chicken (option C), and whether to provide some narrative explanation for it. From the point of view of a company trying to argue that the overcooked chicken should be excluded from an analysis of its underlying performance, the more prominent the disclosure the better, but from an auditor's point of view such prominence should be allowed only if the accounts would not otherwise give a 'true and fair view' (FRS 3, paragraph 5).

If the overcooked chicken is neither capitalized nor treated as exceptional, it must be treated as an ordinary trading cost, or expense (option C). Since expensing an item has the maximum negative impact on a company's reported performance, it is, according to the prudence principle enshrined in Statement of Standard Accounting Practice (SSAP) 2, the default option when no decision has been made to do anything else.[33]

Capitalization

Capitalization was generally the first option interviewees considered, as it represented the status quo in Champion Chicken's accounts. Ryan thought capitalization was acceptable as long as the situation was fully explained in words, although those words could be favourably written: he suggested that Champion 'sell it up a bit' with the 'reasonably open disclosure' that the cost of the roasting facility simply 'includes half a million pounds of stock used to ensure that the best quality stuff comes out'. Ingeniously, Ryan suggested that capitalization in the statutory accounts (satisfying Steve, the finance director) need not preclude treating the same item as exceptional in the management accounts (satisfying Angela, the management accountant).[34] Most interviewees,

Figure 3.1. Sample profit and loss accounts, Champion Chicken, year ended 31 December 2003

Option A
(Item capitalized)

	£(M)
Turnover	200.0
Cost of sales	(100.0)
Gross profit	100.0
Operating expenses	(80.0)
Operating profit	20.0
Interest payable	(19.8)
Profit before tax	0.2
Taxation	–
Profit after tax	0.2
Dividends payable	–
Retained profit	0.2

Option B1
(Item expensed as exceptional below the line)

	£(M)
Turnover	200.0
Cost of sales	(100.0)
Gross profit	100.0
Operating expenses	(80.0)
Operating profit	20.0
Exceptional item	(0.4)
Profit before interest	19.6
Interest payable	(19.8)
Profit before tax	(0.2)
Taxation	–
Profit after tax	(0.2)
Dividends payable	–
Retained profit	(0.2)

Option B2
(Item expensed as exceptional above the line)

	£(M)	£(M)
Turnover		200.0
Cost of sales		
Ordinary	(100.0)	
Exceptional item	(0.4)	
		(100.4)
Gross profit		99.6
Operating expenses		(80.0)
Operating profit		19.6
Interest payable		(19.8)
Profit before tax		(0.2)
Taxation		–
Profit after tax		(0.2)
Dividends payable		–
Retained profit		(0.2)

Option C
(Item expensed as ordinary)

	£(M)
Turnover	200.0
Cost of sales	(100.4)
Gross profit	99.6
Operating expenses	(80.0)
Operating profit	19.6
Interest payable	(19.8)
Profit before tax	(0.2)
Taxation	–
Profit after tax	(0.2)
Dividends payable	–
Retained profit	(0.2)

Note: £(M) = million pounds sterling. Numbers in brackets are negative numbers.

Figure 3.2. Sample balance sheets, Champion Chicken, 31 December 2003

Option A
(Item capitalized)

	£(M)	£(M)
Fixed assets		**300.0**
Current assets	70.0	
Current liabilities	(40.0)	
Net current assets		30.0
Total assets less current liabilities		330.0
Long-term liabilities (bank loan)		(150.0)
		180.0
Capital and reserves		
Share capital		1.0
Profit and loss account		
Brought forward	178.8	
Retained profit for the year	**0.2**	
		179.0
		180.0

Option B1, B2, or C
(Item expensed)

	£(M)	£(M)
Fixed assets		**299.6**
Current assets	70.0	
Current liabilities	(40.0)	
Net current assets		30.0
Total assets less current liabilities		329.6
Long-term liabilities (bank loan)		(150.0)
		179.6
Capital and reserves		
Share capital		1.0
Profit and loss account		
Brought forward	178.8	
Retained profit for the year	**(0.2)**	
		178.6
		179.6

however, rejected the capitalization option. It seemed absurd to be depreciating a highly perishable, useless item over the life of the roasting facility. Daljit, for example, just could not believe that such a large value of chicken being overcooked might have been deliberate, even as a test run.

Interviewees generally thought that the overcooking was most likely to have been a mistake. Alistair found this self-evident: 'Mistakes happen in business all the time.' Liam was more sceptical, though, and wondered whether the chicken really had been overcooked, or whether theft or fraud would be a better explanation of the cost. In any case, he thought there was something fundamentally wrong with 'the control process of the business to have allowed this to happen'. If even a much smaller amount had been budgeted for a commissioning period than what the overcooked chicken eventually cost, that would have demonstrated that a commissioning period was necessary, or at least originally planned, and Liam would have been more sympathetic to management's explanations. Most other interviewees also thought intention was important, and used Champion's budgets as evidence of intention at the planning stage. Sebastian dissented, however, saying that management's intentions were irrelevant to whether the overcooked chicken represented 'inefficiencies' or not.

The common thread through all these reactions is that my interviewees assumed that Champion Chicken's management think in a similar way to themselves. Management might be incompetent, they might make huge mistakes, or they might be corrupt, but nonetheless if they applied their minds to a business problem they would resolve it in the same way as would a given interviewee. The assumption is not unreasonable. Champion Chicken is, after all, in business to make a profit by roasting chickens, and since profit is itself a convention there are conventions concerning how it can be made. Nonetheless, the particular discourse surrounding these conventions simplifies in such a way that human agents seem interchangeable and transparent. There is therefore a presumed similarity between accountants' and auditors' thought: the latter audit accounts prepared by the former to at least some extent by reperforming their thought processes.

When pressed on the capitalization issue, Alistair simplified it with reference to an 'analogy'. If you used some concrete when building an apartment block, the concrete could not be extracted from the asset, and would therefore be part of it. By contrast Champion's overcooked chicken, being physically discrete, is not part of the roasting facility. Alistair's strategy here is to make the issue as simple as possible so that the solution would be obvious to 'even your normal layman. You don't have to be an accountant.' He can then appeal to common sense, and take a straightforward line which does not require too much effort to maintain. Sebastian also simplified, but by exaggeration rather than analogy: 'If the whole place you know, had fallen apart and you had to rebuild it again from scratch, you couldn't capitalize it twice.'

Joe saw his first impressions of the scenario as significant: 'My honest judgement when I'd read it through the one time...was that, in my head I made a judgement you'd have to write it off against profit and therefore anything else is by default, wrong.' Although Joe mentioned judgement, he did so in such a way as to render it opaque. His impressions were merely asserted, therefore, but legitimized by reference to his honesty. Furthermore, he stated his conclusion from 'my very uneducated level', which both denoted deference to the audit partner in the scenario (Geoff), and mitigated his responsibility for interpreting the accounting standards. Even if his conclusion turned out not to concur with Geoff's, Joe could still justify his thoughts by reference to an almost instinctive reaction that was somehow unmediated or authentic, and therefore reliable.

Profit

If Champion's overcooked chicken is not capitalized, it must appear in the profit and loss account, and must therefore reduce retained profit. The only debatable question is then how it does so, and which of the other profit measures are affected.

Profit is the ultimate accounting simplification. Because so much evaluation of a company's past and future and of its management is embodied in that single concept, profit is perhaps the point at which the attempt to portray a company in terms of accounting facts comes under most pressure. As the balancing item between income and expenditure, it is sensitive to all the assumptions made when preparing a P&L account. Gary identified profitability as the key 'fact' in the Champion Chicken scenario, because the need to improve profitability caused the restructuring, and consequently the over-cooked chicken, in the first place. He thought that capitalization would be the wrong option, but reflected the sensitivity of profit by squirming at length before stating a position that would adversely affect it. He would have 'serious concerns' and be 'sceptical' about the treatment. It is something he would 'bring up' with the client, but without being too specific: 'It definitely has to be disclosed somehow.' He said that 'you'd be very hard pressed to justify holding it as part of an asset', and that even if there was 'some small clause in the financial reporting standards which you could possibly bend...I wouldn't feel comfortable' capitalizing the amount. Only after all this indirectness did he feel confident enough to state that the chicken is 'basically a cost that would have to be written off'.[35]

Adrian, like several other interviewees, blamed unsophisticated users of accounts for making profit so sensitive: 'I mean there isn't one number that summarizes a company's position I suppose but people often behave as if there is...even if that is a bit silly.'[36] An item in the P&L can seem more important than the same item on the balance sheet, because on the balance sheet it would make little difference to a company's total assets, whereas in the P&L it could turn a profit into a loss. Adrian countered, however, that a small profit or a small loss should say something similar about the performance of the company.

Several interviewees, particularly those familiar with companies in difficulty, wondered whether Champion Chicken would remain a 'going concern' if it breached its bank covenants.[37] If not, the items on its balance sheet would need to be valued on a break-up basis, or in other words, according to the price that could be gained by selling them off quickly to pay debts, rather than according to the contribution they could generate through Champion's ongoing operations. At the margin of financial viability, therefore, the profit figure might have implications for every other valuation in the accounts. For Tom, the risk to the company made the accounting decision all the more important: 'I mean this is all very very dodgy because at the end of the day, all of these things do tend to come out in the wash around these things, when these companies go down the pan.' His string of clichés strikes a conspiratorial tone, as he tries to secure what is clearly a brittle position.[38]

Some interviewees also took Champion's low profitability to indicate the general incompetence of its management. An alternative explanation is given in the scenario (which relates falling profitability to market conditions), but nonetheless blaming management seemed plausible to interviewees when coupled with viewing the overcooked chicken as an error on their part. Joe doubted that the error itself was very significant. He worked it out to represent about two days' worth of chickens, and concluded that 'the number is huge but the mistake is not huge, and therefore it would be difficult, I think, to justify it as an exceptional item'. However, if the mistake was not huge, neither was it forgivable. 'I keep coming back to this but that's what they do, they roast chickens, and they made a mistake roasting chickens.' For Joe the nature, as well as the size, of the problem makes it unexceptional. Sebastian suggested that 'a lot of exceptional items that appear in accounts could probably be, if you really wanted to, traced to management incompetence', and would therefore be better accounted for as ordinary operating costs.

Just as we saw that Ryan demanded a formal disclosure under the capitalization option but then suggested how its impact might be softened, Daljit, whilst remaining strict about the numbers in the accounts, also offered damage limitation advice to Champion's management:

You've got to manage the expectations of the bank and demonstrate to them, by way of . . . sufficient disclosure in the accounts, that this is a one-off cost. And you know, you could say, 'and during the year, four hundred thousand of stock was written off due to initial', I don't know quite how you'd say it without making it sound horrendous, but 'initial production runs and blah blah blah'.

The importance of getting the profit number right is counterbalanced by a willingness to use the surrounding words to promote a desired interpretation of that number. The overcooked chicken can be glossed as a one-off whether or not it is categorized as exceptional. The subtle distinction between these terms apparently rests on the exceptional being a more exclusive category, which a company's management have to earn or deserve. Although Daljit, like Joe and Sebastian, demands the authority to judge exceptionality in the numbers, he is happy as business advisor to recommend that the events to which those numbers relate be reinterpreted in words on the same page.

Crystallizing fact

Having discussed some of the strategies interviewees used to decide between discrete accounting options, we can now look more broadly at how they crystallized the relevant facts out of the scenario in order to make that style of decision-making possible. How do accountants simplify events such that they can be presented as a finite collection of facts at all? In answering that question with respect to the Champion Chicken scenario, this section introduces issues that will be explored more generally in Chapter 4.

Despite my interviewees' pragmatism, Liam's sentiment is common to most of them: 'In a pure sense, it would be nice to imagine that auditing did not have so many grey areas.' Technical idealists might be cast as soft and unworldly, but not as wrong-headed. Joe, when asked what the facts of the scenario were, retorted: 'From whose perspective?' However, when I asked him whether that would influence his answer, he immediately responded in generic terms. This suggests that the adoption of different perspectives is perhaps tactical, but is not integral to the view of knowledge Joe and his colleagues have. They believe, apparently, in the objective facts of the matter.

Profit challenges this attitude by being so difficult to agree on. Gary used common jargon when he talked of 'recognizing' profit, rather than simply calculating it. Profit can be earned, but recognition implies that social valid-ation is integral to its having been earned. In this light, interviewees' technical framing of Champion Chicken's dilemma appears fragile. I tested its limits by asking Daljit whether anyone at Champion could persuade him that the over-cooked chicken represented a pilot of the roasting facility:

They could persuade me if they had, it's not so much they could persuade me, it's if they demonstrated certain additional information, I would agree that it was a pilot. But what they're not really doing is changing my view, what they're doing is, we're almost trying to find the truth as opposed to, we're trying to find a factual thing as opposed to my interpretation of it. Because in order for it to be capitalized, it has to satisfy certain criteria. If they can demonstrate those criteria, it's fine.

Belief in the pre-existence of facts is bolstered here by the prestige of the accounting discourse. Daljit's inflexibility aims to maintain his independence as an auditor. Its effect, though, is not to eliminate persuasion, but to demand a style in which that persuasion must occur in order to be effective. Either it must challenge existing facts, present new facts, or perhaps argue for a different way of applying the criteria according to which facts are validated. It cannot question the idea of a fact, or the criteria themselves.

In situations where there is acknowledged dispute between possible candidates for factuality, accountants can draw on a raft of evaluative concepts. For example, when I asked Alistair what the facts of the scenario were, he responded:

> I think it's about accounting judgements. It's about people taking different views on certain issues because if you were to look at accounting standards that are prescribed... then you know there are some prescriptions within them that would apply to that particular scenario in terms of interpretation. But it's not necessarily prescriptive in every single way and there's a degree of open interpretation of which some of the characters in this particular scenario decide to interpret in their own way.

> *So what do you think would be the right outcome from this?*

> Well in terms of what the answer is? I would see nothing wrong with treating that... as an exceptional item.

Alistair then went on to defend his conclusion in black-and-white terms. He apparently does think there is an answer, even though a process of contestation is necessary to reach it. One could attempt a taxonomy of his various evaluative terms. In this quotation alone, Alistair refers to judgements, views, issues, prescriptions, interpretations, decisions, answers, treatments, and wrongness. But a taxonomy would risk glossing over the contradiction, for instance, between Alistair seeing some interpretations as being open, and others as being prescribed. Alistair's thinking, fundamentally, is pragmatic: he wants to create an answer, but he wants it to be defensible by more than just assertion, and so he uses all kinds of near-synonyms to describe a process of fact construction acceptable to his peers. In case his defence fails, of course, he hedges: an opponent would find it much harder to argue against the claim that he could 'see nothing wrong' with his conclusion, than against what I pushed him to say, namely that it was right.

Alistair is also resisting the potentially moralistic connotations of my use of 'right' here. Joe did so more explicitly in response to the same question, which took him aback: 'The right, I mean I don't know what right means, but the proper outcome is that they account for their mistake and it's fairly clear and visible in their accounts.' In other words, if the accounting is clear and proper, then readers can draw their own moral conclusions. Accountants' collective desire to exclude normativity from accounting conceived as a technical process may be what makes it possible for an accountant to answer a question with 'I don't know what right means' in such a way as to make the question sound inappropriate. Yet the clarity Joe sought was ultimately not technical. For him, 'the accounting question is potentially a sideshow' compared to 'whether the evidence becomes clear or not', by which he means evidence of a deeper operational reality that underlies accounting technicalities. That reality is surprisingly normative: 'The real issue is, forget finance, the real issue is an operating screw up.'

Interviewees like Joe explicitly styled themselves as non-technically-minded: 'Don't ask me an accounting question for goodness sake.' Joe approached the scenario from what he thought of as a robustly common-sense perspective. He ran through each of the three possible treatments in turn, testing out narratives that would justify each of them. Only if those narratives appeared plausible did he then compare them against the accounting standards to see which were allowed. He made a few attempts to construct a story around capitalizing the chicken, speculating for instance as to whether it was overcooked in one batch or in several, but remained unconvinced, and so did not even consider whether the accounting standards would allow this treatment or not.

Where does the common-sense operational perspective's status derive from? Is it a well-founded reaction against counter-intuitive accounting standards? Or just a set of generally accepted prejudices that are immune from dispute? An oversimplified ethic of performative competence? Or pure pragmatism? The answer is unclear, yet the perspective allows Joe to be outspoken concerning what happened at Champion Chicken at the same time as being somewhat agnostic as to how the event should be accounted for. Liam explained the relation of accounts to reality as follows:

An auditor should actually understand how the business is working and how it's running and have a firm sort of intuitive grasp upon how it is that the company is actually performing, because the portrayal of a company's financial well-being or otherwise in a set of accounts is rather more like a painting than like a photograph.

To 'understand' is important, because accountants construct facts rather than merely recording them: in Liam's terms, they are painters rather than photographers. Yet 'a firm sort of intuitive grasp' sounds anything but firm. Liam is arguing that his understanding pre-exists language, but accounting itself is, after all, predicated on the assumption that understanding can be discursively represented and transmitted. If accountants struggle to use their public, technical discourse to formulate bases for decisions between possible facts, it seems that this leads them to rely in their non-public discourse on an operational perspective that they still cannot articulate. The problem is that this makes it impossible to debate whether that perspective is appropriate, or how it might be improved.

Circumstantial influences

The Champion Chicken scenario includes contextual information that is not relevant to the company's accounting problem in strictly technical terms. Yet when technicalities are insufficient to determine an accounting treatment, accountants do attend to such contextual information, and we will now explore the influence it has over their decisions. Whereas the findings of the previous section will be developed more generally in Chapter 4, the findings of this section will be developed in Chapter 5. This does not mean, however, that the technocratic practice of crystallizing facts can be understood independently of the circumstantial influences surrounding it: on the contrary, the primary finding here is that they overlap and are interdependent.

It is already clear, given accountants' efforts to persuade each other that their decisions are appropriate, that a major test of accounting practice is peer review. Joe, though keen that the underlying communication of Champion's situation should be accurate, nonetheless said that 'if the accounting treatment is solid ... well okay they're always going to choose the capitalization option because you know even if you write a note it's prettier than having losses'. Solidity does not mean objectivity, but being defensible to fellow accountants. Liam argued commensurately that if the overcooked chicken had been separately identified in Champion's draft accounts, Paul (the auditor) would have had a greater responsibility to approach Geoff (the audit partner) about it. It would follow from this that an auditor's view of the facts is framed to a significant extent by the way in which a client initially categorizes and groups the balances in its draft accounts.

Some interviewees did, however, consider the motivations of Champion Chicken's management when evaluating the company's draft accounts. Joe, for instance, cited the finance director's motivation to maintain Champion's funding in order to rule out his accounting proposal: 'Given that motive ... it would seem to me to be dishonest to capitalize it.' Dishonesty, for Joe, is not fully prevented by the accounting standards: he is concerned that Champion may try to exploit flexibility within the standards to hide its mistake from London Money. Joe reaches this conclusion by construing Champion as 'a business in financial trouble looking at getting itself into more financial trouble and within that context there are people who ultimately ... have a reason to hide that fact'. Joe does not ignore his client's motivations in order to focus on the technicalities, but uses those motivations as evidence of how the draft accounts are likely to be biased. Counteracting such bias is a matter of justice as well as technical correctness: when summarizing his reasoning, Joe said under his breath that he wanted to expense the chicken 'more than anything to spite him [the finance director], but that's beside the point'.[39]

It is not clear to what extent Joe's disposition to go against protagonists' agendas would be translated into acting against clients' wishes in real life. Certainly, we have seen evidence earlier in the chapter that other interviewees would be much more amenable. Adrian tried to pin down the limits to such amenability in the context of the Champion Chicken scenario:

By crooked I don't mean doing something illegal, I suppose. I mean someone who'd read this and sit down with a client and try to think up some way of producing some meaningful evidence that they could do what they wanted to do, and stick it on the file so that if it ever came out they could say: 'Well, look, we thought about it, we've documented it, we did this, we thought it was a reasonable thing.' That would not be a professional approach and I don't think many accountants I've worked with would approach it in that way. Whether they would ultimately buckle under or not, I don't think they would sit down at the outset and try to do what the client wanted.

Auditors are paid by those they regulate. Client relationships are important, but so is independence, and auditors must satisfy both requirements. None would be so crass as to take the 'crooked' approach Adrian describes, but the question is how far this is simply a matter of form. If they 'ultimately buckle under', as he puts it, then their professionalism is little more than an elaborate risk management etiquette.

Although Sebastian would not say that the risk of being sued ought to influence which accounting treatment an auditor might accept, he did believe that it ought to influence the amount of attention paid to determining that treatment. Champion Chicken, given its possible going concern issues, would demand significant attention. Liam criticized Champion's auditors for not finding the overcooked chicken sooner, but nonetheless wanted to explain their not doing so in terms of accepted auditing risk management: Was it 'economic' to test in sufficient detail to pick up this item? Liam's question relativizes and proceduralizes the failure. It was a probabilistic error, based on 'statistical likelihood' derived from 'a pragmatic stance'.

The interviewee who most clearly delimited his sphere of responsibility was Tom, whose 'primary thought' about the scenario was that 'I'm in a very fortunate position, never actually having to make a decision on this sort of thing, because all I would do is attempt to get all this information down in a portable format and then it would be up to the senior managers and partners'. He might make suggestions but 'would sort of bow to their greater knowledge and experience basically'. When he said that he would still be happy to defer to the experience of a superior who had signed off on a treatment he was sure was wrong, respect for experience seemed a less immediate concern than being off the hook. But the situation is not quite as simple as Tom abdicating professional responsibility. He inhabits an institutional structure that expects him to act within strict parameters. He is both a professional and an employee, and for him his status as an employee is the more significant. The implications of this for professional ethics are profound, and Tom's comments illustrate something paradoxical about the accountants I interviewed. They are highly adept at constructing and manipulating facts, yet they do so in a way over which they at least perceive that they have little control. For all their art, they do not often think of themselves as being creative.[40]

Conclusion

My interviewees all agreed that the complexities of the Champion Chicken scenario could be unproblematically simplified down to a few clearly defined accounting options. Most believed that there was a right answer, or at least that ideally there should be a right answer. However, as we have seen, they decided between the options by referring to their gut reactions, the alleged intentions and motivations of protagonists, and the likelihood of their decisions being criticized, for example.

There is a disparity, therefore, between the apparent clarity of an accounting decision once made, and the opacity of the decision-making process itself. Interviewees tried to bridge this disparity by using an intricate vocabulary of judgements, views, issues, interpretations, answers, and treatments to gloss a highly argumentative process as if it were technical. Yet that intricate vocabulary is not technical, but rhetorical. In practice, interviewees used it to persuade hypothetical peers that their conclusions were credible, legitimate, possible, acceptable, or conventional much more than they used it to claim that they were technically correct.

The Champion Chicken scenario demonstrates that there is necessarily more to accounting than technical correctness. Yet accounting's apparently factual basis, reinforced by its increasingly rules-based technical standards, obscures the ways in which accounting decisions such as that faced by Champion Chicken must be thought through in practice. My interviewees' technical public discourse leaves them struggling to articulate an ethos that is appropriate to the non-technical aspects of their work. Chapter 4 will show how accountants try to minimize this problem by keeping their work within the bounds of the technical, and will discuss the extent to which this strategy is successful.

4

Technocratism

Chapter 3 offered a specific example of a more general phenomenon that extends beyond accountancy. A contrast between apparently unproblematic facts on the one hand, and the pre-factual controversies through which they are crystallized on the other, is evident with respect to the construction of knowledge in many spheres, including science (see Latour 1987). However in accounting the prescribed form a fact must take structures the pre-factual controversies that can be engaged in. In science, the premises of knowledge are at least in principle negotiable, whereas in accounting, accounting standards establish the allowable form of knowledge in advance. This may seem to be an insignificant distinction given that in practice most 'normal science' operates within given paradigms (Kuhn 1962, 6). Yet it exposes a difference in motivation: where scientists might seek to advance knowledge at a paradigmatic level, professional accountants can in principle concern themselves only to know about particularities in a way that is consistent with their existing knowledge of other particularities.

There are therefore two pictures that could be drawn of the pre-factual controversies which take place in accounting, depending on how the accounting standards are viewed, and this chapter and the next will reveal the tension between them. In the first picture, accounting standards govern the form completed accounting knowledge takes, but not the means by which controversies are resolved. Although some forms of argument might be better respected than others, controversies are in principle conceived as open, and the disputants dispute using the full range of their rhetorical powers. That picture will be the starting point of Chapter 5. Here, however, I want to begin from another picture, in which controversies appear more closed because the resolution of controversy is approached technocratically. I define the *technical* in relation to accounting work as pertaining to techniques of knowledge construction that are generally accepted as resulting in facts. Such techniques may be derived directly from accepted readings of accounting standards, or from generally accepted accounting principles.[41] As Chapter 5 will demonstrate, the construction of facts is not necessarily the result of a purely technical practice; however, a purely technical accounting practice would necessarily result in the construction of facts. By *technocratism*, then, I mean the belief that the best method of crystallizing facts out of controversy is a technical one in this sense. In this second picture of pre-factual controversy, therefore, the structuring of controversies by the pre-scribed forms of the possible facts which might result from them is actively embraced rather than lived with or resisted. Technocratism entails embracing, reinforcing, and even maximizing such restrictions on accountants' methods of argumentation, and according authority to argumentation thus restricted. It is necessary to think in terms of technocratism rather than just of technicality, because, as we shall see, it is not always simply the case that the first picture of controversy represents an earlier stage in a linear process of fact crystallization than the second. My interviewees do make decisions as to whether to approach knowledge construction technically or not.

This chapter will explore how my interviewees' technical argumentation works. I will first establish the analytical vocabulary necessary to that exploration, under the headings of rationalization and framing. I will then look at how accountants delimit and maintain the parameters of the technical, and particularly at how and why they try to keep the technical frame as narrow as possible. I will extend that discussion to show how accountants also use technicality as a means of transcending dispute, or in other words of obtaining agreement whilst implying that no argument has taken place. Finally, I will explore the consequences of technocratism for both the construction and the credibility of accounting knowledge.

Rationalization

We saw in Chapter 1 that the factual status of accounting knowledge is a relatively recent historical phenomenon, and that it reflects the more general ascendancy of quantification as an authoritative form of knowledge in recent times. Contemporary technocratism must therefore be understood against this historical backdrop, the most salient elements of which, for our current purposes, are captured by Max Weber's concept of rationalization.

Weber uses the term 'rationalization' to describe the gradual increase in what he calls formal rationality in modern societies. Formal rationality for Weber refers to the 'calculability of means and procedures' (Brubaker 1984), as distinct from substantive rationality which refers to the value, from some predefined normative perspective, of an end to which formal rationality might be applied. By economic rationalization, I refer to a gradual increase in the 'formal rationality of economic action' in particular, which Weber glosses as 'the extent of quantitative calculation or accounting which is technically possible and which is actually applied' to economic questions (Weber

1968, 85). We will soon see that such rationalization has indeed been taking place. By referring specifically to economic rationalization, however, I avoid claiming that all aspects of modern life are being rationalized. Rationalization in one sphere does not imply rationalization in all spheres, and Weber himself was careful not to overgeneralize.[42]

In a deliberate departure from Weber's vocabulary, I have already referred to disillusionment and compulsion in Chapter 2. Extensive rationalization, I will suggest, results in a form of accounting knowledge that is not compelling, or in other words that fails to draw its creators and users into the perspective from which it describes the world. Disillusionment refers to the experience of accountants who are obliged to create or use knowledge that they do not find compelling. This terminology reflects my view, in contrast to Weber's, that the distinction between formal and substantive rationality is one that rationalization tends to establish but that does not exist a priori.[43] I will demonstrate empirically that the further economic rationalization progresses, the more difficult accountants find it to maintain their commitment to formal rationality as artificially distinguished from substantive rationality, and hence the more fragile the rationalization that depends upon that commitment becomes. Although I seek to explore a phenomenon accurately identified by Weber, therefore, that exploration cannot be concluded in solely Weberian terms.

The recent empirical evidence of economic rationalization is overwhelming. Accounting practice has, for some time, been becoming increasingly complex and increasingly tightly regulated.[44] This trend has been accompanied by an increasing reliance on accounting in the management of organizations, and a corresponding tendency actually to shape those organizations in ways which render them amenable both to accounting-based management and to control through the associated techniques of auditing (e.g. see Matthews, Anderson, and Edwards 1998; McSweeney 1994; Miller and O'Leary 1994; Power 1996; 1997). Such developments in the United Kingdom and elsewhere have made possible an explicit attempt to standardize accounting worldwide, spearheaded by the International Accounting Standards Board (IASB). The IASB's stated aim is to develop 'a single set of high quality, understandable and enforceable global accounting standards' (IASC Foundation 2007a). Both the ambition and the success of this project are striking. Its ambition is for economic activity to be defined and discussed in the same, or in directly translatable, terms everywhere in the world. Its success is demonstrated by the fact that nearly 100 countries already require or permit the use of, or have a policy of convergence with, International Financial Reporting Standards (IFRSs). IFRSs are already in use in all member states of the European Union, for instance, and a convergence project is underway to align international standards and those of the United States over the next few years (Deloitte Touche Tohmatsu 2007; IASC Foundation 2007b).

By claiming that rationalization is taking place in accounting, I do not mean to suggest that the current form of accounting embodies the only form economic rationalization could take (recall my argument, against Weber, that formal and substantive rationality are only artificially separable). Rationalization is consistent, therefore, with interpretations of accounting as constructing and shaping economic realities rather than merely describing them, both in its general design and its local application (Hopwood and Miller 1994; Miller and O'Leary 1994; Power 1996).[45] Ultimately, however, I will argue that advanced rationalization causes an erosion of the legitimacy of the general form of completed accounting knowledge. This is not the same as saying that individual accountants lack the legitimacy to specify what counts as accounting knowledge in particular situations, and therefore does not imply that rationalization cannot be occurring in the first place. The gap between accounting and the economic life it purports to represent is, moreover, sustainable, and may actually widen, because rationalization and disillusionment occur on different levels. Rationalization manifests itself in an overarching system of knowledge, sustained by accounting standards and policies, but it is undermined by disillusionment at a much more local level on the part of individual practising accountants.

Although I will return to discussing accounting's trajectory in the concluding chapter of this book, I am concerned here only with accounting practice at the present moment. Yet insofar as accountants are technocrats who prefer to construct facts according to formally rational standards, that implies at least that they behave in a manner consistent with rationalization. The questions firstly of how far technocratic accountants see themselves as engaged in an explicit project of rationalization, and secondly of whether they actually are the prime movers in the rationalization process or have simply become caught up in it, are more complex and must be postponed until our investigation is complete. In particular, we will not develop a clear view of the ways in which the conflicting impulses of technocratism and disillusionment coexist and interact until the end of Chapter 5. At the very least, however, our terms of reference in describing technocratic accounting practice here need to be consistent not only with the empirical observation that economic rationalization is taking place, but also with the idea that accountants' technocratism contributes to it to some extent.

Framing

The concept of framing is important to the analysis that follows because it makes it possible to discuss the multifarious specifics of how accountants separate facts from value statements in practice, at the same time as positioning their practice within the broader trajectory of economic rationalization.

Erving Goffman defines frames as 'principles of organization which govern events – at least social ones – and our subjective involvement in them' (1974, 10–11). Participants in a frame agree to become involved in it on mutually agreed terms in order to define and simplify their interaction. The more obvious examples of frames include play, theatre, and sport, but accounting can be understood in a similar way. Accountants establish a frame within which economic activity can take place in formally rational terms. In any given situation, this framing of economic activity must be achieved by excluding those aspects of the broader context in which that activity takes place that cannot be fully expressed in such terms (an example might be the social consequences of closing a factory). Determining what is to be translated into accounting terms and how, and what is to be excluded from the frame, is not in itself a formally rational process. What takes place within the accounting frame may appear formally rational even whilst the boundaries of that frame are maintained by means which necessarily go beyond formal rationality. The metaphor of framing therefore makes sense of accountants' paradoxical experience of constructing apparently rational knowledge by means which they cannot articulate in rational terms.

The idea that economic rationalization is taking place through the development of an accounting frame is not uncontroversial, however. Goffman's metaphor of framing is most familiar to economic sociologists through the work of Michel Callon, who borrows it in his edited book *The Laws of the Markets* to argue a position somewhat different to mine (1998a). It will be helpful, therefore, to clarify my own argument by engaging closely with Callon's.

In order to understand Callon's position, it is important to bear in mind that his overall 'point of view... consists in maintaining that economics, in the broad sense of the term, performs, shapes and formats the economy, rather than observing how it functions'.[46] The broad sense of the term here 'incorporates within economics all the knowledge and practices, so often denigrated, that make up for example accounting or marketing' (1998b, 2, 29). Yet Callon emphasizes that the economic frame exists only in relation to the social world from which it is abstracted, and thus that there are 'two diametrically opposed attitudes' that can be adopted towards it. One attitude sees a frame as normal and its unframed consequences, which economists call externalities and which Callon calls overflows, as leaks. The other sees overflows as the norm and framing as imperfect and difficult to achieve. Callon finds the former typical of economic theory, and the latter typical of constructivist sociology. However worthwhile the former attitude may be in creating clarity and frameworks, the latter emphasizes that framing is 'necessarily incomplete: first because a wholly hermetic frame is a contradiction in terms, and second because flows are always bidirectional, overflows simply being the inevitable corollary of the requisite links with the surrounding environment' (1998a, 250–5). If framing is to achieve useful simplification it cannot be either all-encompassing or disconnected from the wider world.

Callon, therefore, uses framing primarily to describe how actors in specific situations create economic calculability out of controversy, whereas I use it to describe accountants' sustained project of defining what counts as economic activity. These usages are not mutually exclusive, and as I read him Callon would agree that framing combines these shorter- and longer-term aspects. However his difference in emphasis leads Callon to make two arguments that contradict my view that rationalization is taking place, and I will now reply to those arguments.

Callon argues firstly that the growing complexity of industrialized societies makes framing more difficult, and secondly that experts are losing their legitimacy with respect to the construction of knowledge (1998a, 261–2). To the first argument, I would reply with the Weberian observation that the evolution of economic complexity has to a significant extent been contingent on the expansion of accounting, and to that extent cannot be seen as a threat to it (Weber 1992, xxxv). Where economic complexity has come first, moreover, accounting has developed in response to it. Framing may be becoming more difficult, but at the same time it is becoming more necessary to large-scale commerce. Complexity does not cause us to give up on accounting, but to resort to it.

Callon's empirical evidence that economic framing is becoming more hotly contested consists of reference to public controversies, for instance over global warming and mad cow disease (1998a, 260–3). Callon argues that there are more and more such examples with respect to which there is no consensus as to how overflows are to be defined and made calculable. He therefore suggests that frames and overflows require ongoing negotiation, and that consequently 'the market' is not 'inexorable' but 'must be constantly reformed and built up from scratch' (1998a, 266). Yet even if such examples are proliferating, increasing difficulties in framing overflows may simply reflect increased awareness of particular kinds of overflows rather than a pressure to reconfigure the economic frame itself. There need be nothing constant about the consequent framing difficulties: once the framing of a one-off public controversy has been resolved there is no reason to believe that it should necessarily need resolving again. The question is more one of how newly recognized or newly problematized overflows are translated into existing commercial terms than of how those commercial terms must be constantly reinvented to allow for them.[47] If awareness of, and debates around, overflows are intensifying as Callon suggests, that may indeed threaten the economic frame, but only from without. Translating overflows into its terms constitutes an attempt to entrench and extend that frame in its existing form, rather than to reform it or to rebuild it from scratch.

Metaphorically, this debate concerns whether economics itself (in Callon's broad sense that includes accounting) is rigid or malleable. Whilst Callon emphasizes the latter, technocratism in accounting emphasizes the former.

Accounting technicalities are by definition within the frame, and the technical resolution of an accounting dilemma proceeds by translating overflows into accounting terms, or excluding them, or not noticing them, rather than by trying to define new forms of commercial relationship which might account for them. As will be discussed in Chapter 5, the pragmatic question accountants set out to answer on a day-to-day basis is not how to accommodate experience within the technical frame, but how to squeeze it into it.

To Callon's second counter-argument, that experts are losing their legitimacy, I would reply that in accounting at least the experts are still accepted as arbiters of what counts as accounting knowledge. Therefore although Callon may be right that there is a problem of legitimacy it would be the legitimacy of the general form of completed accounting knowledge that was being called into question, rather than the legitimacy of particular knowledge constructors acting as experts in particular situations. Callon is right that the sheer variety of economic situations requires accountants to adopt multifarious strategies of what he would call disentanglement to make them comparable (Callon 1998b, 19). However, my interviewees do not only aim for the provisional and temporary simplification that disentanglement implies, but rather for the durable redefinition of commercial experience in accounting terms. Through crystallizing facts accountants aim to construct standardized knowledge, not merely to facilitate exchanges. Disputes over how to do this in particular instances are therefore not disputes in which the accounting frame itself is up for renegotiation.[48]

Callon, therefore, is right to be suspicious of the rationalization thesis, but for the wrong reasons. Rationalization, at least in accounting, is taking place. Yet accounting knowledge is becoming more rationalized at the same time as losing its compulsion. Callon is not sensitive to this lack of compulsion, because he excludes from his analysis the psychological and ethical aspects of economic actors, and without these compulsion has no meaning. Yet it is because purely technical knowledge ultimately fails to command ethical commitment that the more totalizing it becomes, the greater its demand on protagonists' suspension of disbelief, and the more likely they are to surface act, displacing significant debates such that they happen elsewhere and in other terms. Callon wants to liberate economic sociology from the idea that the market is 'cold, implacable and impersonal' (Callon 1998b, 51). Yet he does not need to, because to characterize the market in this way is to say that increasing technicality has itself undermined the compulsion of economic knowledge, which is a failure rather than a triumph of rationalization.

Perhaps Callon's difficulty stems from borrowing Goffman's concept of framing without also borrowing his interest in its relation to actors' 'subjective involvement':

Frame . . . organizes more than meaning; it also organizes involvement. During any spate of activity, participants will ordinarily not only obtain a sense of what is going on but will also (in some degree) become spontaneously engrossed, caught up, enthralled.

All frames involve expectations of a normative kind as to how deeply and fully the individual is to be carried into the activity organized by the frames. (Goffman 1974, 345)

A frame requires 'involvement' if it is to function effectively, because without involvement it is an empty shell that is not taken seriously. Yet the rationalization of the accounting frame increasingly undermines such involvement on the part of accountants.

Goffman talks of frames as transient constructions, existing for instance during a game or a theatrical production. Consequently, the brief period of involvement he refers to might be plausible without the frame having much compulsion for its participants. However the accounting frame is highly durable, and accountants must maintain their involvement in it across their entire careers. Insofar as they do not find the accounting frame compelling, their involvement must be maintained through a constant performative effort, with all the consequences already described in Chapter 2. To a greater extent than would be the case if it were more transient, then, the accounting frame cannot be interpreted without also exploring the nature of accountants' subjective involvement in it.

The metaphor of framing, therefore, offers important insights into accounting work, but in order to develop these insights I will need to apply it in a manner that differs from Callon's in two ways. Firstly, I will retain Goffman's interest in protagonists' subjective involvement in the frame, and secondly, I will focus on the frame's singularity and durability rather than on the heterogeneity of its manifestations.

Limitation of scope

Accountants themselves do not talk in terms of framing, but they do use various strategies in order to achieve it. Liam commented, for instance, that if he was writing a controversial report for a bank he would stick closely to his brief and 'report it in terms which are rife with caveats and limitations of scope'. Limitation of scope refers to the exclusion of possible areas of responsibility from the work to be done for clients, often by means of formal contracts. As well as using limitation of scope to restrict a report's content, Liam used another legalistic concept, duty of care, to restrict the readers who might rely on it. A report may, for instance, restrict duty of care to a company's bankers, and not extend that care to the company itself. This means that Liam's firm would accept no responsibility for any conclusions the company might draw from the report: 'We were writing a report for one party and while that may have been more widely circulated, we actually held no real responsibility to anyone other than our client in a legal sense.' Limitation of scope and duty of care are two very formalized examples of the strategies accountants use to define contentious matters out of their frame. The remainder of this section will describe several other strategies that pursue the same end. For ease of reference, I shall use 'limitation of scope' metonymically to refer to all of these strategies together.

It is worth noting initially that a set of accounts is a very narrowly focused written document. It aims to describe the economic affairs of a single organization at a precise moment in time, and its economic performance over a precise period. The precedence accountants give both to written over oral material and to numbers over words (as we saw in Chapter 3) restricts the scope of what can be considered technical, and therefore makes the technicality of that restricted sphere easier to maintain.

With respect to the Champion Chicken scenario, we saw that Alistair was more willing to say that an accounting treatment was not wrong, than to say that it was right. Francois generalized this negative approach across the profession: 'It's our risk averse nature that we don't like to say something's right, we like to say something's not wrong.' Joe was critical of his colleagues' reluctance to express positive opinions, and illustrated it with reference to the contrast he perceived between financial and operational experts. The latter, with whom Joe tried to identify himself despite being financially trained, were usually direct in their judgements. The former, however, 'will want to institute a whole series of caveats'. I asked Joe if this simply reflected his firm's risk management policy, and he responded that it went deeper:

It's a desire not to give an opinion; people are genuinely constrained about giving an opinion. It's risk management led, I think accountants are risk averse and therefore, it's probably the way they're trained, but it comes through in every accountant we work with.

Joe concluded that one of the most important attributes of a good accountant is 'honesty', but more than that, 'conviction': 'One of the hardest things . . . is standing up and, you know, challenging when you have to.' Fear of giving an opinion compromises honesty in Joe's view, and overcoming it is more important than 'technical' ability. Perhaps because this can be so difficult, Joe later said that 'the one thing I'm recognizing more than ever is, the one thing clients in the end appreciate, is honesty and open challenge'. Joe, like Graham as discussed in Chapter 2, is trying to articulate an ideal of truthfulness which goes beyond honesty defined either as not lying or as managing expectations in the self-interested sense. It is necessarily an ethical ideal: conviction is at once a statement of opinion and a commitment to a performance which asserts that opinion with rhetorical force.

Where my interviewees could transfer the responsibility for giving opinions to others, they generally did. Luke was relieved that a client's actuaries qualified their report on its reserves, because he could then attribute his firm's qualification of its audit opinion to them. Later, discussing the same client, he tried to construe an audit as implying minimal interpretation, since this was the responsibility of analysts covering the company's stock. The reluctance to express an opinion or interpretation is clearly in tension, however, with the monopoly on proper opinions and interpretations claimed by my interviewees. They seemed to want both to be authoritative and not to have to apply that authority.

Luke offered an example that illustrates why the distinction between saying something is not wrong, and saying that it is right, is important. He recalled a client that had, in a metaphor alluding to profligate waste if not wilful arson, almost 'burnt through' its insurance cover with respect to its underwriting business. The client's six-monthly review for the stock exchange, however, made no mention of this. Luke considered the omission to be misleading, but did not feel empowered to object: 'They weren't writing anything which was fundamentally wrong, they hadn't burnt through it, the fact they were within a million of doing so didn't kind of go against what they were saying, so we had to like just say "yes fine".' Luke reassured himself by suggesting that analysts could have worked out the full picture by piecing together information from elsewhere. Liam, in a similar situation, justified helping a client to present its failings 'in their best light' to its regulator by saying that 'an experienced user of that sort of report will probably be able to determine' the underlying situation. He thus downplayed the influence of his presentational advice, at the same time as recommending that his client follow it. But why would the client even want to present a misleading view, if readers of its report could not be misled?

If readers of accounts are postulated as being responsible for, and capable of, reading between the lines, accounting decisions can seem hardly to matter. Ryan emphasized that a bank lending money should always look at sensitized forecasts, which display the relative probability of various possible outcomes. In this context, the decision over Champion Chicken's profit figure loses any absolute significance, and Ryan eagerly washed his hands of it with rhetorical alacrity and considerable relief:

I mean they really should be saying to themselves: 'What if the price of chicken goes up five percent? What if the animal rights people scored some huge victory and you have to allow all chickens access to outdoor light and you can't have boiler houses full of battery hens?' . . . That should be in anyone's mind if they're thinking about the business sensibly. I can't believe that a reasoned investor is going to weigh everything on, what are we talking about, two hundred thousand out of two hundred million, so point one of one percent. Whether it's making a profit of point one of one percent or whether it's making a loss of point one of one percent, will influence some people. And if this is a quoted company, I'm sure there will be private investors who think 'well, that's alright, it's making a profit'. But that's, 'do they deserve protecting from themselves?' seems to be the question. And I'm inclined to say 'no'. I don't think, what can you do? You can't protect people from everything. I'd let them capitalize it.

Although he does not use the term, Ryan's strategy for excluding the differences between the accounting options from his decision-making frame, and thus for allowing the client to account for the overcooked chicken as they want, is to render those differences immaterial. Statement of Auditing Standards (SAS) 220 defines materiality as 'an expression of the relative significance or importance of a particular matter in the context of the financial statements as a whole. A matter is material if its omission would reasonably influence the decisions of an addressee of the auditors' report' (paragraph 3).[49] Determining what would reasonably influence the decisions of an addressee requires the auditor to project, as Ryan does, a normative vision of how it would be reasonable for an addressee to think. SAS 220 offers little guidance as to how materiality might be assessed in practice, because it is 'a matter of professional judgement' (paragraph 4). Interpretations of materiality within audit teams can range in practice from mathematical models to experience-based gut feel, with rule-of-thumb percentages of particular types of balance, or monetary values fixed at the start of audits, being the most common. Yet as Ryan's example illustrates, materiality is often a means of justifying why a problem can legitimately be passed over. Insofar as materiality limits the scope of accounting work by legitimizing prioritization of the use of time, it can seem like a pragmatic consideration which is merely disguised as a technical category.

Adrian, like Ryan, questioned the materiality of Champion's overcooked chicken. 'The point about profit is it's the difference between two potentially quite big numbers. . . . Total income's two hundred million, total expense a hundred and ninety-nine point eight million, does it matter if you're one million out?' Yet the judgemental aspect of materiality is illustrated by the fact that Adrian worried about whether setting a materiality level on the basis of these gross figures would disregard the emphasis users of accounts place on profit. He also suggested that the materiality of an item affecting profit would depend on how that profit compared to previous years. For instance, if Champion had made a £20 million profit in each of the last five years, the difference now between a £0.2 million profit and a £0.2 million loss would seem less material in the context of the huge drop in profitability either figure would represent.

Materiality is clearly a site of controversy. That controversy concerns framing as well as prioritization, as can be demonstrated by juxtaposing such judgements of materiality as discussed above with the scrupulousness with which auditors check and recheck accounts for the slightest arithmetical error or inconsistency. Nothing is immaterial at this stage, the rhetorical effect of which is to imply a spurious precision. Once a framing decision has been made, and an item is either deemed material or immaterial, what falls within the frame receives disproportionate attention, so that it can be presented according to the fiction that a technical practice has resulted in the perfect accounting fact. Once recognized as such, a material item has a status which differs from that of an immaterial one by more than just magnitude. The connotations of the word 'materiality' in general usage, with respect to having material substance or being materialized, are not out of place.

Against these descriptions of the limitation of scope, it might be objected that the scope of accounting has actually increased over time. Statutory accounts now represent increasingly complex items, such as intangible assets and fair values.[50] Some voluntary initiatives go further, for instance 'triple bottom line' reporting, which seeks to account for social and environmental as well as financial costs and benefits (Henriques and Richardson 2004). Yet despite the enthusiasm of their proponents, such adoption as these initiatives have achieved can, to a significant extent, be interpreted as a reluctant response by the accounting profession to external forces. Mainstream accounting displays at least some tendency to exclude difficult controversies (notably social and environmental questions) from the accounting frame rather than seeking to appropriate and resolve them. Technocratic approaches to matters already recognizable in accounting terms might result in an increase in the intensity of accounting's formal rationality, but not an increase in its scope.[51] Even insofar as accountants do welcome the increase in accounting's scope at the level of policy and regulation, this attitude nonetheless coexists with the limitation of scope at the level of day-to-day accounting work.

Transcending dispute

As well as limiting the scope of the accounting decisions they made, my interviewees also tried to make them in such a way that they seemed not to be decisions at all. Technocratism helped them to achieve this by enabling them to claim that their decisions were just the inevitable, factual results of a technical practice, rather than the unpredictable results of controversy.

The desire to transcend dispute became evident when I asked my interviewees to describe the most intense dispute they had experienced professionally. I was given one of two answers in most cases. Either interviewees talked about a dispute which occurred at work but which did not concern an accounting treatment, or they claimed that they had never been involved in any intense disputes at all. From the first response, one might conclude that making accounting decisions was not actually the most important thing my interviewees thought they were doing at work. This is less surprising than it might seem given accountants' focus on their performances as discussed in Chapter 2, and relatedly on pragmatic considerations as will be discussed in Chapter 5.

The second response, on which I will focus here, does not mean that there is no controversy in accounting – clearly there is – but rather that my interviewees strongly resisted my provocation to characterize such controversy as 'intense dispute'.

When I asked Joe about the most intense dispute of his professional life, he described how he had finalized a merger benefits forecast. Merger benefits are the financial benefits derived from merging two businesses, generally through economies of scale, eliminating duplication, operational synergies, and suchlike. They are notoriously difficult to quantify. Forecasting profitability is difficult enough, but merger benefits are the difference between the sum of two forecasts (one for each of the existing businesses to be merged) on the one hand, and the forecast for the combined business (which relies on untested assumptions about how smoothly the merger will go and how the combined entity will operate) on the other. The difficulties are compounded by the fact that forecast merger benefits partially determine any price paid in connection with a merger, and the willingness of banks to finance it. In Joe's case, the two merging companies' directors had a strong interest in maximizing the forecast merger benefits in order to gain funding for the deal. Yet although Joe recalled his meeting with them as a dispute, he did not treat it as such at the time:

> We spent the process of a week going round and asking some very difficult questions and I then got delegated the task of going to a meeting with the two boards of directors and telling them they could have fifty and walking through the model step by step taking them from their number through a bridge to fifty.... I thought we would have hours of argument but they actually accepted the logic and couldn't do too much with it.... They actually couldn't argue with it because we got our facts in order.

Joe approached this dispute as an impartial 'task' or 'process', armed with a formal financial 'model' that he used to define the terms of debate. Facts are 'our facts' rather than 'the facts'. Joe's spatial metaphor of walking through a model and across a bridge illustrates how the directors were made to enter into his discursive frame, and so were rendered unable to challenge it except from within. Joe is not really surprised not to have had 'hours of argument'. Instead, he is claiming that he dealt with a scenario which could have led to hours of argument in such a way as to preclude it.

For Joe, this was a war story concerning the triumph of accounting over personal interests. His logical approach was designed to protect him as 'we'd been warned by various chief executive officers: "You can't do that to us, if you want the post merger work, if you want to be paid."' In order to neutralize such pressure, Joe focused on details of calculation: '"Well you made some calculation mistakes which take off five million; you got their average salaries wrong so you can't have another three million."' Yet forecast merger benefits are inherently debatable, relying on assumptions about all sorts of future possibilities. Joe successfully focused attention away from such assumptions, with respect to which he could be less sure of winning arguments, and in this sense his technical framing was itself an argumentative strategy.[52]

Daljit offered another example of how technocratism can enable controversy to be avoided. When determining whether a client should carry a provision[53] against possible litigation, he recalled (accurately) that paragraph 23 of Financial Reporting Standard (FRS) 12 requires a provision to be made if it is more likely than not that it will be used:

And this is now an area of judgement. Very much so and it's interesting, we developed a test which is quite successful and I was very pleased with, where we said: 'You've got a provision for litigation of two million on your balance sheet. For this to go away, how much would you pay?' And the company would say: 'Oh well, probably pay a couple of hundred thousand.'

'So what you're saying to me is you wouldn't pay a million.'

'No, I wouldn't.'

'Well, if it were more likely than not, you would be happy to pay half the cost by definition. If you're not happy to pay that for it to go away, it's not more likely than not, because you clearly think there's a chance or a strong chance that you won't have to pay it.' And that was the approach we adopted with some success. I remember the finance director even started doing this more likely than not within his report to the board as well. So he bought into that idea if you like. He bought into the application of that theory.

Daljit talks here in the context of having accepted that this is very much an area of judgement. His aim is merely to make that judgement transparent and debatable, which he achieves by simplifying it into a decision rule. He refers repeatedly to the success, not to the accuracy, of his decision rule, and his dramatization of its enactment illustrates that he sees it as a highly pragmatic device. To a large extent he has simply rephrased the question that must be answered with respect to the litigation: determining what one would pay for a potential cost to go away surely entails determining its likelihood, which requires as much judgement as before. But Daljit's rhetoric is technical to the point of quasi-science. He refers to the development of a test, and the application of a theory, and in so doing makes the adoption of his approach persuasive to the finance director.

Daljit's test aimed to ride out a change in accounting standards. FRS 12 was introduced to prevent companies from holding large provisions and then releasing them to boost profits in years when operating earnings were low (a practice known as 'profit smoothing'). The introduction of this standard in 1998 required a culture shift for Daljit's client because 'it goes against their whole psyche of preparing accounts on a prudent basis', and therefore of keeping ample provisions. That psyche, though encouraged by the earlier Statement of Standard Accounting Practice (SSAP) 2 (1971), was for Daljit intimately bound up with the desire to smooth profits. He was confident enough that this was his client's motivation to argue 'tooth and nail' against any creation or release of provisions they might suggest. His scepticism was such that he seemed tempted to define his stance as an auditor simply in opposition to the client's perceived strategy, rather as Joe did with respect to the Champion Chicken scenario.

During the time that Daljit worked for this client, the partner he reported to changed. The first partner was keen to implement FRS 12 strictly. The second, however, 'was from the old school and said: "There is no risk to us or to you if you carry a certain level of provisioning."' This change demonstrates the level of discretion available to auditors even with respect to an apparently prescriptive standard. The latter partner's emphasis on risk harks back to SSAP 2's prudence principle, adopting the view that if you have provisions and are careful about how they are released, then there is a limit to what can go wrong. As Terry put it: 'You're never going to get sued for being over-prudent.'

I asked Daljit whether, if he told the company to release a provision, they would just think up a new provision to replace it. He agreed that this would happen to some extent, but as an auditor Daljit thought he should consider each proposed provision separately, rather than in the round: 'If they can justify it, that's fine and we all know that companies have pluses and minuses, that they can always bring things to the forefront.' Technocratism focuses Daljit on detail, and leaves him without a basis for critiquing the whole.

Daljit tried to assert his authority by giving his client one year to adjust its provisions to an appropriate level in accordance with FRS 12, and after that allowing provisions to be released only when the company could 'absolutely demonstrate' that its circumstances in respect of the provided item had changed. However he acknowledged that such absolutes are elusive, and therefore used the presentation of provision movements in the accounts as a further check against profit smoothing. The movements were separately itemized in a note on provisions, and totals for new provisions and for releases were shown in a separate exceptional column in the profit and loss account. Daljit saw this as achieving a transparency which was some consolation for the figures disclosed not being those he might have preferred: 'Admittedly, your profit figure is still the figure they wanted to get to, but people can see what comes from operations and what comes from exceptionals and write-backs.'

Daljit's discussions of provisions with his client became ritualized performances after FRS 12 had been in place for a few years: 'They were well rehearsed and so were we by the end of it.'[54] Daljit did not claim to have changed his client's way of thinking, but rather to have 'agreed on a way forward'. The technical device he established was rhetorically appealing to the client, because when the finance director presented his results to analysts they could be shown to be 'sensible', to 'tie in', and to have 'internal consistency'. It does not, however, seem to have succeeded in becoming the frame of reference within which the client actually thought about what provisions it should make, and how it should disclose them. Despite all of Daljit's efforts to implement FRS 12, he still suspected, at the time of his interview, that the client would have successfully engaged in profit smoothing in the two years since he had last worked on their accounts.

Daljit's style of reasoning is typical of how interviewees tried to deal both with the Champion Chicken scenario and with debates they reported from their own experience. They tried to simplify their representations of economic life by generalizing their method of doing so across different situations. This suggests a self-fulfilling prophecy: accounting describes a regular world because it sets out to construe commercial situations as comparable to each other. As Joe put it when I asked him if one client was in the same industry as another: 'No, this is financial services but it's the same principle in everything.' Universalizing their way of thinking was a means by which interviewees maintained their claims to impartiality as auditors. Most at least began by saying they would ignore the interests of Champion Chicken's management when considering how to account for the overcooked chicken, and technocratism is a way to claim to have done so. However, impartiality thus conceived can also legitimize reluctance to enter into debate. When Gary could not unambiguously determine an accounting treatment, his solution was simply to disclose the various possibilities. By making known his uncertainties to readers of the accounts, he deferred responsibility for crystallizing facts to them. In this way, the accounting frame can be preserved almost by definition: if accountants cannot resolve a question within their frame, then it is not a question for accountants. Insofar as accountants can exercise jurisdiction over what is knowable or unknowable in accounting terms, they can avoid being compelled to enter into the negotiations that might otherwise take place when framing becomes problematic.

The consequences of technocratism

Accountants do often have to stand their ground with clients. As Gary put it, referring to a basic disagreement over whether a batch of caravans could be said to have been sold or not, 'it's only worth getting in an argument if you think you can change their opinion or they can change yours'. It is difficult to see how Gary could deal with such a dispute other than simply to insist on the technical definition of a sale. The issue at stake, therefore, is not the existence of a technical sphere per se, but the effect that a generalized sense of technocratic authority has in situations where it is not clearly grounded. We have already seen that technocratism can foreclose legitimate as well as spurious debates. This section will explore the consequences of technocratism in more detail.

In both the previous section and in Chapter 3, we saw that the technocratic assumption that all accountants think similarly discourages engagement with unfamiliar viewpoints. The accounting frame's exclusivity in this sense is, moreover, generally experienced as a source of prestige rather than as a limitation. For Sebastian, to say that a client was using 'a fairly non-accounting argument' implied that the client's argument was ephemeral and unsubstantiated. Jason felt the prestige of accounting's perceived technicality acutely, saying that 'I feel I'm technically inferior to my colleagues',[55] and later that 'I'm a qualified accountant but my technical skills and knowledge of [the accounting standards] have slipped so much I almost think I'm a fraud in some cases'. He retains these insecurities despite having deliberately moved into less technical work because he found it more interesting. Francois displayed the arrogance which is the flip side of Jason's insecurity: 'I suppose that's why clients employ us, to go in and be technically superior.' Graham similarly did not see any need to engage seriously with those outside his profession: 'I don't know how much they really need to know about what you're trying to do, you know.' The implication, as for instance where Graham dismissed non-experts' 'stupid questions' at an Annual General Meeting, is that those outside the profession simply need to learn from those within it. In a more guarded instance, Graham discussed a lay reader of accounts not as being wrong, but euphemistically as being likely to form a different 'opinion' about a company if only he knew how to 'interpret' the accounts. His approach here is almost evangelical: all comers are appreciated, but for their potential to think more like him rather than for how they think now.

Liam offered a quintessential example of technocratic authority, having acted as an expert witness in court. Yet he described the expert witness as a role he could play well enough by surface acting, rather than as an ideal character he aspired to embody. He said that 'expert witnesses actually have a responsibility to the court rather than to the parties, however they, inevitably being appointed by one side or the other, take specific sets of instructions and represent things as they have been shown them'. This language uses technicality to dissociate a witness from the effects of his or her conclusions. Witnesses are passive: they are appointed, carry out instructions, represent things without influencing them, and deal only in specifics. Their responsibility is circumscribed as a matter of legal fact. Liam's speech is carefully constructed of complex, layered clauses, like a legal document. Yet all this technical rhetoric is being used to justify the conscious bias that surface acting makes possible. Liam implies that 'things as they have been shown them' need not constitute an impartial view, but without having to say this.

Liam did distinguish between being 'misdirected' to the wrong areas of enquiry, for which he takes no responsibility, and being 'swayed' in how he approached the areas he does look at, which he said would never happen. He therefore accepts responsibility for how he acts, but not where. He is concerned to perform appropriately within a frame without being concerned about what falls within or outside of that frame. Liam went on: 'Our role is as a support to one particular line of the litigation and therefore we will direct our work to favour that or allow our work to be used in a manner which does not necessarily reflect every aspect which it might do.' He is therefore prepared to assist in the framing of his work to suit his client's case. Liam treats it as 'accepted within the system' that even expert witnesses have their own interests and paymasters and so approach the court from biased positions. Technocratism can make such bias immune to legitimate sanction, since it recognizes no basis on which to adjudicate between technically allowable positions.

Alistair took technocratism a stage further by adopting a very narrow definition of what might count as fraud. I asked him at what point he thought it would become fraudulent for a client of his not to make a provision in its accounts against non-recovery of a debt. He argued that it was legitimate not to provide against a debt even if, say, the debtor was in severe financial difficulty and the debt was very unlikely to be recovered. Only if the debtor had become insolvent and been wound up, and there had not been sufficient money to pay the debt, 'then that's factual, that supports that the debt's non-existent. Then that clearly would be a case of fraud'. To be called fraud, misrepresentation needs to be factual, and however strained a judgement or interpretation may be, if it is not indisputably counterfactual, it is not fraudulent.

Greg was preoccupied with what he called the neutrality of accounting. He did argue that a profit made by a fair trade coffee company, for instance, was qualitatively different to a profit made by, say, a tobacco company. However he sought to reconcile this view with seeing profit as a formally neutral device, and with expecting nothing but amorality from those who sought to make it. For example, he proposed taxes 'linked to the inherent good or badness of an industry' as 'one of many different triggers that us in a society and governments can use, or different stakeholders can use, to encourage good corporate behaviour or encourage bad corporate behaviour'. Good and bad are placed in the same grammatical positions here, in otherwise identical clauses. Inherent goodness or badness may be recognizable to people within an industry, but the distinction is functionally irrelevant. It is the role of an omniscient civil society or government to establish a framework within which the functional irrelevance of the distinction between good and bad still results in a socially desirable outcome. Commercial organizations simply react mechanically to stimuli. Ethical agency for Greg can be exercised either through one's selection of occupation, or through one's political influence over the commercial world, but not through one's behaviour within that world.

Perhaps Greg is simply rationalizing the uncomfortable truth that to survive in commercial life one has to observe severe constraints on one's ethical autonomy (Jackall 1988). He talked clinically of 'a match or a mismatch between my values and what the clients are asking for', which was beyond his capacity to influence. He observed that his firm would help almost any business in any industry to improve its profitability: 'The business model's neutral.' But Greg's problem, that he finds this formal neutrality stifling, remains. 'It doesn't link in with my own values, my own approach, I like organizations, I like people who have a sense of their own direction, who have a sense of identity, and aren't neutral, aren't amoral, they have a purpose bigger than just making a certain amount of profit.' Greg can see a rationale behind what he calls neutrality, but cannot accept it ethically, or at least not without considerable effort. He later described working in a 'numbing environment' in this respect.

To put his difficulty in Weberian terms, Greg is struggling to maintain his commitment to the formal rationality of accounting as a generally applicable means. His job is to make such means available to the users of accounts, whose substantive ends are no business of his. Yet Greg seems almost aware that the distinction between formal and substantive rationality is an artificial one, and that the formal rationality his accounting facilitates makes some substantive ends visible and pursuable at the expense of others. In his words, there is a link between 'the way people's minds work' in accounting, and a failure to engage fruitfully with the 'broader issues of community building and motivation and being a responsible business':

It's not who they are as people, I think if they went off on a retreat and started doing team-building courses for ages and started painting. . . I think their brains would change slightly. But the grooves people's brains are in, in the professional services firms and a lot of multinationals, are such that they don't slot into that way of thinking.

It is not necessary to take on the amateur psychology here to see that for Greg thinking as an accountant is a mechanical experience, which makes his brain feel like a mere object which can be moulded into grooves and slots.

FRS 5 makes a distinction between form and substance which is not the same as Weber's. It characterizes form as the legal form of a transaction, and substance as its commercial effect. FRS 5 requires accounts to represent substance, but nonetheless states that 'the FRS is not intended to affect the legal characterization of a transaction, or to change the situation at law achieved by the parties to it' (paragraph 46). The accountant's perspective is seen simultaneously as more factual than, and as subordinate to, the lawyer's. The peculiar negotiation of the boundary between the two which thus arises in practice is best illustrated with respect to my interviewees' work regarding tax. Adrian argued that a lot of tax work involved 'inventing commercial purposes' in order to avoid tax. As long as there was a commercial purpose behind an action aside from avoiding tax, any tax saved by that action would be considered avoided rather than evaded, and so the saving would be legal. Simon recalled his firm having helped a client to set up a series of transactions solely for tax avoidance rather than for commercial purposes. It had, however, advised the client on the risk that the tax authorities might see the transactions as tax evasion. In the event, the courts determined that they were evasion, but Simon's firm was not implicated because it had not *intended* to assist evasion. As Simon put it, very pragmatically, 'we thought we were putting in place...a structure that worked'. The underlying desire to save tax here is thought to be distinct from both the legal form and the commercial substance of the case, both of which have evolved into malleable formal categories with technical definitions. As a result, trying and failing to 'invent commercial purposes' to avoid tax can seem a legitimate activity. FRS 5's distinction between form and substance therefore has the effect, contrary to its intention, of creating another layer of technical artifice, rather than grounding accounting in commercial reality.[56] Yet this difficulty seems insurmountable insofar as accountants experience their work as a purely formal exercise. Accountants' technical framing systematically derecognizes not only the substantive viewpoints of non-accountants, but also of accountants themselves.

Conclusion

This chapter has shown that accountants are technocrats to a significant extent. As we also saw in Chapter 3, they often adhere to a technical means of constructing accounting knowledge because they believe that this is the best way to do so. However, accountants' technocratism has several problematic consequences. Through the limitation of scope, it can engender a narrow conception of their responsibilities in relation to the construction of knowledge. When accountants seek to transcend dispute, a generalized sense of technocratic authority can deny alternative viewpoints a hearing. Technocratism can encourage a mechanical way of thinking, legitimizing the impression that only absolutes matter, and that in grey areas anything goes. Accountants' technocratic authority, nonetheless, enables their disengagement to seem not an abdication of responsibility, but an ethically principled stance in itself. Those who express no opinions can seem not to be passive, but to be above the fray.

The technocrat clearly embraces, and to some extent furthers, economic rationalization. Yet paradoxically, as the rationalization of accounting knowledge advances, technocratism becomes a harder mindset to sustain. The abstraction of formal from substantive rationality makes accounting facts seem ethically neutral and therefore superficial. Accounting knowledge itself then seems less compelling even to those who create it, as they find that what seems most important to them about the events they account for cannot be described in technical terms. Accountants therefore find themselves obliged to construct knowledge that lacks truthfulness in their own eyes. Their frequent response to this, I shall argue in Chapter 5, is to abandon technocratism, and to approach their work with a pragmatism that simply brackets the question of truthfulness out of everyday consideration.

5
Pragmatism

Pragmatists privilege ends over means, for instance by manipulating systems or relaxing standards in order to get a job done. Unlike technocrats, pragmatic accountants admit various possible means by which a controversy might be resolved depending on the end in view. This does not mean, however, that technocratism cannot be pragmatically motivated: we saw in Chapter 4 that the adoption of technocratism is itself often a strategic choice.

Although I will argue that the distinction between technocratism and pragmatism is ultimately an artificial one, there are nonetheless several factors which serve to reinforce it. Accountants' training tends to establish a distinction between technical knowledge that can be transmitted in a training centre's classroom, and a capacity for judgement that can only be acquired on the job.[57] Additionally (and ironically), the more complex and technocratic accounting regulation becomes, the more pragmatically accountants must approach their work in order to get anything done. Yet this chapter will show that pragmatism in accounting runs deeper than that. Highly rationalized accounting leaves its users and creators disillusioned with it, and inclined to exploit it as an abstract construct rather than to sustain it as a compelling system of knowledge. Insofar as accounting knowledge itself is not compelling, then the manner in which it is created and used is more likely to depend on what else seems important in a given situation.[58]

Graham illustrated the extent to which accountants can become disillusioned with accounting knowledge, when he explained why he rarely bothered to enter into accounting disputes: 'Ninety-nine per cent of the time, if it's not perfect, no one's really going to know, and no one's really going to care. So no, I haven't really come across anything where I've had a fundamental disagreement with someone about how things are being treated.' Graham retains a technocratic sense of what would be 'perfect', but technical perfection seems increasingly irrelevant from a practical standpoint. He justified himself on the basis that published accounts are not very important anyway: 'I'd be quite surprised if people actually do read a set of accounts.' When I asked Graham if he had a final word at the end of his interview, he concluded with a reflection on auditing: 'It's useful but limited, limited in its use [laugh]. But I'll still carry on working [laugh].' He is aware of the tension in his position, but his disillusionment leaves him unable to address it. He resorts instead to a hollow resolve to keep going on, doing his job for no other reason than that it is his job.

If accountants were limited to a straightforward choice between technical correctness and a pragmatism presumed to be incorrect by contrast, Graham's comments might be the logical conclusion of their disillusionment with rationalized accounting knowledge. Yet we saw in Chapter 2 that accountants must make decisions about where to focus their technical attention, and in how much detail to work, which are negotiated in performative terms. By contrast to the technical conception of accounting that appears to be explicitly literal and self-sufficient, the performative conception of it seems more clearly metaphorical, with accounting being described more or less explicitly as theatre. This chapter will build on Chapter 2 by discussing three further prevalent extended metaphors which cast accounting practice as strategic, sporting, and familial. I group these metaphors under the heading of pragmatism because they were most often invoked when my interviewees described how their actions deviated from those prescribed by their default technical discourse. Yet we shall see that the metaphors express much more than straightforward deviance, because they embody competing perspectives on accounting practice.

We saw in Chapter 4 that even apparently technical resolutions of accounting dilemmas are rarely the result of a technical process, and often cannot be so. In any case, the contrast between the metaphorical and the technical is not clear-cut, because the technical itself could be seen as an extended metaphor likening accounting to science or economics. However the metaphors of performance, strategy, sport, and family are less publicly and explicitly accepted as appropriate ways in which to conceptualize accounting work. Consequently, conclusions drawn in their terms are potentially more controversial than those drawn in technical terms. Nonetheless, explicit disputes over metaphorical perspectives never occurred in the reported experience of my interviewees. I will suggest that this is because metaphorical conceptions of accounting work are not seen as sufficiently concrete to be rigorously argued for or against. Therefore, although we shall see that particular metaphors express much more than pragmatism, when differences between them arise they do tend to be resolved in inconsistent ways according to the demands of pragmatic expediency.

Many of this chapter's empirical conclusions could be drawn without contextualizing them within a discussion of the extended metaphors of strategy, sport, and family. Yet doing so reveals that although the choice between metaphorical perspectives may be pragmatic, those perspectives are at least somewhat coherent in themselves. Appreciating them as metaphors helps to bring their coherence to the fore, to validate them as rival perspectives alongside technocratism, and to provide a richer understanding of accountants' ethical thought and practice. Yet there are two prior assumptions entailed in attaching functional significance to such metaphors: firstly, that language can influence thought, and secondly, that users of metaphorical language often cannot readily reduce their meaning to a literal equivalent. Before proceeding, I therefore need to defend these two assumptions.

Metaphor and thought

The anthropological linguist Benjamin Lee Whorf studied cultures that use languages radically different to English. By comparing their languages to ours, he argued that linguistic variations across cultures cause corresponding variations in how people think (see Whorf 1956, especially 84–5). He found language to be influential both over which ideas are easiest to grasp when explained, and over which ideas are most likely to develop at all.[59] Whorf argued that languages do not become dominant simply because of their functional superiority, but also through association with dominant cultures. He therefore associated differences in language with differences in world view, and consequently with different priorities for action.[60]

The argument of this book that accounting language both affects the ways in which accountants are able to evaluate their actions, and could be different, relies to some extent on a Whorfian argument about the relation between language, culture, and thought. Whorf's position has been much debated in linguistics, and significantly undermined by those who emphasize the universal elements to human cognition (e.g. Chomsky 1988; Wierzbicka 1996; for an overview see Gumperz and Levinson 1996). The result of these debates, however, has been to make positions at either extreme seem increasingly untenable, and the compromise conclusion that language can have at least some, but not total, influence over thought is sufficient for our purposes here.

Insofar as accounting is a discourse conducted in pre-existing languages such as English, rather than an independent language in its own right, it is distinguished not as a language but as a particular way of using language. Insofar as Whorf's argument is correspondingly applied to language in use rather than language as such, it gains both a broader and a weaker applicability, since regularities in language use are more likely to derive from communicative conventions than from constraints built into the language itself (see Clark 1996, 353). Emphasizing language in use therefore localizes the debate. Precisely how much influence a discourse has over thought varies according to the discourse in question. It seems reasonable to suggest that the accounting discourse's influence is enhanced by the profession's explicit efforts at standardization and simplification, and by its possession of some of the attributes of a distinct language (such as its own concepts and vocabulary). Empirical evidence of its influence will appear in the sections that follow.[61]

An epistemology, particularly with respect to metaphor, follows from this view of language. Where the belief that objective reality can be clearly and unambiguously described in language might privilege the literal, a constructivist view that our perception of the world is inherently mediated by culture and language would not create such a clear hierarchy between literal and nonliteral statements. Andrew Ortony relates the two classic views of 'metaphor as an essential characteristic of the creativity of language; and metaphor as deviant and parasitic on normal usage' to the two sides of this broader debate about 'the relationship between language and the world'. 'Since, for the constructivist, meaning has to be constructed rather than merely "read off," the meaning of nonliteral uses of language does not constitute a special problem. The use of language is an essentially creative activity, as is its comprehension' (Ortony 1979, 2). This view is consistent with seeing the distinction between accountants' technical language, which styles itself as literal, and the metaphors which are the subject of this chapter, as an artificial one maintained through a process of framing. As Willard Quine puts it:

It is a mistake . . . to think of linguistic usage as literalistic in its main body and metaphorical in its trimming. Metaphor, or something like it, governs both the growth of language and our acquisition of it. What comes as a subsequent refinement is rather cognitive discourse itself, at its most dryly literal. The neatly worked inner stretches of science are an open space in the tropical jungle, created by clearing tropes away. (1979, 160)

This chapter highlights the importance of tropes to an accounting language which obscures them.[62] By referring to sporting, strategic and familial conceptions of accounting as metaphorical I do not intend, therefore, to trivialize them by implying that the equivalence between term and referent is somehow less direct than when accounting interactions are cast as technical. I intend simply to highlight the richness and opacity of accountants' language and thought by contrast to the transparent directness that a rhetoric of technicality implies, despite itself being at least somewhat metaphorical in any case. I therefore define metaphor as I. A. Richards does: 'In the simplest formulation, when we use a metaphor we have two thoughts of different things active together and supported by a single word, or phrase, whose meaning is a resultant of their interaction' (1936, 93). This definition does not assume that one of the thoughts is literal and the other fanciful, but that both combine to produce a meaning which did not exist until the combination.[63] Indeed, a metaphorical argument can be successful on its own terms only if its audience does not assume that it could be made more literally.

We shall see in this chapter that accountants' use of metaphor goes beyond the comparative. They do not, for instance, think of accounting as being like sport, but rather they make a sport of accounting. When they use metaphorical terms to describe what they do, those are often the primary terms in which they conceptualize their work.[64] Therefore, although in the sporting example we might say that sporting vocabulary applies less directly to accounting than it does to sport itself, nonetheless the metaphor of accounting as sport results in meanings which are not reducible to a comparison between accounting and sport. Accounting being conducted as sport transcends the literal question of whether or not accounting, otherwise described, is like sport.

Metaphor thus offers a way for accountants to think themselves into a particular kind of practice. To make a sport of accounting is to develop a particular orientation to that work. Losing the capacity to assess the metaphorical against the literal might seem to suggest a loss of purchase over tropes. Yet the factual is not the exclusive preserve of the literal, or of the apparently literal. In accounting, technocratism merely makes it seem so. If particular metaphors are defined out of accounting's factual frame, then claims made in terms of those metaphors will inevitably appear as value statements between which the frame itself offers no basis for adjudication. In what follows I shall therefore suggest that a less technocratic approach to the construction of accounting facts would make the knowledge embodied in the non-technical metaphors accountants use more legitimate, more debatable, and therefore more useful. The evaluation of different metaphorical perspectives is both difficult and important, as Wayne Booth explains:

[I]f rational criticism of values is possible, however difficult, then we have an immense obligation to build and improve our repertory of standards and our ways of talking about standards. In this perspective, criticism of metaphoric worlds, or visions, becomes one clear and important – perhaps the clearest and most important – instance of a general human project of improving life by criticizing it. And it is a project that will necessarily entail the use of metaphor; literal propositions will not be adequate to convey many of the judgments that our criticism must attempt. (1979, 63–4)

My aim in this chapter is to make the metaphors on which accountants rely explicit, and hence to open them up to this kind of criticism.

Strategic pragmatism and risk

Strategy is the metaphor that comes closest to articulating the pragmatism I have suggested accountants appeal to in order to select between competing metaphors. It is also the metaphor they are most likely to defend explicitly as an alternative to the technical conception of accounting. The strategic metaphor, then, both exemplifies the pragmatic approach that accountants disillusioned with accounting knowledge tend to adopt, and constitutes the terms in which that approach is often justified.

Alistair rejected the vocabulary of my interview questions where it might have threatened his pragmatism. For instance, when I asked him for examples of when he had not told the truth, he responded: 'I wouldn't say not told the truth, but not given them the story, if you like.' Strategic pragmatism is also deeply embedded in accounting slang. Sam, for instance, called a loan a 'funding solution', and Simon's euphemism for a company losing money was that it had incurred a 'cash-flow disadvantage'. Sebastian talked of being 'on strong technical ground rather than weak technical ground'. A Freudian slip by Graham illustrated that, for him, technicalities can simply be a gloss on pragmatic disputes: 'If there was a big enough situation then you know, sorry a big enough error or difference, then you know I hope I'd be brave enough to stand up to people.'

A subset of the strategic metaphor relates to military strategy, and many of my interviewees referred to their work in warlike terms. With respect to the instance discussed in Chapter 2 when Jason resigned from a previous job over a fraud, he called escalating the matter to the audit committee 'a bit of a nuclear option' and speculated that he did not do so because he was not 'brave' enough. Eventually, he said, the matter 'blew up in their face out of all proportion really'. Gary recalled 'beating [a client] about the head with the rules', but cautioned against 'fights with the management' even when 'they think they can strong arm you'. Undisciplined fighting is something clients may try to draw accountants into, but to which they should respond with the more prestigious discipline of a strategic military campaign. Jason thought it important not to 'burn bridges' between himself and possible informants. Sebastian, however, had found himself 'bored' by 'regimented [auditing] work', and glamorized his current non-audit role in terms of individual military heroism rather than communal military organization: 'the opposing side will cut you down' if you 'chance your arm' instead of behaving with 'brutal honesty'.

Liam commented that if there is fraud in a company 'we will go in', and that it is important to 'take a firm stand' in support of correct accounting treatments. This imagery asserts the heroic accountant against the depravity and mutability of his or her environment. Barry had a similarly heroic self-image, describing himself as a man of action, 'sleeves rolled up working with people', physically 'closer to the management team than just a consultant', 'in there with the finance director', and, like a sheriff from a Western movie, prepared to 'give . . . both barrels'. Having one's sleeves rolled up and commenting that 'you could drive a bus through these forecasts' appeals to a no-nonsense working-class pragmatism, which was also postulated in my interviewees' appeals to operational reality and the man in the street with respect to Champion Chicken. Terry similarly described the core of his department's activities as its 'bread and butter' work. The military virtues of strength and physical heroism, and perhaps a particular style of strategizing, also reinforce a stereotypical masculinity. That masculinity can then be threatened by failure or embarrassment. Simon, with respect to a dubious tax avoidance scheme, commented that 'I certainly don't want to be caught with my trousers down advising a scheme like this'. In a professional environment highly sensitive to self-presentation, such metaphors of physical exposure and disgrace are extremely powerful.

Pragmatism, however, legitimates compromise. As Gary put it, 'you have to make a balance between being fair and allowing the business to actually operate'. He takes technocratic dogmatism as a sign of immaturity, and looks back on the time when he would have said ' "it's wrong, therefore you don't do it" ' as an early stage of his development: 'I mean you also have to be reasonably commercial, you have to take a view on small differences which don't distort the financial statements, it's not worth sort of falling out over.' To 'take a view' is common accounting slang for making a decision on limited evidence, or letting something pass which is not worth arguing over, and these two senses have a tendency to merge. Adrian recalled an unusual situation in which a clean group audit opinion was signed for a French conglomerate with no year-end audit work at all having been done on one of its UK subsidiaries. The subsidiary was inherently low risk, it had been audited in previous years and the audit partner knew the people involved. Although the audit of the subsidiary was a significant part of the work done by the UK audit team, it was not expected to reveal any figures material to the group. Adrian therefore reflected that, given pressures of time, 'the partner was right to feel fairly confident that nothing had gone wrong with that business', but he nonetheless wondered whether 'it makes a bit of a mockery of it, I mean if the partner... can make that judgement why bother doing the audit?' Adrian lacked the partner's experience, but as he saw it the partner's authority to take a view, based on experience, was being extended beyond its legitimate bounds.

There are, nonetheless, situations in which a willingness to take a view seems necessary if accountants are not to be paralysed by technical uncertainty. Joe recalled that when he was working on a company valuation for one party to a corporate merger, the firm working for the other party 'got booted off the job because they just didn't get it, they couldn't bring themselves to sign an opinion on something which was so intangible'. Joe mocks the technocratic sensibilities of the rival firm by contrast to the simple violence of being 'booted'. As was the case here, many accounting valuations are based on assumptions about the future that cannot be verified technically. It may be necessary to assume, for instance, that an asset will last for a certain period of time, that debts will be recovered, that stock can be sold, or that a business is a going concern. In such cases, as Barry put it, 'all you can do is challenge someone's assumptions... the more robustness you can get around the assumptions the better'.

Technocratism and strategic pragmatism are not always directly opposed, however. Within accountancy and business more generally, the discourse of risk management has become increasingly influential in recent years (Hutter and Power 2005; Power 2007; more broadly, see also Beck 1999). Risk bridges the divide between technicality and strategy by making strategy a technical matter. As Michel Callon puts it: 'Seeing risks everywhere...tends to make very different situations homogeneous.... The idea, for example, of distributing risks between social groups or different actors is a technocratic dream' (Barry and Slater 2002, 288–9). The discourse of risk extends the technocratic project of making things comparable by legitimizing the appraisal of possibilities in terms of probable consequences. Quantified probabilities coexist as aspects of a known present, despite their mutual exclusivity as possible futures.[65]

Niklas Luhmann contrasts the risk-based style of dealing with possibilities with a different style which, he says, preceded it. 'The individualism of risk-calculating merchants, learning from experience, attentive to news, making decisions on the basis of a well-judged mix of trust and distrust, replaces the individualism of the hero holding out against all kinds of danger and fit for all manner of unhappy surprises' (1988, 100). Luhmann's distinction between danger and risk emphasizes the consequences of risk-taking being the direct responsibility of the risk-taker. Risk management reduces the scope of possibilities that risk managers are prepared to respond to, but renders them responsible for their pre-emptive management of those possibilities, rather than merely for their preparedness to deal with them if they arise.

Perhaps the peculiar kind of responsibility associated with risk management explains why an audit partner Kumar worked with, for instance, worried so much about the non-accounting consequences of a difficult audit decision. He found himself beset by risks: Would his firm lose the audit? Would his reputation be damaged? Would his career suffer? The partner apparently thought of himself as being responsible for all of these possible consequences of his decision. A strategist, it seems, forfeits the possibility of innocence. Responsibility of this type encourages a risk manager to exclude what he can from his purview, and hence from the assessment of his performance. Such an approach was discussed in Chapter 4 as limitation of scope.

Accountants talk a lot about risk, and risk management is enshrined as a principle of audit work in the United Kingdom by Statement of Auditing Standards (SAS) 100. Although the relevant risk is formally that of material misstatement in accounts rather than of being sued (SAS 100, paragraph 12), or in other words of error rather than punishment for error, the two were often conflated in the minds of several interviewees. As mentioned in Chapter 3, Sebastian described the commercial risk of being sued as self-evidently being an appropriate indicator of how much work he should do in order to be sure of an accounting treatment.[66] The discourse of risk, then, may make strategy technical, but it also tends to legitimize the resolution of technical disputes according to the imperatives of strategic pragmatism. As the next section will show, accounting can develop so far in this direction as to take on the character of sport.

Accounting as sport

Games played to win are strategic, so the sporting metaphor I shall discuss in this section is closely related to the strategic metaphor. My interviewees frequently described their work in sporting terms. Graham, for instance, commented that 'it's quite enjoyable when you get a result' and referred to a summary of unadjusted differences (a list of the issues found during an audit) as 'our score sheet'. The most successful accountants, according to Sebastian, are those who can 'win the work' in the first place. Such sporting references are very general, and although my interviewees alluded to a variety of specific sports, such specifics seemed incidental to their meaning. What is noteworthy about my interviewees' language, therefore, is not that they use sporting metaphors as such, but the frequency with which they do so and the influence those metaphors have over how they view their work.

It is worth noting at the outset that there are peculiarly English connotations to sport which go beyond the parameters of any given game. Helen Kanitkar, reviewing adventure tales written for English boys before the First World War, noted that the ideal sporting boy was a privately educated member of the upper class, fit and skilful, but also instilled with qualities of loyalty, pride in achievement, leadership, and teamwork (1993, 186–8). It is a matter of debate as to how much influence such a version of sporting masculinity still has, but undoubtedly it has some. It certainly seems to have retained considerable resonance in the 1950s, when an emphasis on accounting principles over rules could be credibly defended in such terms as these:

In this country we do not favour written codes. As a nation, we prefer a man to be judged by his peers rather than be condemned by the written word and we can still pride ourselves upon knowing instinctively what is 'done' or 'not done'; what is 'cricket' or 'not cricket'. (D. V. House, a past president of the ICAEW speaking in 1956, cited in Millerson 1964, 160)

Although I will postpone discussion of the complex relation between rules and professionalism until Chapter 6, this background nonetheless helps to clarify the kind of sporting analogy my interviewees presumed between accounting rules and the rules of a game. A certain scepticism about rules survives in their milieu, as does a shared sense of propriety, albeit in an altered form.

Alistair remembered preparing a set of accounts according to German accounting standards. He consistently described them not as clearer or more precise than the English standards, but as 'strict'. He saw the German rules as limiting discretion, rather than defining appropriate action. Alistair wanted to know what could 'actually be potentially shown' in a certain way. Like a sportsman, he respected the rules at the same time as seeking to exploit them. He saw himself as operating within a formal structure, but nonetheless as being allowed and indeed required to play at the limits of the rules. Ryan, similarly, looked on his colleagues' attempts to slide their proposals past his firm's risk management team as a matter for indulgent satire rather than criticism, reflecting his view that 'the firm needs people who can say yes when it is just on the right side of the line'.

The deference to rules implied by conceiving of accounting as sport is therefore somewhat different to that implied by technocratism. In Chapter 4, we saw that Alistair was willing to accept an accounting treatment as legitimate so long as it was not explicitly forbidden by the rules. The sporting metaphor establishes a different, though clearly complementary, threshold of legitimacy, by merely requiring that an accountant construct an argument, however tenuous, that a proposed treatment is compatible with the rules. Kumar, in an unguarded moment, even commented that 'I don't necessarily think there's anything that's sort of impossible in terms of what you can or can't do'. The way in which possibility can be stretched is further illustrated by Liam's comment that 'I don't think I'm likely to be corrupted, however, at a certain stage I think it is possible that the arguments in favour of taking an illegal or an unethical view would be possible'. Liam's talk of a possibility becoming possible aims to make its probability seem remote. However, the rhetoric of possibility actually makes the matter binary rather than probabilistic: something is either possible or it is not, and Liam concludes that his corruption is possible. If an argument is possible, it is as useful as any other possible argument, however tenuous. Liam implies that possible arguments pre-exist him, being part of the field of play established for him by the rules of the game, and thus being factual rather than subject to evaluation. Kumar, however, discussing a controversial accounting treatment, recalled that 'there was a huge amount of time spent on disclosure type arrangements . . . that was almost another way of sort of being able to take that position'. Kumar meant that by providing supplementary information in a set of accounts, he was able to justify an accounting treatment that might have seemed misleading in the absence of such information. His cleverness with disclosure made the accounting treatment possible. He was 'able' to use the controversial treatment in the dual sense of possibility and also, because he created that possibility, of skill.

It is clearest with respect to tax accounting that the exercise of skill in creating possibilities can tend towards obfuscation. Several interviewees found tax avoidance work exciting, associating peak performance with pushing boundaries in a way that is reminiscent of the ethos adopted by Enron's accountants and managers, as discussed in Chapter 1. Where tax liabilities are uncertain, for instance, accountants can write to the tax authorities asking for their opinion. Simon said that in practice doing so can be used as an opportunity to gain permission for tax avoidance: 'There are various clever [things] you can do in your letter to try and pose it in such a way that they don't realize they're agreeing to that, but that's to do with the skill of writing a letter.' Adrian described his involvement in tax avoidance schemes as follows:

When I was producing accounting advice [as an auditor], I would give a very clear explanation, 'this is what is happening, there are various different transactions which relate together in this certain way', and I don't think those clear explanations of what was going on would be what they [the tax advisers in Adrian's firm who worked for the same client] would submit to the Inland Revenue.[67] I think what they would submit to the Inland Revenue would be, erm, as confusing as possible, you know.

Adrian concluded: 'I don't know how the system works, I don't know if the Inland Revenue can say, "show us an explanation of what the fuck's going on, this is too complicated, show us something a bit more sensible". I don't know if they can do that.' He assumes that the Inland Revenue work in terms of similar conditions of possibility to those through which accountants conceptualize their activities as sport.

The sporting metaphor also helps to explain some aspects of accountants' interactions with clients. A partner in Luke's firm had been repeatedly preparing his client's reports for the Lloyd's insurance market on time, despite receiving the necessary information from the client at the last minute. On one occasion Luke described, the partner had his team complete a report on time by working all night. However the partner then held the report back for a couple of hours, missing the deadline and causing the client to be fined, or in Luke's words 'penalized'. Luke did not otherwise describe the incident in sporting terms, but the sporting metaphor nonetheless helps to articulate what happened. The client's repeated refusal to play fair by providing information sufficiently in advance led the auditors to try to reassert the rules of engagement. Completing the work on time remained highly important, however, even when the client was not playing fair. Winning the game in this sense had intrinsic value in an almost heroic sense: 'We got it done actually, we got it done.' Only in victory did Luke's partner then feel self-confident or self-righteous enough to make a highly symbolic gesture to his client's directors, audit committee, and shareholders. Moreover, the gesture was construed by his staff not as wasting their nocturnal labours, but rather as rewarding them. They had earned a delicious conspiratorial moment with him, which Liam remembers vividly: 'The partner...was like "no, let's wait", so we waited until one [pause], one thirty and he said "right, now give them clearance".' This experience cannot be explained simply in terms of commercial self-interest, because the client was never told that the report was actually completed on time. Concerns over control, authority, achievement, and fair play in relation to clients are operating here beyond what is relevant to optimizing the profitability of the client relationship.

We can now generalize about accounting conceived as sport. Sportspeople are judged according to whether they win, or in the financial world, whether they make money. The importance of winning makes competitiveness not only socially acceptable, but prized. To talk of skill in competition implies that interactions are threats or opportunities to be overcome or exploited. Yet particularly in large firms, accounting is a team sport. Good players are team players, who respect the hierarchies within the team, and are disciplined in pursuing team objectives. They all think in a similar way, and being on the team is an opportunity to learn that way of thinking. The team is gendered, and assumes a shared masculinity.

Accounting as sport emphasizes playing within and stretching the limits of the rules, rather than evaluating the appropriateness of the rules to any given situation. However, there is a strong unwritten ethos of fair play to which everyone is expected to adhere. Sportspeople also take pleasure in their sport for its own sake, enjoying the personal challenge of improving their performance. Nevertheless, however engrossing it might be, sport is ultimately about play. Sport is confined to the sports field, and is not thought to overflow. Events on the pitch have limited consequences off the pitch. Sport is serious only within its own terms, and accounting, therefore, can seem like a game that can be played without broader moral consequences.

Firm as family

The final group of metaphors I want to discuss primarily concern accountants' relationships with colleagues in their firms, rather than with their work. These are distinct from their relationships with clients, which, although touched on above, will be more fully discussed in Chapter 6. I will focus on the paradigmatic example in which relationships with colleagues are described as if they were relationships with family members, although as we will see there are several variations on this theme. In the narrow case of the metaphor – accounting firm as family, accountants as children – the comparison is not to a realistic family but to basic folk stereotypes as to how families ought to work. The fact that the metaphor only crudely reflects its source domain, however, does not undermine its importance in making sense of several aspects of accounting practice.

Before looking at the clearly familial metaphors used by my interviewees, I will begin with their more general fraternal language. Barry related to his boss as courtier to king, talking about what it was 'within my gift' to do and about who could be brought into the 'circle of confidence' on a delicate matter. Jason, who did not receive a position of responsibility he had expected within an audit team, said he had thought he was 'being groomed . . . to take over' and was concerned about the 'discourtesy' of someone being 'catapulted in over [his] head'. As might be expected given the importance of appearances in accounting as at court, he was concerned primarily because of his loss of face in front of his peers.

Such heightened courtly language was unusual amongst my interviewees, but the sensibilities it describes were not. Daljit commented in a revealing juxtaposition that his firm was 'very cosy, very hierarchical and you can just keep plugging away . . . for most people who stay there, it's their one and only job in their life'. The large accounting firms themselves are pyramid organizations, with many hierarchical layers and very significant differences in remuneration between them. Hierarchical positions are taken very seriously. Adrian, for instance, talked of successful people as 'people who get through to partner', as if the period spent doing so simply entailed overcoming a series of incidental obstacles to hierarchical progress. Extravagant respect for those above, however, can imply the opposite for those below. Luke, for instance, recalled getting 'really really pissed off' with two juniors who got a straightforward task wrong: 'I said "look, I bloody well told you what I wanted you to do".'

Given such a discrepancy between how my interviewees viewed those above and those below them in the hierarchy, it is unsurprising that their own status was ambivalent. Francois exemplified this. He was sure that Champion's over-cooked chicken should be expensed, and when I asked him how he would react if Geoff, the audit partner, told him to ignore it and leave it in fixed assets, he replied: 'I'd like to understand his reasons for it being treated as such' and went on to restate his own view. Nonetheless, he was not prepared to say he would contradict Geoff, despite disagreeing:

I'd feel less comfortable in my role as it is, if I thought Geoff was going to dictate that 'this is fixed assets, you will treat it as such', no questions asked. I'd like to feel there was some degree of interaction there to be able to get consensus, as opposed to just him making that decision. Although I suppose I appreciate that in certain situations calls have to be made and Geoff, as the person who is going to sign these accounts, is the correct person in our organization to make that call.

Clearly Francois would bow to Geoff's hierarchical authority if pressed. Yet he cannot quite take this eventuality seriously. His language is layered with conditional qualifiers, and he talks about himself hypothetically from an external point of view, for instance 'if I thought Geoff was going to' and 'I suppose I appreciate that'. The idea of a partner overruling him summarily and without explanation can perhaps only be resisted from his subordinate position through an attempt to make it seem unthinkable. Or perhaps Francois' disbelief is genuine, and Geoff behaving in this way simply does not ring true for Francois in the context of how he relates to partners in practice.

The perception that the large accounting firms are places to learn was widespread amongst my interviewees, and hoping for 'some degree of interaction there to be able to get consensus' is similar to hoping for the partner to be willing to teach. When Adrian likewise said that he would approach an accounting problem in a particular way 'because I think that is the way that partners look at it', he may have been being somewhat craven, but was also trying to learn.

Consistently with his deference towards Geoff, Francois commented with respect to Champion Chicken's accounting dilemma that 'consultation is a large part of my answer' and later admitted that 'to some extent I suppose I'm looking for a bit of a comfort blanket of "somebody thinks this is the right way to treat this"'. Michel de Certeau articulates the problem that arises here in a more general context:

Replacing doctrines that have become unbelievable, citation allows the technocratic mechanisms to make themselves credible for each individual *in the name of the others*. To cite is thus to give reality to the simulacrum produced by a power, by making people believe that others believe in it, but without providing any believable object. (Certeau 1984, 189)

A consensus can, in this way, evolve without anyone consciously affirming it. My interviewees looked almost anywhere they could for sources to cite in order to produce consensus. Peers were sources, but so were precedents, industry norms, perceived investor opinion, and various forms of independent advice, for instance. Consensus-seeking was encouraged by interviewees' heightened awareness of risk management, concern not to be wrong rather than to be right, and reluctance to commit themselves or to criticize colleagues. An emphasis on consensus is also encouraged by the homogenizing influence of my interviewees' working environments and socialization.

Greg discussed his behaviour towards superiors explicitly in familial terms. He commented of someone who behaved unconventionally that 'she was exceptional, she wasn't brought up in the [firm] system'. The early years of professional life appear here as a second childhood, and Greg commented that 'the corporate culture is...quite sort of parental, patriarchal, so that corporate, that hot-desking, very neutral culture pervades the group still'. Greg's firm is conceived of not only as a family but as one with a particular parenting style. That style is authoritarian, hierarchical, and distant, with male dominance simply presumed.[68]

In this context, my interviewees' anxiousness to please superiors who are, metaphorically, demanding parents, takes on more psychological substance. Greg thought it necessary to be highly cautious when contradicting parental wisdom, and his recollections of how his institutional parents dealt with one of his transgressions is revealing. As already mentioned in Chapter 2, Greg offended a partner in his firm's tax practice by emailing that partner to criticize what he saw as an unethical action, and after a series of Chinese whispers through the hierarchy the news reached his line partner, who 'called me into his office and gave me a bit of a wrist-slap'. Greg described the Chinese whispers as a comic palaver, recounting how several senior people in various parts of the firm passed the complaint on to other senior people before it eventually reached Greg's line partner. A 'wrist-slap', by contrast, is comically informal, and through this juxtaposition Greg reacts to a demeaning disciplinary experience by satirizing it. He describes the 'wrist-slap' his partner gave him as follows: 'He was passing on the message. Basically he was saying "this is what's happened, you've got lots of important people saying negative things about you, this is how the organization works, be careful, you're not doing yourself any, you're not doing anyone any favours really".' The wrist-slap was, as the phrase implies, a combination of admonition and conspiratorial pep talk. Greg's partner did not dilute the force of what seems to have been the firm's considerable overreaction to Greg's naïve behaviour. Instead, he channelled it into teaching Greg how to behave strategically within the firm. Greg learnt his lesson, and reflected that instead of adopting a critical tone, he 'should have said: "Oh I've seen this, you might want to be aware of it, we're getting bad publicity, you might not be aware of it, love to know what's actually happening here, I hope things are going okay in [your department], love and kisses, Greg."' Next time, he would play happy families, and make his point, if at all, under the guise of filial love and concern for his family's well-being, rather than for the well-being of those outside it. He would not presume to directly criticize, but would couch his evaluative perspective in terms of appearance to a third party, thus distancing himself from it. 'Love and kisses' is mocking because Greg recognizes the dysfunctionality of the situation, not because he has failed to learn his lesson. He would not broach an ethical matter so carelessly again.

My interviewees' desire to be accepted by their metaphorical parents magnifies their seniors' power over them. Simon candidly acknowledged that in an ethical grey area he could be influenced 'if someone more senior was persuading me to do it and therefore ultimately it would affect my performance as an individual.' He sees his actual performance as being affected, not merely the perception of his performance: he absolutely accepts the legitimacy of his seniors' judgements of him. 'So basically I suppose ambition within the firm, wanting to do well, wanting to be accepted and appraised positively by my seniors, might encourage me to do something.' Corruption here would not be a matter of simple greed. Simon wants to be 'accepted', to be part of the group. His firm polices his group membership, and grants or denies him the identity he craves on the basis of whether he can prove himself to be a good boy within its terms of reference.

Conceiving of one's firm as one's family, then, implies that accountants' views should not be their own, but those of their firm. Accounting facts derive their authority from their consensual nature, and individuals should not go out on a limb. Accountants' institutional status has a legitimate influence over whether their concerns carry weight with respect to accounting decisions, and senior accountants must be treated with deference and courtly respect. More junior accountants should learn from them how to behave as full-fledged members of their firms, and particularly to make accounting decisions as they would do.

The metaphor of firm as family foregrounds the relative youth of accountants employed by the large firms. Assuming KPMG to be representative, the majority of the firms' UK workforce are in their twenties (KPMG 2004), and there are far fewer people at senior than at junior levels. Consistently with this, a study of the mentoring relationships between junior and senior staff in the firms' US offices has found that those relationships are highly influential in shaping accountants' identities, and even reports a recently retired international senior partner still describing a regional partner as his 'grandson' (Covaleski et al. 1998, 320; see also Dirsmith, Heian, and Covaleski 1997). The identities built in this way can become intensely important to the individuals concerned, and there are clearly broader questions to be asked about whether it is healthy to identify with one's work to the extent that the metaphor of firm as family implies, and whether professional independence can be maintained in the context of such identification.[69] At the very least, we might expect a certain pragmatism in the pursuit of the firm's interests to become legitimated. However at the same time as legitimating that pragmatism, the metaphor of firm as family also limits it. Like the sporting metaphor, it offers accountants an ethical identity in terms of which appropriate behaviour is, albeit unclearly, circumscribed.

Conclusion

Each of the extended metaphors examined in this chapter helps to illuminate a different aspect of the complex way in which accountants construct knowledge. It is implausible to claim, in this light, that accountants conceive of their work solely as a technical enterprise, and that all these metaphors are merely obsolete turns of phrase that linger on. Why, then, has technical language accrued such authority? As well as the reasons given in Chapter 4, we might consider Friedrich Nietzsche's argument that human psychological and cognitive limitations compel all of us to create the illusion of a certitude which, nonetheless, can never be real:

Only by forgetting that primitive world of metaphors, only by the congelation and coagulation of an original mass of similes and percepts pouring forth as a fiery liquid out of the primal faculty of human fancy, only by the invincible faith, that *this* sun, *this* window, *this* table is a truth in itself: in short by the fact that man forgets himself as a subject, and what is more as an *artistically creating* subject: only by all this does he live with some repose, safety and consequence. (1911, 184)

This chapter substantiates Nietzsche's view insofar as accountants clearly do have a strong desire to create facts in which they can place faith for the purpose of simplifying their day-to-day work. Yet we cannot quite call such facts truths, if 'truths are illusions of which one has forgotten that they *are* illusions; worn-out metaphors which have become powerless to affect the senses; coins which have their obverse effaced and now are no longer of account as coins but merely as metal' (1911, 180). We have seen that to a large extent accountants' desire to create facts is an active, conscious intent, rather than an unarticulated psychological reaction. Metaphors structure my interviewees' practice in ways which are not directly articulated, but which are not unconscious either.

Whether or not accountants would say that they think of what they do metaphorically, or would agree that they think of accounting as a sport or of their firm as their family, are questions of limited interest given that some aspects of their practice only make sense in such terms. It is not, as Nietzsche might have it, that one extended metaphor or set of compatible metaphors has gradually come to define what seems literal. The accountants I interviewed behaved in accordance with different metaphors in different circumstances. They did collude in order to maintain their technical accounting frame, but often with only provisional investment and belief in it. Nietzsche would therefore be right to say that metaphor underpins accountants' very conceptions of truth, but not to say that they cannot apprehend the provisionality of that truth. Though they might have denied it for strategic reasons, my interviewees were comfortable with, and even exploited, that provisionality when faced with pragmatic problems that they needed to solve.[70]

The plurality of metaphors required to adequately interpret accountants' practice indicates that the richness and creativity Nietzsche attributes to metaphorical understanding persists in accounting, and is far from becoming a mere etymological relic. In Quine's words, the tropes have not been entirely cleared away. That accountants' metaphors are incommensurable and sometimes mutually exclusive means that, just in order to practise as accountants, they have to field ethical questions that cannot simply be resolved by quasi-utilitarian decision conventions. When is it appropriate to treat fact creation as a game? How far should I be loyal to my colleagues when their interests conflict with the technocratic ideal? Should strategic imperatives override sporting and familial expectations? These kinds of questions, which are simultaneously epistemological and ethical, are integral to accounting practice.

Although such questions must be resolved by accounting practitioners, however, they are rarely made explicit, and we have seen that they are therefore vulnerable to being resolved according to pragmatic imperatives. This tendency is exacerbated by accountants' disillusionment with highly rationalized accounting knowledge, of which we have seen evidence in this chapter and Chapter 4. Accountants' ongoing commitment to accounting as a system of knowledge (their technocratism) coexists with their exploitation of it as an abstract construct (their pragmatism). These two impulses are in tension, and the uneasy balance between them, I have argued, tends to tip towards pragmatism when rationalization is far advanced. Formal accounting knowledge comes to seem abstracted from, and irrelevant to, the substantive business of life. At a local level, accountants might attempt to maintain the compulsion of accounting knowledge in particular contexts by limiting its scope. More generally, however, they become disillusioned with accounting as a system of knowledge, and consequently become more inclined to exploit it pragmatically for reasons couched in other terms.

Nonetheless, we have now seen that those other terms are complex and multifaceted. A variety of extended metaphors offer alternative perspectives to that of pure pragmatism. These metaphors, though not explicit, are embedded in accountants' decision-making vocabulary, and embody ethical imperatives which are not always reducible to mere expediency. For instance, accounting conceived as sport legitimates pushing legal boundaries, but also demands adherence to an ethos of fair play. Pragmatism is, however, the default when the other aspects of such metaphors are not invoked. Making the various aspects of accounting's motivational metaphors more explicit could, therefore, be a step towards enhancing the ethical reasoning accountants use at work.

This chapter has not attempted to make specific prescriptions about which metaphors might offer the most appropriate framing for which aspects of accounting work.[71] We have seen that different metaphors are suited to different purposes, and that each could be developed in various ways. Instead, I have sought to highlight these metaphors' potential as a resource, and to make their influence over accountants' thinking explicit and therefore debatable. With the richness of accountants' language now more clearly in view, Chapter 7 will look at how ethical questions are worked out in their explicit discourse of ethics, and at whether that discourse is as sophisticated as it might be. First, however, Chapter 6 will look at my interviewees' professionalism, and particularly at whether it offers them a frame within which they can adjudicate between the competing priorities discussed here.

6

Professionalism

The concept of professionalism is central to understanding the creation of accounting knowledge. This is not only because accounting is governed by professional institutions, and because accountants' professional status inspires trust. Professionalism also enables accountants to articulate an ethical orientation towards their work, which, as we have already seen, my interviewees found it difficult to do in other terms.

In the conclusion to this book, I will ask what future role the professional ethos might have to play in accounting. This chapter, by contrast, will analyse the present situation by exploring when and how my interviewees invoked and practised professionalism. In doing so, it will complement the few existing ethnographic studies of professionalism in British accounting (e.g. Anderson-Gough, Grey, and Robson 2002; Coffey 1993; Grey 1998; Harper 1988). There is a different but larger body of work on the position of accounting and other professions within the social structure, which I do not propose to duplicate here, but will draw on as necessary to interpret my interviewees' specific experience (e.g. Abbott 1988; Freidson 1986; Hanlon 1994; Larson 1977; Matthews, Anderson, and Edwards 1998; Parsons 1954). The chapter will look at my interviewees' professionalism in relation to expertise, commercialism, and client relationships, with the aim of discovering the distinctive significance professionalism has for them beyond what could be reduced to these three categories. First of all, however, I will prepare the way by looking selectively at the recent intellectual history of the idea of professionalism, and then at the historical development of the accounting profession in particular.

The idea of professionalism

It is small wonder that my interviewees did not use the term 'professionalism' in a consistent or rigorous way. Professionalism means many different things to different people, and much scholarly effort has been devoted to defining it (a few of the many examples not already mentioned include Carr-Saunders and Wilson 1933; Elliott 1972; Haskell 1984; MacDonald 1995; Millerson 1964; Tawney 1920). Such definitions are always problematic, though, because they require that a position be taken with respect to several fundamental debates in social theory. Is professional work to be analysed descriptively or normatively? Is professionalism a question of behaviour, or of personality, and how are these related? Is a profession to be defined in the first instance according to its institutions, its membership, or its members' spheres of work? Are professionals distinguished by their knowledge, their skill, or their approach? Explicitly or implicitly, answers to all these questions are embodied in any given usage of the term professionalism, and those answers, moreover, are rarely clear-cut. Because the term professionalism is so multifaceted, attempts at a straightforward definition struggle to exclude its other associations, and insofar as they do succeed in doing so they tend to impoverish its meaning.

Sociological interest in the activities of professionals can be traced back at least as far as Max Weber's *Economy and Society* (1968). The specific field of inquiry that became known as the sociology of the professions only began to take shape, however, with the publication of Carr-Saunders and Wilson's *The Professions* in 1933. Having surveyed the development of a wide range of professions, they concluded that 'the application of an intellectual technique to the ordinary business of life, acquired as the result of prolonged and specialized training, is the chief distinguishing characteristic of the professions' (1933, 491). Carr-Saunders and Wilson criticized professionals thus characterized as follows:

[I]t is not...that professional men are innately reactionary or unprogressive, but that they lack vision. They do not grasp the essential features of the social and economic structure and the place of the professions in it. Moreover, in so far as they do interest themselves in matters outside the development of their own technique, they often fail lamentably to display the same standards of exactitude and judgement as they demand with rigour in their immediate spheres. The pity of it is that their opportunities are so great and that they have so large a part to play, if only they would open their eyes and summon up courage to act in the larger issues of contemporary life. (1933, 498)

However accurate it may be as a description, this criticism is naïve in its call for action, because it takes too little account of how professionals' powers are restricted by their socialization and by the contexts in which they work. Several subsequent studies reacted against this individualistic approach, beginning not from a descriptive survey of professions but, by contrast, from social theories that work at a more general level even than does the concept of a profession itself. Two examples are particularly noteworthy: Larson's *The Rise of Professionalism* (1977), rooted in Marxism, and Abbott's *The System of Professions* (1988), rooted in systems theory. Larson does not seek to assess whether particular groups live up to what a profession should or could be, but instead to expose how the ideology of professionalism legitimates 'a collective project which aims at market control' (1977, 50). Abbott returns to a more knowledge-based definition of a profession, proposing 'the very loose definition that professions are exclusive occupational groups applying somewhat abstract knowledge to particular cases' (1988, 8). He argues, however, that previous theorists have adopted the wrong starting point, and that constructing and comparing narratives of the development of professions imposes a continuity that does not exist (1988, 320). Instead, professions develop when what Abbott calls jurisdictions become vacant, and a profession has an opportunity to colonize a new area of work. Professions in this view are reactive rather than proactive. A profession is distinguished by being able, by virtue of its abstract knowledge, to enter new jurisdictions with authority (1988, 9).

A comprehensive analysis of the sociology of the professions is beyond the scope of this study, but the above definitions exemplify some of the positions within it that will help to illuminate my empirical findings. However, it is conspicuous that all these positions are consistent with an overarching narrative of the demise of professionalism in the face of commercialization and rationalization, at least in the private sector. It has come to seem reasonable to believe that the larger claims of professionalism – as a benchmark of integrity, for instance – are not inherent to the concept but are mere sales patter.[72] Most recently, such claims seem even to have lost their importance as sales patter, since the 'legitimation' of professions has shifted 'from a reliance on social origins and character values to a reliance on scientization or rationalization of technique and on efficiency of service' (Abbott 1988, 195). Any distinctive meaning professionalism might have had is then lost: 'If technical competence (either as the sole or the major factor) is to be the criterion of professional status, then the term "profession" is likely to become a rather meaningless appellation since it will no longer differentiate among work groups' (Pavalko 1971, 30).[73]

The remainder of this chapter will challenge this historical story, and the understanding of professionalism associated with it, by demonstrating that professionalism does have continuing relevance and meaning for accountants. It may well be the case that the distinctive ethos of professionalism has been in decline for some time, and I do not mean to understate the importance of such a trend. Yet what matters in the present is not what has been lost, but what remains. Rather than assuming that professionalism is dying a very slow death, we should instead ask why it has endured at all in an environment that is apparently hostile to it. Answering that question will enable us to see what potential remains latent in the concept. The discussion first needs to be contextualized, however, relative to the historical development of the accounting profession in England.

The English accounting profession

Accounting only became formally professionalized in England in the latter part of the nineteenth century, so its history as a profession is much more recent than that of double-entry bookkeeping as discussed in Chapter 1. Professionalization perhaps took so long because of the low regard in which commercial activity, and by association bookkeeping, was traditionally held. Associations of accountants were formed in Scotland in the 1850s, in response to the legal system's demand for demonstrably reputable accountants to manage the affairs of those deemed unfit to do so themselves. Subsequently in England, changes in the law during the 1860s resulted in demand for reputable receivers, liquidators, and auditors. An association of accountants was formed in Liverpool in 1870, followed quickly by associations in other cities, which consolidated themselves into the Institute of Chartered Accountants in England and Wales (ICAEW) in 1880 (Carr-Saunders and Wilson 1933, 209–11; MacDonald 1995, 192–6).

Almost from the outset, the ICAEW required its members to undertake professional education and to sit for exams (Boys 2005). Whilst examinations were an accepted prerequisite of professional status across many occupations, however, the ICAEW was very much in a minority in seeking, from very early on, to regulate its members' moral conduct. It aimed, perhaps, 'to promote public confidence in an occupation otherwise assumed to consist of disreputable, untrustworthy, incompetent characters' (Millerson 1964, 125, 163). Nonetheless, despite the ICAEW's examination requirements and ethical codes, it 'hesitated to pronounce on technical matters, fearing resentment by members or embarrassment to them'. The first Recommendation on Accounting Principles was not issued until 1942, and formal accounting standards only began to be issued in the early 1970s (Boys 2005).

The early part of the twentieth century saw the consolidation of accounting firms, and an increasing focus in London. Both these trends responded to demand from increasingly large London-based clients (Hanlon 1994, 39–41). As commerce and its regulation became more complex, accountants increasingly distinguished themselves by the portfolio of skills they could offer in response to this complexity, rather than by their unique possession of any single one. To claim the latter distinction would have been difficult in any case, as most specific accounting skills had always been shared by others such as lawyers, company secretaries, and less qualified clerks. More recently, the ICAEW has attempted to merge with various other accountancy institutes in order to maintain its representativeness of the profession. It has also established specialist faculties in order to encourage practitioners engaged in those specialisms to remain associated with the ICAEW, rather than turning to more specialist institutes (MacDonald 1995, 201–7). Although self-regulation remains central to accountants' professional status, it has become increasingly difficult to defend in the context of the increasing state regulation of commerce more generally (Cooper et al. 1994, 293).[74]

The most straightforward interpretation of these events might suggest that accountants' primary aim has always been financial gain. 'Maybe all that has happened is that these firms have finally ditched any pretence to their being public spirited in the light of the ideological shift of the 1980s' (Hanlon 1994, 150). But is professionalism really just a pretence? Its nineteenth-century leaders actively sought to establish accountancy as a profession, and in doing so tried to absorb into it what were already, by then, a confused collection of behaviours and attitudes that a profession was supposed to embody. The explicit collective self-interest of accountants therefore led them to engage, from the outset, a range of other motivations. Larson's way of putting this is to argue that professionalization in the nineteenth century incorporated some residual pre-capitalist elements. In particular, she identifies an ideal of universal service, a distaste for commercial pursuits, and a work ethic derived from ideals of craftsmanship according to which good work is an end in itself. Larson suggests that these elements were specific to individuals of high social status, and that as professionals shifted from being independent practitioners to being salaried employees of large organizations, their work came under pressure of commodification. Professionalism offered an ongoing strategy by which to resist such commodification, but it obliged professionals to entrench a cluster of values which were increasingly at odds with their commercial project, and which therefore became ideological illusions both for accountants and for those outside the profession. Hence 'the fusion of antithetical ideological structures and a potential for permanent tension' (Larson 1977, xviii, 63, 220–2).

My interviewees negotiated a variety of tensions and contradictions in order to give meaning to the idea of professionalism. Neither a structural nor an individualistic general theory can fully characterize this process. Their agency itself was highly problematic for most of them, and they were incessantly testing it and working it through. Although my interviewees often dismissed professionalism as superficial or ephemeral, they rarely seemed happy doing so. The role of the professional was one they tried to play and thought ought to be played, but were not sure how to play. Most interviewees thought of professionalism as opaque to them, or as absent from their milieu, rather than as a vacuous notion in itself. The insubstantiality of their performance of professionalism was for them embarrassing or regrettable, rather than a matter of indifference or of calculating self-interest.

The remainder of this chapter will therefore elaborate what professionalism means to my interviewees in practice, and by doing so will reveal what form of professionalism survives in contemporary British accounting and why. In the next section, I will discuss the notion of expertise which bridges, to some extent, the professional and the technical. I will then discuss how my interviewees reconcile professionalism with commercialism, in their capacities both as employees and as providers of services to clients. I will conclude by exploring the appeal professionalism has for my interviewees as a source of self-worth, and by prefiguring Chapter 8's discussion of the role it might therefore come to play in future commercial life.

Professionalism and expertise

My interviewees were less comfortable talking of expertise than of technical or professional skills. Expertise was seen as a very high benchmark, with the expert being taken to know everything about a particular subject, or at least to know more than anyone else. Yet expertise was not highly prized. Francois articulated a common perception that experts have a narrow field of vision, and are therefore to be distinguished from professionals who can take a wider view. This perception substantiates MacDonald's suggestion, cited above, that professional accountants define themselves as being able to apply a mix of skills to complex situations, rather than as having a monopoly over any single skill. By association with narrow expertise, accounting or auditing work in general tended to be disparaged by interviewees. Broader analytical or strategic roles, such as those of a consultant or business adviser, were preferred to the point that Greg, having moved away from audit work, took offence at being called an accountant.

Expertise is, therefore, both a very high benchmark in the minds of my interviewees, and one against which they are wary of defining their own value. The reason for this is that as technocrats they respect the abstract knowledge signified by expertise, but they also realize that what differentiates them from others is not their knowledge as such, but their capacity to apply it to specific cases. If even such application is understood solely as a matter of know-how to the exclusion of ethics, then accountants become merely functionaries whose personal engagement with their work is irrelevant to the work itself. Abbott explains what is at stake: 'To ask why societies incorporate their knowledge in professions is . . . not only to ask why societies have specialized, life-time experts, but also why they place expertise in people rather than things or rules' (1988, 323). My interviewees were keen to maintain a clear answer to this question because, as I shall argue below, their self-respect as well as their social status depends on it. However their task was made more difficult not only by their own technocratism, pursued for different and more immediate ends, but by the evolution of increasingly detailed accounting rules.

For Graham, the ascendancy of rules in accounting had reached the point where he could say that 'having quite a large body of rules and regulations as to what you're supposed to do, and having a reasonable knowledge of those rules, that's what makes you a professional'. Jason articulated a common view that attempts to reform accounting following recent scandals have tried to 'create you know a particular atmosphere . . . when we go out to audit business units they want the message to go out that we are inflexible . . . there's no room for interpretation, the rules are what the rules are'. Clearly this constitutes a shift from expertise residing in accountants to expertise residing in rules, which is occurring despite most of my interviewees' awareness that reliance on rules has clear disadvantages. As we have seen in previous chapters, this awareness generally tends not to undermine my interviewees' deference to the rules, but rather to undermine the value they see in the accounts they use them to produce. Rules encourage and justify technocratism without reference to the ultimate usefulness of the rules-bound activity. They create the illusion that ethics are irrelevant to the detail of accounting decisions, and therefore justify accountants in bracketing ethical questions off from technical ones. Greg, for instance, despite all his frustration with what he saw as the soulless-ness of accounting, argued consistently, as we saw in Chapter 4, that the work his firm did was morally neutral in itself, and that the only appropriate moral evaluation of it concerned for whom, and in what circumstances, the work was done. This orientation is clearly opposed to a professionalism which situates expertise in people rather than rules, and which therefore has the potential to make the interrelatedness of knowledge and ethics explicit.

Ryan succinctly stated a common myth amongst UK accountants as follows: 'American regulation is much more rule-based than European professional regulation is' and consequently, when preparing accounts acceptable to both jurisdictions, 'it's part rules, legislation and Americans, and part common sense principles, European thing'. However, the above discussion at least suggests that this distinction is limited. The principles invoked in the United Kingdom are often now treated as technical in practice, and the trend towards rules-based accounting is increasingly a global one.[75] The relocation of accounting expertise from people to rules, as Abbott would put it, is already well advanced in the United Kingdom, with corresponding relocations of the sources of authority and ethical agency. My interviewees' preference for a discourse of skill rather than expertise, and their attempts to define expertise as non-technically as possible, are strategies of resistance to this change which are significant despite contradicting their own frequently technocratic behaviour. In this light, accountants' technocratism, by which they resort to rules to sustain their influence, can be seen as a symptom not of the strength but of the weakness of their professional authority (see also Porter 1995, 89–90).

Professionalism and commercialism

Simon said at the start of his interview that 'I'm a VAT [value added tax] consultant, so that basically involves advising businesses on how to minimize their VAT tax liability or how to treat transactions correctly for the purposes of their compliance'. The use of 'or' rather than 'and' to link these two aspects of his role foregrounds the conflict between them. Commercialism – which for my interviewees roughly means the pragmatic alignment of their behaviour with their firms' and their clients' profit-making – seems to demand a different orientation than does expertise. In sporting terms, accountants might be seen to occupy an unstable position between being players and being referees, with their commercial side reflecting the former role, and their expert side the latter. In the next section, I will show how professionalism sometimes offers a way to merge these roles, but here I will focus on the relation between professionalism and commercialism specifically.

Two possible perspectives on the relation between professionalism and commercialism arose from the brief review of accounting history set out above. The first was Hanlon's argument that professionalism retains little meaning beyond commercialism, and the second was Larson's argument that the two constitute different frames of reference which coexist in permanent tension. I will demonstrate empirically that Hanlon's argument is incomplete, because my interviewees do continue to use the concept of professionalism in a distinctive way. Nevertheless, Hanlon is right that commercialism is extremely important in modern professional life, and this does at least undermine Carr-Saunders and Wilson's view, for instance, that 'the incompatibility of profit-making with professionalism is ceasing to be an obstacle in the way of the spreading of professionalism throughout the world of business' (1933, 493). Carr-Saunders and Wilson thought that workers need not act commercially when employed by large companies, except in the very indirect sense that those companies as a whole need to make money. Talcott Parsons (1954) similarly thought that professionals were able to define success differently than did businessmen, as a result of the different social structures in which they operated. Yet even if this was the case when these theories were put forward in the 1930s, it no longer holds. My interviewees were very clear about how closely focused they and their superiors now have to be on budgets and profit targets. We will see that the form of professionalism that survives under these conditions is not, therefore, simply in permanent tension with commercialism, but is intimately interconnected with it. The empirical analysis that follows will therefore take us beyond both Hanlon's and Larson's perspectives.

Commercialism was prized by all of my interviewees, to the point that Greg played down a client's misstatement of its reported profitability: 'Bookkeeping wasn't their objective, they were very commercial, their eyes were on actually setting up the project and not recording it.' Gary said he worked in his firm's internal finance department because 'it's a more commercially based role compared to audit', by which he meant that it was more proactive, analytical, problem-solving, and long term. He continued:

I think you'd definitely be working in our team to be more than just sort of a financial reporting unit. We're definitely more of a business consulting unit. Anyone can produce a set of numbers. It's being able to interpret them and provide valuable suggestions and judgements on them which is what's important.

Gary is dismissive of mere accounting, which anyone can do, and attempts to forge a more exclusive identity for his team. Yet insecurity is built into that identity. Gary must constantly prove that his work is commercially 'valuable', and doing so depends entirely on validation by others. As he put it later in his interview, in more personal terms: 'It's a more interesting challenge if you try and make things work better. You feel more valued.' His job satisfaction and his evaluation by his peers are indistinguishable. His team are constantly 'working...to be' valuable, always trying to prove themselves against a latent accusation that they are, indeed, doing no 'more than...financial reporting'. The implication, consistently with accountants' disillusionment discussed in Chapter 5, is that to 'produce a set of numbers' is not to do anything of much value at all. Such disillusionment clearly increases accountants' vulnerability to the idea that their work has only commercial value.

Gary's talk of 'valuable suggestions and judgements' reflects a broader motivational cliché in accounting, that of 'adding value', which is not reducible to increasing profit. Commercialism concerns profit, not some broader conception of value, but the discourse of adding value nonetheless enabled my interviewees to dignify their profit-maximizing behaviour with broader meaning. Sebastian recognized 'adding value' as a cliché, but still described it as the only possible source of motivation: 'I wanted to...have a chance to have my own personal input more and be sort of I guess more valued. Because adding value, that great term, is the only thing that's really going to motivate you at the end of the day, I guess.' Adding value and being valued are conflated here. Jason even equates adding value with the altruistic cliché of 'making a difference'. Yet slogans like 'making a difference' and 'adding value' disguise an underlying vagueness as to what should be different and what is valuable. Their allusion to broader meaning beyond profit is spurious, and so they are not ultimately able to transform commercialism into a secure basis for self-worth.

The desire to be seen to add value, combining, as it does, commercial competitiveness with an identity dependent on the appreciation of others, leaves Jason unable to understand how unpopular workers can sustain their self-respect. Alluding to the widespread worry amongst auditors that clients see audits as unhelpful impositions on them, he commented:

If at the end of the work I've done that is still their perception, they haven't seen us as being anything of value...I wouldn't feel particularly good about myself even if I knew I'd done a very professional job.... I think it's hard to feel self-respect if nobody else respects your profession. I think you need to be a particularly robust individual to be that type of person. It's the traffic warden syndrome, you take great pride in being a traffic warden but everybody hates your guts. Personally I probably couldn't do that.

Even when he himself knows that he has 'done a very professional job', Jason feels obliged to persuade clients that he has added value by doing so, not only in order to gain respect for his profession but to be able to respect himself. Needing the approval of colleagues and clients results in a disposition towards dependence rather than autonomy, in the context of which being well paid becomes a necessary reassurance. As Luke put it: 'I want to be recognized as someone who's quite good at what they do, and then of course I want the reward that comes with it, just because you know, reward and success and respect are all kind of linked aren't they?'

My interviewees' problem would seem to be one of how to generate self-respect, independently from the validation of others, whilst lacking confidence in the value of their work when done well. Professionalism offers a possible solution, if 'the professional takes the stand that the service he performs is not to be judged by the results it achieves but by the degree to which available occupational skills have been proficiently applied' (Goffman 1969, 215). If one's work is judged independently of its results, the achievement of results can no longer offer a straightforward antidote to self-doubt. Yet perhaps, in the absence of confidence in the value of those results, that price seems worth paying. It might at least become possible to insulate some kernel of professional work from the evaluation of outsiders, and so to resist commercialism's demands that outsiders' evaluations be taken ever more seriously.

The problem is exacerbated because commercialism encourages accountants to do just enough and then move on, rather than to dwell on things. Doing good work as an auditor at least is defined in terms of producing a satisfactory output in a given time as much as by the quality of that output itself. Despite attempts by accounting firms to persuade clients of the value-added aspects of auditing, it can be something of a limiting case, where the output is a signature and, at least from the client's point of view, the key measure of performance is cost, which translates directly into time. How could a concept of quality be applied to this type of work? Can accountants, like fruit pickers or production-line workers, be asked to build self-respect on their pace of work, defining that as its quality? If so, accounting knowledge must become a commodity the quality of which, beyond a minimal and conventionalized standard, is of far less interest than the speed of its creation. In the big four firms, Greg suggests:

People do things because they believe there's a business case for it, but when that business case changes it changes, so there's not that consistency, there's not that stability, there's not that sustainability about the type of organization. They're very shape-shifting, they're fluid, they're not going to be there in ten, twenty, thirty years' time. Professional services won't be there in that form . . . and probably the more enlightened partners, maybe most of the partners, they know that.

Commercialism imposes a logic which is short term and reactive. The business case is simply a given. What reason is there, then, to become deeply and ethically engaged in the creation of knowledge, let alone in the long-term development of a system of knowledge? To do so would contradict the logic of modern commerce. Commercial narratives of self-worth depend on the evaluation of those with whom an accountant comes immediately into contact, either as paying clients, current or potential employers, or colleagues, rather than of a broad and stable professional peer group. Such evaluations are fleeting, and those who rely on them therefore remain insecure.

In Greg's view, professionalism does not offer a solution. He takes being a 'professional' simply to mean having 'a good in inverted commas job', a phrase that gently mocks the professional's conformity and undermines the moral and social status that Greg sees the term 'professional' as claiming. Greg's institutional frame of reference is his firm, not his profession. He explicitly refuses to personify the accounting profession or to attribute an ethical style to it, arguing that those professional functions he does recognize, such as stand-ard-setting, are relevant to practitioners' ethics only insofar as they influence the cultures prevailing within individual firms. Yet many interviewees did have a more substantial concept of professionalism than Greg's, as the next section will show.

Client relationships

Qualified accountants' stable employment in large firms, their ability to con-struct career narratives, and their professional status set them apart from most service workers. Yet on a day-to-day basis they work in fluid teams serving demanding clients. This section will examine how accountants construe their relationships with clients, and will show that although those relationships are commercially motivated, accountants like those I interviewed do attempt to engage in them in a distinctively professional way. The terms 'client rela-tionship' and 'professional relationship' are often used interchangeably by accountants, who seem to aspire to an ethos with respect to such relationships in which commercialism and professionalism are fused.

An understanding of professionalism based on client service can be entirely consistent with commercialism. Tom's description of acting professionally at work, for instance, largely concerns timeliness and use of time in the service of clients:

If work needs to be done, then I'll work till ten, eleven o'clock in the evening to get it done. I'll work overnight as has happened in the past to get it done if I have to hit a deadline . . . whereas, we have non-technical staff, secretaries and things like this, you'll ask them to do something for you, and if they haven't got it done by five o'clock, well then it doesn't get done until the next day. It will be done the next day regardless of when you need it. . . . So that's what I consider the difference between being a professional and not being a professional.

Professionalism consists for Tom in taking responsibility for client service, and even support staff who accept less responsibility are experienced as an insult to Tom's work ethic. His professionalism here is not about being an accountant, but behaving in a particular way – he expects everyone in his firm to behave professionally, accountants or not. Lack of regard for his 'need' is effectively lack of regard for his clients' needs and therefore an affront to the premise according to which Tom defines himself as professional. It also contradicts the ethic of team play. Perhaps Tom's example answers the question of how pride can be taken in work when that work's quality is defined in terms of time – when a gift of time is demanded, a greater gift can be given, and self-worth created through that generosity. Yet it is hard to exceed expectation in this regard: as we saw with respect to Luke's client in Chapter 5, consistently near-impossible deadlines could only be challenged very subtly and at a partner's instigation.

There is, nonetheless, an important difference between client service and client relationships. Focusing on the discourse of 'client service' in accounting firms foregrounds the commercial aspects of interactions with clients, and these are important (see Anderson-Gough, Grey, and Robson 2000). Yet client service is provided in the broader context of a relationship, particularly where audit engagements are repeated year after year. The full picture is therefore more complex. We will see that client relationships can be a sphere in which accountants work out and exercise their professional authority, even though the service-oriented aspects of these relationships do, by definition, compromise that authority.

Client service is an important means by which profitable client relationships can be created and maintained. Simon, a tax adviser, talked repeatedly of 'building' client relationships, seeing them as having a very tangible value in terms of 'regular little queries that you bill for every month'. On this view, a relationship is an illusion constructed to gain loyalty from a client valued only for the fees it pays. Simon wanted to 'bill for value', not for 'just a standard product'.[76] To enable him to bill for value, Simon said, 'the client needs to feel that they can call on you. They need to feel you know their business. They need to feel that they can rely on you and all the rest of it.' Simon advocated the development of such self-consciously false pseudo-friendships with clients as a generic ideal.

Daljit similarly sought to develop relationships as a route to profit, but after his interview he distinguished a professional from an ordinary salesman, since a professional sold himself and his colleagues rather than a product.

Daljit identified the characteristics of a good salesman of himself as insecurity, helpfulness, and a desire to be liked. The emotional labour implied by striving to be professional in this sense clearly entails reliance on the approval of others for one's self-respect. By associating helping with selling, Daljit reconciled it with transacting commercially: 'You try and find out how you can help, and that's obviously the selling process.' Yet the fact that Daljit wanted to talk in terms of helpfulness suggests that it matters to him. Associating it with selling might therefore have been a rhetorical device by which to do so without appearing commercially naïve.

Kumar described how he would determine an accounting treatment in the context of a client relationship. He would 'construct an argument' for each possible treatment, and then 'attempt to make some assessment about which one of those seems the more convincing argument'. He would then

take into account what the client wants to do because there are these sorts of relationship angles as well. So it's not necessarily a sort of straight 'these are the two arguments, which one's more reasonable'. . . . I've seen clients get away with, well get away is probably the wrong word, but I've seen clients do things which we ideally would not want them to have done, but from a sort of relationship angle and because it's not wholly unreasonable for them to do that, I suppose, they, we tend to allow them to sort of take those, to adopt those treatments.

Client relationships, therefore, do affect the information my interviewees produce, whether as auditors or as advisers, despite accountants' rhetoric of 'professional scepticism'. Particularly where accountants aim to give independent opinions, the clear commercial motivation behind maintaining good client relationships creates an inevitable conflict of interest. Jason even went so far as to say that clients 'are our paymasters, and therefore, to a certain extent, we articulate their views in potential grey areas'. However, my interviewees' attempts to approach client relationships professionally sometimes mitigated such conflicts, or even gave rise to more robust accounting than would have been possible with no relationship at all. The remainder of this section will explore what can be learnt from such instances.

Gary described how a client had accounted for some of its sales in the wrong accounting period in order to inflate its reported profitability (a practice known as 'window dressing'). Although this practice is deceptive, and was found incorrect by Gary's firm in this instance, the client's accounts were not adjusted as the numbers involved were small. The client was, however, warned that ' "you've got to keep this under control because when it becomes material, we're going to have to pull you up on it" '. This reflects an aspect of auditing best practice known colloquially as 'no surprises', according to which auditors are expected not to surprise clients with accounting requirements at the end of an audit. No surprises promotes a cooperative approach to anticipating and planning for a potential accounting issue, which has clear advantages for both client and auditor. Yet a consequence of the no surprises approach is, ironically, that Gary's firm cannot remain technocratically aloof. It has become intimately involved in the development of its client's accounting policy, and eventually in determining how far the client can push the rules.

Barry, like several other interviewees, was more concerned with getting the accounting right than with maintaining good client relations: 'If it means falling out with the client it means falling out with the client.' Clearly, that this needs to be said indicates how serious falling out with the client would be. Yet if accountants try to avoid being forced into either/or choices between correct accounting and client relationships, it is nonetheless too simplistic to say that client relationships always lead auditors and advisers to be lenient. Several interviewees even defended going against a client in relationship terms. Francois suggested that clients might respect auditors more for standing up to them. Sam saw a good relationship as making it more likely that auditors would be able to get their way on accounting matters, both because clients were more likely to think about points made by people they knew and liked, and because having a good relationship with a client would make an auditor aware of how best to broach tricky issues with them. Looking back on his time as an auditor, Luke did not distinguish between his pride in having good client relationships and in reaching agreement on accounting treatments: 'I...got on quite well with my clients, quite good relationships, good banter and you know things always got resolved, I don't recall any major disputes.' Good client relationships enable accountants to exercise subtle influence, backed up only in extremity by regulatory power.

Jason articulated a complex view of appropriate client relationships, describing himself as 'professional in my approach':

I think it's just the way you, you know, approach people, you plan, you organize, you interact, you just do present an image, do the right thing, you dress in the right way...if you have an ethical concern about something you express your concern about it...part of being a professional is also being pragmatic, so it's not entirely black and white...it's a state of mind as well as the technical qualification.

The apparent contradiction between appearance and reality, presenting an image and doing the right thing, is denied by their grammatical equivalence here. Since both are manifestations of the same underlying disposition, presenting an image is not deceit, but part and parcel of doing the right thing in the right way. Jason is trying not to view professionalism as a site of contest between ethics and commercialism, but as a sophisticated way of working of which both are constitutive. A professional knows how to manage such contradictions, which is a kind of practical know-how that is inherently difficult to articulate: 'You just do.'

Taking the above discussion together with the discussion of performance in Chapter 2, it is clear that appropriate self-presentation and behaviour around clients is an important aspect of what professionalism means for accountants in the big four firms (see Anderson-Gough, Grey, and Robson 1998a, 85–91; Grey 1998). Yet examples such as Jason's suggest that professionalism is more meaningful for at least some of those I interviewed. It is not just a matter of self-presentation, but of self-formation and self-definition. Insofar as this is the case, moreover, the behaviour observed must be reinterpreted. Professionals, in the sense that Jason uses the term, are deep acting, and are doing so at least partly out of an ethical commitment to the role rather than out of necessity. It is this commitment that makes professionalism an actual and potential formative influence over the ways in which accountants perceive accounting questions and construct accounting knowledge.

We are now in a position to reappraise Larson's view that by appealing to non-market values for purposes of legitimation, professions accidentally make these values central to their professional projects, resulting in 'the fusion of antithetical ideological structures and a potential for permanent tension' (1977, 63). This is not the whole story, because my interviewees are sensitive to that tension and seek to overcome it in practice. Adding value, no surprises, client relationships, and most notably the very idea of professionalism itself are used to work across what might otherwise be incompatible performance imperatives. This argument also complicates Hanlon's 'commercialized professionalism' thesis (1994; 1999). Hanlon is surely right that professions like accountancy have always been somewhat commercial in orientation, and that the enterprise culture of the 1980s caused them to become more overtly so. Yet my interviewees' attempts to fuse commercialism and professionalism do not look like attempts to appropriate professionalism's remaining authority to commercial ends. Instead of commercializing professionalism, they seem instead to want to professionalize commercialism, and in so doing to maintain the relevance of the professional ethos in an environment which demands that actions be justified in commercial terms.

Conclusion

The empirical analysis in this chapter has contrasted starkly with the theoretical review with which it began. The contrast is one of scale. My interviewees approach the question of professionalism far more myopically than does the sociological literature on the professions. To some extent this is to be expected – practising accountants deal in practical situations, not theoretical generalizations. However the contrast is cautionary for both sides, reflecting overgeneralization by sociologists as well as reinforcing Carr-Saunders and

Wilson's frustration with the lack of vision of the professional person, however naïve their exhortation of professionals to 'open their eyes' might be.

For my interviewees, we have seen that the term professionalism is complex and multidimensional, and it would be a mistake to try and pin down what it means for them in a single definition. In different contexts and for different individuals, it can carry any of the meanings suggested in the sociology of the professions, and more. In particular, technical competence and proficient self-presentation are important aspects of the term. I have not focused on these matters here, however, because they are discussed in the chapters on technocratism and performance respectively. My aim instead was to explore those aspects of professionalism that cannot easily be articulated in other terms, and to discover what meaning my interviewees themselves tried to give to professionalism as distinct from the meaning given to it by their firms, by their regulators, or by anyone else. My interviewees' inarticulacy about professionalism made the analysis more difficult, but also more interesting. If accountants find professionalism so problematic, why do they want to accord any meaning to it at all? What are they trying to express through it that they cannot express through the more user-friendly discourses available to them?

In order to answer these questions, this chapter has looked at how my interviewees invoked professionalism in relation to expertise, commercialism, and client relationships. It has shown that professionalism enables them to resist the idea that they are merely functionaries of, respectively, a technical system, a profit-maximizing employer, or a client. Professionalism does not enable them to avoid playing the roles of technocrat, employee, and service worker. However it does enable them to modify those roles to some extent, and to do so in ways that make them less dependent on validation by those employers or clients before whom the roles are played. Accountants continue to invoke professionalism not only as an assertion of their marketable skills, therefore, but also in order to specify and sustain an ethical relation between self and work. Professionalism enables them to situate themselves relative to the accounting frame, and to articulate why they matter to what happens within it. Consequently, this ethical aspect of professionalism is particularly important with respect to the construction of accounting knowledge.

All this is not to say that professionalism promises accountants personal autonomy with respect to their work. Such autonomy would be both impossible and counterproductive in the context of the collaborative and interpretative relationships through which accounting knowledge is produced. Professionalism is not an individual but a collective ethos. My interviewees' attempts to specify it were always attempts to generalize for all accountants, not to express a personal opinion from which others' dissent would be inconsequential. Nonetheless, a professionalism that articulates an ethical relation between self and work does entail a degree of independence from employers' and third parties' interests. This kind of independence is not always achieved, but it matters not only to accountants but to their clients and to the general public as well. Professionals must be trusted by clients to perform on their behalf in spheres where those clients are not competent to operate themselves, and they must be trusted by the public to do so with due regard to the overall consequences of their actions. We have seen in previous chapters that a system of accounting rules cannot remove the need for this trust. There is little practical alternative but to place significant reliance on the collective ethos which accountants adhere to when conducting their work, and which is sustained and reinforced by professional discourses and institutions. It seems reasonable to suggest, therefore, that becoming worthy of such trust through the cultivation of a distinctively professional ethos could indeed offer a substantial basis for the sense of self-worth my interviewees crave. It also seems reasonable to suggest that if the accounting profession could nurture the collective ethos which is already latent in its members, and if its members could more readily articulate it, then that ethos could play a much more influential role in modern commercial life.

7

Ethics

This book has already made frequent mention of ethics. We have seen how the ethical, broadly defined,[77] infuses many aspects of accountants' work, ranging from technical framing to client relationships and from career narratives to risk management. Here, however, the focus will change. Whereas preceding chapters have looked at practices which accountants do not discuss in explicitly ethical terms, even when they arguably should, this chapter will explore how and when they do employ ethical language.

My aim here is not to superimpose a moral vocabulary on accountants' practice, and then criticize accountants for the lack of fit.[78] This is what the congressional investigator Levin did, for instance, when he talked of 'deception' in the quotation given in Chapter 1. As we saw, Levin's criticism lacked meaning for those to whom it was directed, and so could not change the way they evaluated their own actions. Neither will I take as my starting point the professional guidance issued to accountants which is labelled as relating explicitly to ethics. Where this guidance is couched in terms of general principles, my interviewees found it difficult to relate to the intricacies of modern accounting practice. Conversely, where the guidance is more specific in respect of particular issues such as fraud and money laundering, my interviewees tended to perceive it simply as a series of hoops to be jumped through. Instead of adopting either of these two approaches, therefore, this chapter will begin from the more consequential ethical discourse that my interviewees actually use on a day-to-day basis.

'Ethics' itself has come to function as a fairly narrowly defined technical term in accountancy. Therefore before looking at how accountants use the word ethics, I will first explore how they engage in more general debates about right and wrong. I will then go on to discuss my interviewees' explicit ethical discourse, and will review the various forms of equivocation they use in order to avoid taking ethical positions or discussing ethical matters. I will conclude by analysing my interviewees' answers to the direct question of how they could be corrupted, and will relate their difficulty in taking a clear stand against corruption to their difficulty in articulating why their work is important to them and therefore worth doing well.

Clearly I use the term 'ethics' differently than do my interviewees. Yet I am not simply making the circular argument that if only accountants defined ethics to include all that I define it to include, then their ethical vision would become clear. What is of interest is where accountants' shared conception of ethics perhaps promises more than it delivers, seeming to articulate an area of meaning which it does not articulate, and thus leaves a vacuum as a result of which accountants lack the language to discuss matters pertinent to their work. Discussing accountants as ethical actors in my broad sense is a strategy for exposing the limitations of their own collective ethical discourse. It will become clear that accountants are often individually aware of these limitations, and often think in more sophisticated ways than they feel comfortable articulating amongst their peers. They therefore find themselves groping beyond their collective understanding of ethics, but in idiosyncratic ways. These already present but latent resources, I suggest, offer a more appropriate starting point for the enhancement of accountants' ethical discourse than could my own, or anyone else's, unfamiliar terms. My approach is therefore to present and explore empirical evidence that ethics has the potential to mean something more, or something different, to modern British accountants than what it means in their discourse at present. The conclusions the chapter then leads to concern the directions in which accountants might develop their own existing conception of ethics.

Right and wrong 1: employee ethics

This section and the next will explore the ways in which accountants determine whether their actions at work are right or wrong. I will reveal that, when doing so, accountants are strongly influenced by factors which they believe to be out of their hands. This is so much the case that the sections can be divided according to the external influence in question. Here, under the heading 'employee ethics', I will discuss how conceptions of right and wrong are influenced by the roles my interviewees play within their accounting firms. In the next section, under the heading 'legalism', I will discuss how they are influenced by my interviewees' perceptions of the law.

The significant influence employers have over employees is sometimes manifested in their telling employees what to do, but more subtly employees are often expected to act on their own initiative to further their employers' interests or objectives. Consequently, responsibility for employees' decisions is transferred, to a greater or lesser extent, from them to their employers. When employees embrace such a transfer, they adopt what I shall call employee ethics. In accounting, employee ethics is particularly consequential because the responsibility being transferred is responsibility for decisions relating to the very construction of knowledge.

My interviewees were often explicit in their adoption of employee ethics. Graham, for instance, told me that 'certainly there's quite a lot of relief in someone else, the partner, senior manager, manager, whatever, taking the decision', and Sam reflected that 'I'm probably lucky because I'm at a stage in my career that I can generally defer upwards'. Luke, like several other interviewees, pointed out that since partners sign accounts, they are the ones legally liable for mistakes, and argued that they should therefore be deferred to with respect to accounting decisions even when their decisions seem wrong. As Liam succinctly put it: 'It's their firm, it's their money and it's their reputation.'

What is striking about these attitudes is that they do not rely on the technocratism discussed in Chapter 4, for instance, to imply that there is actually no decision to be made. It is not quantification that makes these interviewees' actions indisputable. Their actions' indisputability is not even attributable to bureaucratic 'rule by Nobody' in Hannah Arendt's sense that 'in a fully developed bureaucracy there is nobody left with whom one can argue, to whom one can present grievances, on whom the pressures of power can be exerted' (1970, 81). Responsibility is taken to reside in individuals, but only in those individuals at the very top of their institutions.[79] Everyone else apparently operates in a different moral environment comparable to that described in a corporate context by Robert Jackall: 'As a former vice-president of a large firm says: "What is right in the corporation is not what is right in a man's home or in his church. *What is right in the corporation is what the guy above you wants from you.* That's what morality is in the corporation"' (1988, 6, emphasis in original). This ethos encourages subordinates to be uncritical. Employee ethics assumes not only that the judgement of those at the top must be appropriate, but furthermore that an assumption made by a more junior accountant about what the judgement of those at the top would be, if exercised in a given situation, must be appropriate. We have seen in previous chapters that my interviewees often assessed their actions against what they thought a partner would have done, deferring as much to an idea of a partner as to any actually existing partner.

Adrian commented, moreover, that at least up to a certain point in his firm, the people who were successful and well regarded as auditors could often be

people who are quite good at organizing stuff but are actually quite crap at accounting, and I wouldn't be inclined to say they were good accountants, I'd be inclined to say that they were good at their job, but that their job is not likely to involve them uncovering any mistakes. It's about getting through the process.

Accountants who focus on 'getting through the process' are adhering to employee ethics by saving time and thus acting in their firms' interests, yet doing so must clearly compromise the overall quality of the audits they perform. Daljit made a similar point in more judgemental terms, observing that the most successful of his colleagues generally possessed 'an element of selfishness that allows them to look after themselves and the interests of [the firm] as opposed to looking after the client solely'.

Simon extrapolated employee ethics to its logical conclusion. He absolved himself from evaluating the overall 'fairness' of the way in which he pursued his firm's interests because, as a corporate tax advisor, he was merely 'a cog in the wheel that ultimately ensures a fair taxation system':

It's up to the business to try and maximize profits and for the government to try and make it fair. Do you see? So they just have separate roles that compete to make it an efficient system, and I just happen to be on the side which is peddling something which you know, could be funding schools and hospitals.

When pressed, Simon said defensively that he did believe this, and it is a common justification of the profit motive in business.[80] But his phraseology here is provocative. The pejorative verb 'to peddle' being used instead of 'to sell', and the shorthand reference to all that is worthy in British society in the form of 'schools and hospitals', seem designed to provoke me into offering a credible retort. A few moments before this quotation, Simon commented sarcastically that he was 'paid to short-change the Revenue as far as possible'. The 'schools and hospitals' cliché captures well the tedium of worthiness, admittedly, and Simon's sarcasm cuts both ways. However, his portrayal of his role as part of a larger system here seems to plead for refutation, as if he does not want to see himself this way. In the context of his own belief that he is acting 'against the spirit of the tax,' his justification of doing so seems like a veneer of self-deception which enables him to ignore the implications of his underlying views. Cynicism, perhaps, is a strategy for avoiding vulnerability: if Simon knows he is doing wrong and feels powerless to do otherwise, cynicism helps him to resist demands that he exercise a power he thinks he does not have.

These examples illustrate that whilst some types of instrumental responsibility (e.g. to meet targets) are devolved to lower-level staff when they work in client-facing teams in accounting firms, those same staff do not assume ultimate social responsibility for their actions. As John Hendry observes, this is not a paradox, but a direct consequence of greater responsibility for profit-related performance being delegated and dispersed. 'Bureaucracies have often been criticized for disabling people's moral faculties by taking ethical decisions out of their hands, but flexible organizations simply crowd those faculties out' (2005).[81] Accountants experience both of these phenomena. Their ethical thought is crowded out by flexible working in client service teams, as well as being subordinated to hierarchical authority. Taken together with commercialization, rationalization, and the difficulties accountants have in

articulating their professional independence, these factors can not only encourage, but also legitimize the adoption of a restricted ethical perspective.[82]
We have seen that accountants often embrace such restriction: translating
ethical matters into solely commercial terms, for instance of salesmanship,
career, or client service, can become a strategy of self-alienation through
which accountants abdicate from an ultimate responsibility they feel unable
to discharge. Nonetheless, if a firm can define what it means to be good at
one's job as an employee, it does not thereby gain jurisdiction over what it
means to be a good accountant in professional terms. In Adrian's words above,
being good at one's job may be more highly rewarded than being a good
accountant, but the two are not assumed to be the same. Yet although Adrian
might regret that good work and success do not go together, his conception
of good work is not robust enough to become the definition of success. Simon,
similarly, might wish that I could contradict his approach to his tax avoidance
work, but he knows that I cannot do so in terms which are plausible amongst
his peers.

If accountants are indeed functionaries until they reach the highest levels
of their firms, how can they then fulfil the ethically exacting demands of
senior positions? How can they suddenly learn to think independently according to complex ethical principles if they have been socialized not to think
in such terms throughout most of their professional lives? In this form, employee ethics raises the more general question of whether a person can really
be absolved of responsibility as a result of acting under the direction of other
people or institutions or discourses. If so, can anyone really be charged with
righting institutionalized wrongs?

Right and wrong 2: legalism

Like employee ethics, the legalistic mindset leads my interviewees to situate
the evaluation of right and wrong outside of themselves. By legalism, I mean
willingness to defer to legal or regulatory definitions of right and wrong.
Legalism implies adherence to the letter of the law without concern for its
spirit. Previous chapters have already shown that accountants often interpret
the accounting standards legalistically, and here we will see that they tend
to take a similar approach to the law in general.

Adrian described a striking example of legalism at the very end of his interview. He was auditing the accounts of a bank, based in the United Kingdom,
which regularly received dividend income from abroad, on which it incurred
'withholding tax'. Withholding tax, at its simplest, is tax deducted by the payer
of a dividend in advance of paying that dividend to its recipient. It does not
apply to dividends originating in the United Kingdom, but is charged on some
dividends overseas. A tax question then arises: Can a bank based in the United

Kingdom recover withholding tax paid overseas from the domestic tax authorities? For Adrian's client, it turned out that the answer was 'no' if the relevant part of its business was managed on the mainland United Kingdom, but 'yes' if it was managed on the Isle of Man (an offshore tax haven).[83] Adrian was clear, however, that 'in order to get that they need to actually manage this business on the Isle of Man, and it's not managed on the Isle of Man, it's clearly managed in London as far as I can see'. Adrian's emphatic repetition builds up to a clear statement of his own view. Yet although he is sceptical of his client's tax avoidance scheme, he articulates his scepticism not in terms of moral acceptability but in terms of instrumental action and reward: 'In order to get that they need to . . . '. Tax avoidance here is an achievement rather than an entitlement.

The UK tax authorities, Adrian recalled, would accept that a business was managed on the Isle of Man if its senior management function took place there. The prevailing interpretation of this in Adrian's scenario was that 'I think that so long as the directors fly out to the Isle of Man and do their meetings there then it's alright, or some bullshit like that'. Adrian's verdict of 'bullshit' is appended to a statement it cannot interrogate. If 'it's alright', if you can get away with it, there is nothing more to be said. Adrian does not know what to do with his own critical sense, and as he remembers the scenario better he transmutes it into dry humour:

In fact, what it is, no, they've got a small branch on the Isle of Man anyway that does something else, and the guy there is normally in charge of that, but he actually came over to London to meet some of [us] to explain what this business did. It was a total farce, because he met the people in the finance department in London in the morning, they explained to him what the fuck he was supposed to do, what was going on [laughs]. And they were quite up front about this to me, at any rate, about this being slightly ridiculous. He came over in the morning, had it explained to him, and met my colleagues in the afternoon, whereas it would have been a lot more sensible for my colleagues just to meet the people [in London who actually ran this business], you know. This is all part of creating the perception that he was [the manager of the business], but then he talked quite a lot of shit as well, because he hadn't really understood it in the morning, I mean he clearly [laughs]!

This example illustrates a whole group of professionals colluding to do something that none of them actually believes to be right. They expect each other to go along with it, because they reason collectively in a legalistic discourse which they individually agree to be 'slightly ridiculous' and to promote actions which are 'a total farce'. It almost seems that they are taken over by the craft work of creating a discursive 'structure', the merit of which consists in manipulating the moral reasoning embodied in law. Perhaps this explains the appreciation and even excitement that Luke, for instance, expressed with respect to a 'very complicated claim leasing transaction, it's all cutting edge and it's all highly illegal where you go through some very dodgy tax loopholes, it's very sensitive'. To be cutting edge alludes to scientific advancement, the development of a technology. The metaphor of sensitivity implies both the delicateness of a highly refined instrument and at the same time vulnerability to criticism. The technological achievement of Luke's transaction is to construe a tax avoidance strategy in such a way that it sidesteps criticism. The sensitivity is performative, it is sensitivity to failure, to seeming incompetent, to losing money, but it is not sensitivity to being found to have acted illegally. There is nothing intrinsically wrong, in this discourse, with illegality. Of course, if I had interjected at this point, Luke would have clarified that he was not acting illegally but at the limits of what was legal. That he loses this distinction when he gets carried away with the work, however, demonstrates that it is not in itself of prime importance to him. Yet this is not a straightforward criticism of Luke, because we will see that the law, as it appears to accountants, often seems unworthy of their respect.

Returning to Adrian's example, what did he mean by 'creating the perception' that his client's business was managed from the Isle of Man? Clearly, that perception was not actually created either for him or for anyone else involved. The perception was for the auditors' file, a perception they could document and defend in court if it came to that. That perception was deemed to have been created by virtue of assumptions made about what counts legally as being believable. A certain level of scepticism in the eyes of the law is assumed, because otherwise the client could just have said the business was managed on the Isle of Man without making any effort to substantiate that claim. However, there are clear conventional limits to the law's imputed scepticism, and the arrival of a manager from the Isle of Man to explain the business, regardless of whether he was known to have been briefed by managers in London before meeting the auditors, or whether he knew anything about the business, is seen to allay legal scepticism. The law is personified as a suspicious idiot rather than as a reasonable man.

It is clear in the extended quotation above that his client's staff agreed with Adrian 'about this being slightly ridiculous'. They even seem to have drawn the scheme's ridiculousness to Adrian's attention. Did they want him to challenge it? Or did they want to use his reaction as a test of whether it would work? Adrian commented that the client was sufficiently unsure whether it 'works' to have 'reserved most of the withholding tax because they've said "we can't recognize this income because it's all quite dodgy"'. In other words, the client had entered a provision in their accounts against having to pay the withholding tax they had recovered back again. Even if Adrian is only referring to his client's internal accounts, the perception they have taken such trouble to create seems yet further abstracted from any humanly realisable viewpoint. Adrian himself did raise this matter with the relevant partner in his firm, but despite being worth 'a few million pounds' to the client in recovered withholding tax, it was not material to their consolidated accounts, and so could not be challenged on that basis. Adrian also tried to argue that 'it was a sort of reputational risk thing, that the client would clearly want us to investigate this further', but did not succeed in persuading the partner of this. Ultimately, he had to accept the tax avoidance strategy not because he thought it was right, but because he lacked a sufficiently credible discourse in which to challenge it from his subordinate position. What was right or wrong was out of his hands.

Adrian was not the only interviewee to experience an antipathy towards the moral reasoning he felt obliged to use at work. Liam recalled a situation where he was writing a report for a client to use in court, but did not agree with the client's case. 'That may be my personal view, but really there's no one to go to, there's no laws being broken, there's nothing really intrinsically wrong with writing a report which slightly favours the other side.' Liam's accumulating clauses imply a coherence of argument which does not exist. There being no one to complain to does not mean no law is being broken, and no law being broken does not mean that nothing is wrong. Liam knows this, and the rationale he articulates comes across as a somewhat exasperated attempt at self-justification. Its truth lies in Liam having no way to operationalize his personal view as anything other than personal idiosyncrasy, and accepting this situation to such an extent that he subordinates his own assessment of intrinsic wrongness to the institutional and discursive framework which renders his personal view idiosyncratic. 'If by leading us to particular areas of investigation and not to others they could fake their case, that's up to them.'

Accountants can be highly sophisticated thinkers in some respects, such as in commercial strategy, so why not in legal matters? Can it be inevitable that the law is personified as idiotic rather than reasonable? One might expect the latter question to seem bizarre to a lawyer, given that the personification of the reasonable man is enshrined within the law itself. Christopher Stone, a corporate lawyer writing about the effectiveness of law in regulating corporate behaviour, argues that laws could be written which required organizations to do their best, rather than to meet a minimum standard. However he acknowledges that such laws would be difficult to implement and enforce. 'For one thing, to do so would put outsiders (including juries) to the task of judging how well any particular person or institution could perform – a harder job than deciding what is reasonable' (1975, 102). Reasonableness, at least in this corporate lawyer's vocabulary, is indeed a minimum standard, a baseline rather than a requirement to make any kind of positive effort. It is a small step from here for accountants to take legal reasonableness as connoting a cap on the sophistication of thought which is relevant to formal justice. Reasonableness then becomes conventional rather than compelling. As Liam put it, reflecting on the limits to debates over right and wrong amongst his colleagues: 'It should be just, you know, is this a reasonable way of things proceeding, and we'll discuss that outside the context of whether it's, you know, our opinion one way or another. It's just, just separate issues.'

Jason appealed to professionalism in order to contradict the legalistic approach. He commented that, when making an audit decision, 'there is a sort of undercurrent of almost respect of what the situation is, and you're a professional person and therefore you know or should know what is ethically right and wrong'. Yet he knew he was talking beyond his established professional discourse: 'I'm sounding pompous and self-righteous but I guess you know in your heart of hearts what's right and what's wrong as an individual irrespective of any overlay of professional training.' Jason makes clear assessments of right and wrong which he thinks others should also adhere to. Yet in the absence of a shared ethical discourse in which to couch them, disputes over those assessments would be personally wounding, and Jason's self-deprecation guards against this by defusing his own words. Jason is perhaps, therefore, the exception who proves the rule. As we saw in Chapter 2, even when taking an ethical stand he assumed that doing so put him on weak ground. Although confident in himself, he was not confident of himself in dispute with others: he did not challenge his seniors over a fraud but left things as they were and moved jobs.

The meaning of 'ethics' in accounting

Accountants' discussions of appropriate action, particularly with respect to complex accounting matters, very rarely make explicit reference to ethics, as we have seen both in the sections above and in previous chapters. Why is this vocabulary not used? Is it because it contradicts a technocratic characterization of accounting facts? Is it because mention of ethics connotes high-minded condemnation rather than constructive engagement with a practical problem? Or is it because ethics in accountancy has come to label a small group of uncontroversial procedures? By discussing how my interviewees responded to questions framed in ethical terms, I will argue in this section that all of these reasons and more combine to explain the absence of ethics from accounting discourse.

To accountants' ears, my questions about ethics were potentially impolite, if not rudely intrusive. Kumar, typically of most interviewees, thought of ethics as a personal matter which had little influence over how he did his job. He argued that it was not that he and his colleagues avoided discussing ethics, but that ethical questions just tended not to arise. Discussions of his own standards of ethical behaviour, when they did 'occasionally' occur, would 'be more like a sort of hypothetical discussion in the pub after work type of arrangement'. Ethical matters are abstracted from accounting practice here both by translation into analogous hypothetical situations, and by taking place out of work time and off work premises. At the end of his interview,

Kumar said he had found it interesting and unfamiliar to think about the issues I raised, 'in a hypothetical sort of situation'. Even in our anonymous discussion, he did not want to be engaged directly on an ethical level.

The difficulty of ethical discussion may help to explain how Adrian's sensibilities, as well as, apparently, those of most other protagonists in the withholding tax avoidance scenario discussed above, could differ so markedly from the practical action they all agreed upon. Greg stated the general case: 'I wouldn't say that each individual themselves had a shallow moral sense, but I'd say that the way the individuals interact together as a collective in a working environment creates a shallow corporate culture, where it's more difficult to discuss openly about values.' When my interviewees did discuss ethics, they tended to do so in very specific and procedural terms, which made ethical debates seem simplistic or trivial. I asked Alistair whether he discussed corruption, deception, and suchlike with his colleagues, and he replied by telling me about the email updates he received, and the electronic training package he had completed on the prevention of money laundering. He then went on to describe how his colleagues tended not to bother with the training, and just skipped to the multiple-choice questions at the end and guessed the answers. The training was a marginal annoyance to be sidelined as quickly as possible, and such transgressions were 'more of a joke rather than taken seriously'. At the end of his interview, however, Alistair paused for thought:

I think the thing is a lot of things don't often come up for debate. It's almost as if, you know, it's the way things are done. You know, you're prescribed a way of doing things and you always just follow that way of doing things until someone questions the status quo which is not very often in fact. . . . If it's something say like you have to spend three hours doing the money laundering course which you feel is a complete waste of time because you think it's never going to happen to you, then you kind of informally discuss with colleagues in the pub and say to them 'it's a big waste of time, you know, I didn't need three hours, I didn't spend three hours reading course notes, I just guessed the answers to the questions'. So there's not really any sort of formal discussion about it. Not really questioned it really. You know, and I've certainly not raised it with our money laundering officer, and said 'actually I know this person has not read the course notes and just guessed the answers'. And I'm sure if I did, those colleagues would probably get in trouble.

These are reflections on a system which Alistair does not feel a part of, but which he operates within. Underlying the behaviour he describes is a sense of camaraderie amongst peers who create their personal bond in spite of the impersonal institutional apparatus that brings them together. Colleagues are almost conspirators against the systems of their employers. Ethical training delivered as an auditable electronic formality distances rather than engages people on a personal level. It would be socially unacceptable for those working within such a system to report a colleague to an authority that exerts power over them but remains external. Serious discussion, in this context, would be 'formal', conducted under the auspices of a discourse of control that feels disconnected from day-to-day practice. Consequently, it tends not to take place.

Earlier in his interview Alistair described another practice, known as 'phantom ticking', that sustains peer-group camaraderie by reinforcing behaviour that is acknowledged as being wrong. Junior auditors often do a lot of repetitive checking work, for instance looking at the dates on samples of invoices to confirm that they have been entered in a client's accounts during the correct accounting period. Phantom ticking means ticking in an audit file that such things have been checked without actually checking them. Alistair mentioned it in the context of a discussion about truth-telling:

I've certainly done some phantom ticking in the past [laughs] this is audit, yeah, yeah, sure, everyone has. You know, you're coming to five, six, seven o'clock, you're thinking, 'Oh Christ, I'll just tick the box there'. Sure, that's an element of lying.

And what makes you think that that's okay?

Erm, I mean it quite clearly isn't okay.

But you're grinning and laughing about it.

Erm [laughs] well only because you know, we've obviously shared the experience in the past. And I'm sure that everyone has done it, partner included. But it's obviously not something that everyone actively mentions.

Alistair looks back on his phantom-ticking days with nostalgia and a certain mischievous glee. His justification is a substantial one, in that for many auditors phantom ticking might seem the only way to avoid working excessively long hours as a matter of course, but the hours he refers to are not particularly late. Alistair seems more interested, therefore, in evoking the feeling of boredom induced by the work: of course no one takes it seriously, 'this is audit'. Alistair is so confident that everyone phantom ticks that he assumes I must have done so as well, and it seemed to me that I would have lost face and undermined a bond between us if I had chosen to deny it.

Alistair went on to comment that phantom ticking was, like money laundering training, something to be discussed with peers in the pub, but 'obviously' never with partners. I asked him whether, perhaps, he just did not take statistical testing seriously as an audit approach, but he rejected that excuse, and defended the technique when properly carried out. So why, then, did people phantom tick? 'You know, reality is it does happen, it does happen. Laziness, carelessness, or just wanting to go home.' Alistair thus demonstrates the tension between technocratism and disillusionment described in Chapters 4 and 5. Whilst the technical accounting and auditing standards cannot be argued with, they coexist with different practical standards that govern how much effort it is worth putting into their implementation. Those practical standards cannot be argued with either, because no one cares about the argument and they would lose credibility if they appeared to care about it. A shared sense of the otherworldly idealism of the explicit professional standards creates a bond between disillusioned practitioners. When such a bond sustains practices like phantom ticking it may, for instance, become impossible to make things auditable by quantifying and standardizing their description, even when the auditors themselves say that they support this project.

Spheres of acceptable deviance, such as phantom ticking, are quite clearly circumscribed, however. Tom recalled a conversation amongst peers in the pub where a colleague admitted deleting audit steps he did not understand.[84] 'I thought that was a fantastic approach to take, but I think everyone around the table was pretty much as genuinely shocked as I was...it was really memorable because it just made me laugh.' The colleague, who had recently joined the firm, had not yet learned which transgressions were acceptable and which were not. He tried too hard to fit in, and thus managed to be funny, shocking, and fantastic at the same time.

Joe found himself disagreeing with another kind of collective transgression in which he and his colleagues engaged. Joe's firm might, for instance, be working for three bidders wanting to buy the same target company. Because these bidders would be bidding against each other, any breach of confidentiality between them could have serious commercial consequences. To prevent such a breach, non-physical barriers known as 'Chinese walls' would be erected between separate teams working for each bidder, meaning that the teams would not be allowed to communicate, share work, or even know what each other were doing. However, Joe still said it would just make no sense to do the preparatory work on the target three times.

So does it get passed round? Probably. Should it be? No, because we're effectively billing clients three times for work. We've promised not to give inside information to any one of them and we probably do...people justify it as not being a big deal...it's like copying someone's homework, it's seen as a minor, you know, felony.

Copying homework evokes the same conspiratorial spirit as Alistair's phantom ticking. It also draws out the juvenile aspect of these transgressions and thus trivializes them, exploiting the metaphorical sense discussed in Chapter 5 that my interviewees are young learners who are not yet fully responsible for their actions. A felony is just mischief, not serious crime. 'It's not a clear breach of major rules, people will be uncomfortable breaching rules like that in public or breaching major major rules...people kind of like eat away at the sides so, I'm not saying I agree with it, but that is the justification process.' Joe does not approve of the justification, but by characterizing it as a process he both distances himself from it and keeps his criticism impersonal.

Joe might have justified this justification process. Ideally, perhaps, clients would know and accept what was happening and the same work would not be billed for three times over. Even in the situation Joe describes there could be a pragmatic case for sharing work as long as confidentiality is not severely breached. Joe made no such positive argument, however. He disagreed with what was happening but succumbed to peer pressure, knowing that if everyone thought and acted like him then nothing would change:

What stops me is [pause] awful to admit but it's probably kind of like a herd instinct that you know I don't want to be the one going against the grain. . . . Why would I want to make such a big fuss of it when no one else is? It's probably just about alright.

In order to relieve his conscience, Joe then went on to interrogate himself in tedious rules-based detail about another iconic ethical issue, expense claims. Did he, as he thought most colleagues did, put in fraudulent expense claims, because below £30 receipts were not needed? No. Did he charge his entire mobile phone bill, even personal calls, on the basis that it was not worth the time to split them out? No, but rather than count up all his personal calls, he made an estimate. Was that the morally right thing to do? The existence of a rule makes even the slightest exercise of judgement morally dubious. For Joe, whether to reclaim the cost of an underground ticket is a moral question 'because you make it moral by questioning it': when you call a question moral it inevitably becomes so, simply because you have started to think of it in those terms. Like most other interviewees, Joe does not seem able to reconcile morality with materiality. Whereas he can very clearly identify which commercial decisions really matter, he has no way to determine which ethical decisions really matter. Ethical reasoning must therefore entail obsessing about details, and being commercially effective must entail leaving such details to one side.

Difficulties in assessing the relative importance of ethical questions perhaps explain why concern with ethics appeared dogmatic to many interviewees. Ryan described being 'ethically prevented' from doing a particular piece of work, and then looking for 'another piece of work that we could do which would achieve substantially the same result but which doesn't offend any of the ethical principles'. Ethical principles for Ryan here are not really principles, but irrelevant yet irritating formalities. They are personified as quaintly prudish in their susceptibility to offence, and naïve in their abstraction from practice.

In some interviewees' discourse, the dogmatism of ethics was described almost in terms of religious fundamentalism. Alistair, for instance, rhetorically dismissed the idea that he might have intervened when colleagues ignored their money laundering training by saying 'I've not tried to preach anything'. He sees 'preaching' as so self-evidently inappropriate that no further explanation is required. Adrian, seeing himself as being quite tough with clients on ethical matters, said: 'I've been quite self-righteous about this kind of thing, because it's fun [laughs].' Yet later, when we discussed a specific practice within his firm, he felt unable to object to it because 'I think a lot of people would have felt that that would be pretty self-righteous'. Self-righteousness, rather than righteousness, implies egocentricity. Taking an ethical stand is a selfish act, clearing your own conscience at the expense of the group. The 'fun' Adrian refers to partly consists of pleasure in righting wrongs, no doubt, but also connotes a reckless irresponsibility.

The dominant discourse in accounting, therefore, does not take ethics particularly seriously. Ethics, as conceived within the profession, does not guide accounting practice in general, but merely prescribes or prohibits specific actions. To get past a negative conception of ethics as an onerous checklist would require a significant change both in my interviewees' collective ethical discourse and in how they feel able to use it. Yet it is less clear that it would require a major shift in mindset for all of my interviewees as individuals. The discrepancy between my interviewees' personal and collective ethical orientations will become increasingly apparent as we discuss their tendency to equivocate and their vulnerability to corruption. As with professionalism in Chapter 6, I will argue that this discrepancy potentially motivates accountants to develop their collective ethical discourse beyond its current limits.

Equivocation

My interviewees most commonly dealt with the difficulty of discussing ethics by avoiding doing so, tending either to sidestep ethical questions, or to fudge their answers to them. This is not surprising given my interviewees' more general use of technocratic and pragmatic strategies to short-cut debates. Although their equivocation was discussed in earlier chapters, this section will look specifically at the form it takes when my interviewees clearly know that an ethical question is at stake.

Alistair employed some familiar techniques of equivocation when he recalled a story he had read in a newspaper. Three of the big four firms had, he said, been sued for routinely claiming back travel expenses from clients without subtracting rebates that they later received from their travel agents. Whatever the facts of the case, Alistair's discursive approach to it is illustrative. He discussed the practice in a technocratic way which ameliorated its ethical implications. For instance, he referred to it firstly as 'misclaimed expenses', implying procedural error, and later as a failure to act – 'not saving the client money' – rather than a wrong action. He emphasized form over substance, claiming that the ticket prices before rebates were meaningful because the gross ticket price had actually changed hands. He also argued that the rebates were immaterial with respect to each individual travel ticket, despite their cumulative value. Alistair's choice of an example from the public domain reflected interviewees' common preference for discussing ethical matters generically rather than specifically. Although he did go on to relate the newspaper story to his own experience of the same practice, Alistair evaded personal challenge by implying that everyone engages in it. He employed all these strategies of equivocation, moreover, despite having brought this practice up as an example of clients not being told the whole truth.

Ryan recalled a practice that he called 'the VAT [value added tax] scam'. 'The VAT scam' sounds like a slang name for something well known in the office. Its name blends ethical disapproval with indulgent respect – whoever thought it up did well. The 'scam' involved reports, written for banks' use, being addressed to, and paid for by, the banks' clients rather than the banks themselves. The VAT paid on the cost of the reports could then be recovered from the tax authorities by the clients, even though the banks could not have recovered it if they had paid for the reports directly. It was eventually established, very straightforwardly, that a report should be paid for by whoever used it, and VAT charged accordingly. However, Ryan commented that 'it has actually taken a bit of a while to actually work out what on earth you're meant to do with it', whilst in the meantime VAT was being wrongly recovered. He thus ameliorates the 'scam' into a matter of procedural uncertainty. The uncertainty does not appear to have been insincere exactly, but rather to have been consciously or unconsciously sustained over a longer period than was warranted by any underlying ambiguity. The uncertainty was sustained, furthermore, alongside the broader awareness that something of a 'scam' was being propagated.

Simon explained, in more general terms, how he avoids the dogmatism associated with ethics:

> I don't know, I'm not a highly ethical person because ethical implies, well I am ethical but ethical implies dogmatic which I'm not. So I find that, just personality-wise, I am capable of flexing my ethics to anything that's justifiable. So frequently if I'm asked to do something, I will find reasons why that's okay and be happy with it and not feel like, not feel guilty.

That Simon is 'capable of flexing [his] ethics' renders them something external to himself, which he can work upon. To do so requires the professional skill of managing one's own feelings of happiness and guilt in ways that one does not finally believe in.

The naïve, fundamentalist connotations of ethical stances in accounting make it unsurprising that my interviewees preferred equivocation to the adoption of such stances. If ethical debate is socially unacceptable, moreover, that has to make it difficult for accountants to develop their ethical perspectives. The verbal fog several interviewees created in response to some of my questions was so incoherent that it could hardly have been systematic equivocation: their own ethical behaviour was opaque to them. Luke even commented that he had benefited from his interview with me because 'it's always nice to, er, my psychologist or something'. By comparing the interview to being psychoanalysed, Luke implied that it had probed subjects which he ordinarily repressed and, moreover, that it had been therapeutic in doing so.[85] For Greg, however, avoiding ethical discussion was a matter of deliberate self-preservation: 'Being open about your values, your personal things, can make you vulnerable... being open and allowing that vulnerability, although it probably is socially quite good, isn't necessarily the best idea in an aggressive corporate atmosphere.' As we saw in the previous section, Greg criticizes his colleagues' 'shallow moral sense' as a collective rather than an individual phenomenon. However, he feels its impact very personally. His comic exaggeration and mockery of his own sensitivity tries, but fails, to conceal that impact:

What is the evidence that there's shallowness of corporate culture? It's just from the way that the office is physically set up, to the way that the resourcing works, the bureaucracy, to the fact that you don't get people challenging things, its just from the beigeness of the walls, to the way that you hot-desk every day, it's so many things scream out shallowness of culture and the organization. No heart. There's no heart there. Where's the soul?

Corruption

The last question I asked my interviewees was whether or how they could be corrupted. Two initial observations are relevant to interpreting their answers. Firstly, I found that if I asked 'Could you be corrupted?' I was more likely to get a straightforwardly negative answer than if I asked 'How could you be corrupted?' In the latter case, interviewees adopted their now familiar approach of trying to think up ways in which something could be done, rather than arguing that it could not. Because it yielded more interesting responses, I tended towards using the latter form of the question as my interviews progressed. Secondly, corruption is an umbrella term which covers a multitude of sins. My interviewees rarely challenged the idea that the word appropriately identified an area of common ground between such sins, and most answered my question in general terms. However, when our discussions got into more detail regarding what interviewees would do and under what circumstances, that generality quickly broke down, raising doubts over the generally accepted meaningfulness of corruption as a blanket term.

It would be easy to read corruptibility into all sorts of interviewee responses when it would be inappropriate to do so. In broad terms, my interviewees did not think of themselves as corrupt or as likely to be corrupted in the future. Sebastian's statement that he would change how he accounted for something if he was corrected rather than corrupted, for instance, was to his mind a broad and significant distinction rather than sophistry. Daljit's initial response to the question – 'phew!' – reflected surprise at its even being raised in relation to his behaviour, rather than indicating guilt. Kumar, having circumspectly discussed how he might be corrupted, then commented that he had been surprised by the question, and that his instinctive reaction had been that 'well actually, I'd hope not to be'. Hope here does not imply doubt, but that corruption is unconscionable.

The majority of interviewees did nonetheless say that they could be corrupted in some very unlikely way, apparently because they felt obliged to say this. Adrian said 'I gather that everyone has their price so I probably do as well, but I've no idea what it would be'. Being bought off in this way is inconceivable to Adrian – he has 'no idea' about it – yet he defers to a general, more cynical wisdom which he sees as being beyond dispute in his milieu. Liam said 'I wouldn't try to pretend that I'm incapable of being corrupted'. Such pretence would signify the fundamentalism which we have seen is associated with a naïve ethical orientation. Liam wanted to show that he is both more modest and more sophisticated than that. His being 'capable' of corruption also renders it a skill, like Simon's skill of flexing his ethics discussed above. Ethical certitude would signify incompetence, and Ryan argued that a lot of people who claim they could not be corrupted are 'deluding themselves'. Human nature is assumed to contain a propensity towards corruption which enlightened accountants must simply accept in themselves and in others. Alistair offered the least tortured reply when I asked how he could be corrupted: 'Oh, pretty easily [laughs]. Yeah, give me a million pounds, I'll turn a blind eye quite easily on quite a few things [laughs]. . . . Yeah, I'm sure a lot of people would quite easily take the money, just sort of run with it.' Running with it implies accepting something already being done, and plays down the corrupted accountant's agency.

Adrian thought that he would be 'reasonably difficult to corrupt'. However he described how, on secondment to his firm's corporate finance department, he had found himself doing accounting work to support various 'tax wheezes'. A 'wheeze' is a mischievous scheme, for engaging in which clever, enterprising youngsters might expect to be superficially admonished but more deeply respected. Adrian commented:

I do regard that as all pretty immoral and borderline corrupt, I mean, reading the Finance Act every year and thinking of ways round it, although that wasn't particularly my part in the process, but . . . I pretty much regard that as corrupt. I mean, I thought it was quite interesting to do for a couple of months, but to do it for the long term, that would be sort of, erm [pause].

Adrian justified being caught up in this work in terms which are now recognizable. It is a process, which he contributes to, but does not take overall responsibility for. It is also a learning opportunity, and viewing it as such postpones the question of its rightness. Adrian responded to his discomfort by moving within his firm, rather than by challenging the work itself. He sees the work as 'borderline corrupt' in moral terms, but it is not illegal, and the tax authorities know how the game works anyway. Adrian therefore rejected the role of whistle-blower: 'I think I would have felt I would look slightly ridiculous.... I don't think people's reaction would have been "fucking hell, you've caught us at it", you know, which would be the conventional "whistle-blower's discovered cheat" sort of response, wouldn't it?' Adrian assesses his action against how his colleagues would perceive it, even when that perception entails an assessment of their own corruption. He respects their sense of the game even when he does not respect their way of playing it. For Adrian, therefore, his colleagues' imputed responses can still be a good guide to what is and is not an exposure of foul play. Adrian's dispute is ultimately with an aspect of the game itself, not with the players. The role of whistle-blower is, metaphorically, that of referee, existing within the terms of the game. In Adrian's words it is 'conventional', another role already available to be played on the field, rather than a standpoint from which to criticize the game.

Unlike Adrian, many interviewees tended not to perceive a proximity to corruption in their day-to-day work, but like him they felt that they would need a situation to be very black and white if they were to take a stand against corrupt practice. This is a high benchmark, as we saw in Chapter 4, and it seems even higher given my interviewees' readiness to be persuaded that a situation is not black and white. Oliver played safe by sticking to an extreme and unrealistic example, saying 'I'd like to think I wouldn't' be corrupted by 'a hundred grand in a suitcase'. His turn of phrase leaves room for doubt out of modesty more than anything else: he is confident of his morality in this clear-cut situation. With respect to real-life situations, however, Ryan thought that he would be 'innately' more likely to engage in a doubtful practice if a personal or professional relationship was involved. Jason expressed the general view when he suggested that he would be 'vulnerable to unethical persuasion'. He would want to feel persuaded of a point, but is aware that persuasion would have a high chance of being effective, even when it perhaps ought not to be.

'Vulnerability to unethical persuasion' can be enhanced not only by a reluctance to criticize anything which is not incontrovertibly wrong, but also by personal ambition. As we saw in Chapter 5, Simon acknowledged that he might be corrupted by his superiors as a result of wanting to do well. He also admitted being less likely to challenge his superiors' actions for that reason: 'You want to progress in the firm, you probably don't end up being Mister Anal who goes "I think you'll find technically what's supposed to happen right now is", you know, you say "phew, yeah, alright, okay".' Furthermore, it emerged in our conversation after his interview that his ambition is very unspecific. He wants to do better than those around him, rather than to do any particular thing well.

Consequently, he is vulnerable to being persuaded that success should be defined in a particular way, or can be achieved by particular actions.

Liam, conversely, stated that he would be less likely to be blatantly corrupted as a representative of his firm than he would as an individual:

Would I be corruptible as a representative of the accountancy firm in order to pass something through which then benefited me as a result of a backhander? Highly unlikely, but if you asked: 'How many millions would it take to get me to work for the Mafia?' I'd have to have a long think about it [laughs].

Working for the Mafia is not being entertained as a realistic prospect here, and its appeal may be as much about self-image as about money: to someone who fears that doing the right thing might render him a stereotypical dull accountant, such a role could seem like enviable forbidden fruit. Yet the fact that blatant corruption is more thinkable on an individual level than as a representative of Liam's firm illustrates, once again, the moral subordination of the individual to the firm. Such a claim might seem to contradict Liam's discussions earlier in his interview of how reports prepared by his firm can be biased in favour of clients. Yet this bias occurs within tacit limits, and it is beyond those tacit limits that Liam can more easily imagine going on a personal basis than as an employee. As an employee, more than as an individual, he would be prepared, in Simon's words discussed above, to flex his ethics, rather than to break them, perhaps in order to improve his own performance. His organizational context encourages such flexibility, but at the same time it also discourages more blatant wrongdoing.

Aside from accepting suitcases full of banknotes, however, it can be difficult to pin down what would actually count as blatant wrongdoing. Gary had heard a rumour that 80 per cent of frauds were committed by ex-auditors, and found that statistic entirely plausible 'because I mean I've often looked at companies and thought "this is going to be so easy to defraud this place" '. He seems to recall being excited by this prospect, although clearly as fantasy rather than as something he would actually do. The only way a fraud perpetrated by someone who knew the controls of a business well would be picked up, Gary said, was if the fraudster was 'greedy', by which he meant if the fraudster tried to take a sum too large for the auditors not to notice. The condemnation that 'greedy' might imply is reserved for inept fraud, rather than being applied to all frauds, reflecting the respect for cleverness shared by most of my interviewees. Luke revealed how such an attitude can slide away from being hypothetical. He was beguiled by the sheer cleverness of a tax avoidance scheme which he knew was dubious, and developed an almost aesthetic sense of awe towards it. He hoped that it would fall just on the right side of the law: 'I just think it's a fantastic way of doing it.'

Important work

Much of this chapter is consistent with a view of accountants as alienated workers. Such a view implies that of course accountants are not ethically motivated by their work, because they engage in it instrumentally; it is not important to them for its own sake. Yet although several interviewees (particularly the auditors) thought that their current line of work was not important, they nonetheless aspired to do important work within the accounting field. Others argued that they were already doing important work, for instance when offering investment advice to banks, or engaging in decisions upon which a company's future depended. However, the meaning of such claims was undermined by the presumption that even such important work is technical and therefore not subject to moral evaluation.

When I encouraged Terry to distinguish between strategic and moral issues, he initially restricted his conception of the moral to include only matters of broad public policy very distant from day-to-day accounting practice. Yet the irrelevance of moral issues to accounting work was not clear-cut:

I mean the importance of the work I do certainly in terms of, I don't know, I don't associate it with being a moral issue, of course yes there is a moral issue to it, but I guess in the realm of moral issues if you could rank moral issues I think it would be somewhere down the bottom.

Terry tried to argue that commercial success is important, but not morally important. He wants to do important work, but not morally important work. Such important work involves decision-making, but a very technocratic form of decision-making, which could ultimately be appraised in terms of correctness. Yet Terry himself, in the above quotation, clearly senses that these distinctions are weak. I pressed him further:

I'm struggling, why do I think it's important? My mind's going blank, why is what I do important? I don't know it's just, part of it's the preconceived idea I have that doing what I do somehow, I don't know, if I had a league table of decisions that people make or businesses make I'd say the things that I get involved with are decisions that come higher up the league table. . . . I don't know, for instance, my dad's a caretaker, I look at my dad and I think being a caretaker's not as important as ensuring the long term financial stability of the largest electronics group in Denmark.

Terry's reference to a 'league table' here recalls the sporting metaphor discussed in Chapter 5, and this, as well as the strategic and particularly the military metaphors accountants use, perhaps helps to explain why they might think of their work as important without being able to directly articulate why. Terry's particular problem is that although he can articulate why his work is important in technocratic terms, he cannot describe why he therefore wants to do it. If Terry is just going through the motions and acting correctly, why does it matter to him that he, rather than someone else, is doing so? To say that Terry was arrogant, and simply thought himself more competent than anyone else, might be part of an explanation, as might his earlier comment that 'I feel as though I get recognition from other people if I'm involved in those important decisions'. He later reflected that 'I guess the types of businesses I like to work on are ones that . . . tend to affect a lot of people, so may be that's the way I calculate importance, I don't know'.

Something is still missing here. Terry does not see the term 'moral' as being part of his professional vocabulary. He sees morality essentially as adherence to universal definitions of right conduct with respect to highly important matters. If the term moral is reserved to denote issues more important than accountancy, then of course accounting is not a moral issue. But neither, as previous chapters have demonstrated, is it merely a technical activity, if such activity were possible. Between the abstractly moral and the technical, then, is a gap which might be described as ethical if the meaning of that term in accountancy was not restricted in the ways discussed in this chapter. For Terry to articulate his sense of the importance of his work, he would need an interstitial language which did not imply that an accounting decision mattered in the same way as a decision to embark on nuclear war, but which nonetheless recognized that questions of right conduct were raised by it, and that not being matters of public moral debate such questions could only be answered with reference to his own ethical orientation towards his work.

The role of such an interstitial language could be fulfilled by a vocabulary of motive as conceived by C. Wright Mills. Mills, reacting against the Freudian conception of motives as a set of individualistic, internal drives, argued instead that there are varying vocabularies, associated with particular social contexts, through which motivation is understood (1940). Professionalism, commercialism, and technocratism could be understood as such vocabularies of motive. However, we have seen that these vocabularies can cast accountants as surface actors, performing one-dimensional roles for one-dimensional reasons, and so can demand their adherence without commanding their respect and therefore their ethical commitment. Yet such commitment is necessary if accountants are to determine right conduct rigorously in unique and unforeseen situations, when neither rules-based morality nor technicality offer sufficient guidance. Although existing vocabularies of motive might help Terry to work out what to do, moreover, he would still lack a reason to believe that the action thus decided upon was important. A vocabulary of motive cannot in itself give such a reason; a connection between such a vocabulary and Terry's ethical sense of self would also be required.

In Erving Goffman's terms, the problem is that vocabularies of motive emphasize performance to the exclusion of character. In *The Presentation of Self in Everyday Life*, Goffman postulated that for the purposes of research an individual might be 'divided . . . into two basic parts: he was viewed as a performer, a harried fabricator of impressions involved in the all-too-human task of staging a performance; he was viewed as a character, a figure, typically a fine one, whose spirit, strength, and other sterling qualities the performance was designed to evoke' (1969, 244).[86] Accountants, as we have seen, are performers. However, their performances, unlike those Goffman considered typical of everyday life, are not designed to evoke the attributes of a character. No wonder, therefore, that the accountants I spoke to could not answer questions such as: what do I think of the prevailing consensus about what is important? Why do I want to be the one doing important work? To answer such questions, they would need to experience themselves as characters, and furthermore, as characters who mattered.

What would be the ideal character of an accountant? The metaphors discussed in Chapter 5, for instance, illustrate some aspects of such an ideal by different names. Yet that ideal is not fully formed in the minds of my interviewees, and so cannot be clearly espoused. Perhaps, for instance, the rhetoric of excellence in accountancy is an attempt to define the ideal accountant's persona. However the definition is a flawed one in that excellence is defined outside the self, in terms of rules or of performance. The appeal of cleverness and sharpness similarly offers an aspiration which does not fully satisfy its adherents. What might an alternative formulation look like? For accountants, in their capacities as accountants, to be noble, to be beautiful, or to be wise, for instance, is not currently plausible. If aspirations like these made sense in accounting, perhaps accountants could more easily articulate their engagement with their work as something personal, creative, and important to them.

Conclusion

Accountants enjoy being clever in a technical sense, and appreciate such cleverness in others. In a technocratic environment, cleverness is almost a technique of survival of the kind imagined by Michel de Certeau:

In these combatants' stratagems, there is a certain art of placing one's blows, a pleasure in getting around the rules of a constraining space. We see the tactical and joyful dexterity of the mastery of a technique. . . . Like the skill of a driver in the streets of Rome or Naples, there is a skill that has its connoisseurs and its aesthetics exercised in any labyrinth of powers, a skill ceaselessly recreating opacities and ambiguities – spaces of darkness and trickery – in the universe of technocratic transparency, a skill that disappears into them and reappears again, taking no responsibility for the administration of a totality. (Certeau 1984, 18)

Accountants' behaviour does resemble the exercise of 'skill' whilst 'taking no responsibility for the administration of a totality'. Accountants do reduce broader issues to technical specifics, as we have seen with respect both to ethical and legal matters. By narrowing their field of vision, they render such matters localized puzzles, resolvable by cleverness. Their ethical equivocation apparently evades any challenge to this reductionism. Nonetheless, it would still be wrong to assume that this is the whole story.

The image of accountants as clever manipulators suggests that they have no personal stake in the discourse of accounting, but instead are independent agents, working around it rather than with it. There are then two options: either criticize accountants for exploiting a discourse they are employed to maintain, or criticize the discourse for restricting accountants' freedom to get on with what really needs to be done. However, such an image overlooks the complexities of the ethical relationship between accountants and accounting. We have already seen, particularly in Chapter 2, that accountants seek meaning in their work through their adherence to standards of truthfulness which necessarily surpass the pragmatic demands of a given situation. In this chapter, we have seen that there is a high level of consensus amongst accountants as to the importance of substantive audit testing, for instance, which coexists alongside, and imposes unwritten limitations upon, the alienated practice of phantom ticking. In Certeau's terms, ignoring the totality of accounting as a system of knowledge would make no sense to accountants, because their project of simplifying and standardizing commercial information depends on it. Accountants, therefore, do not reduce their work to the local application of a skill or technique in the way Certeau describes. They retain, as we have seen, an inarticulate sense that their work is more broadly important. Ethical questions are not so much ignored as displaced onto the practical sphere, where tacit consensus between peers comes to define what is right and wrong. Adrian's deference to his peers as to when whistle-blowing might be appropriate demonstrates that this consensus goes beyond a shared appreciation of, or even aesthetic pleasure in, skilful tactics.

Accountants, therefore, are in a difficult position. Those I spoke to, at least, wanted to engage personally in their work. It was this desire that distinguished them from Certeau's tacticians, driving them as it did to take ideals such as truthfulness, professionalism and good work at least somewhat seriously. However, the dominant discourse in accounting tends to trivialize such engagement, and loses the respect of practitioners by doing so. It also renders the tacit ethical consensus between peers ephemeral, and so leaves it vulnerable to erosion. Insofar as the law is an idiot, my interviewees certainly found it expedient to behave commensurately. However they also felt obliged to do so out of self-preservation. In a profession that measures performance according to the simplification of information and the strict management of time, self-preservation necessitates expediency, making it hard to differentiate between lazy and constrained behaviour.

I have argued that ethical myopia is counterproductive for individuals, organizations, and society. Yet the technocratic culture in accounting obscures ethical vision. Accountants need to be interpretative to overcome the limitations of their explicit professional discourse, yet that discourse makes it difficult for them to construe themselves as ethical characters whose interpretations would be legitimate. As discussed in Chapter 4, a good accountant is traditionally someone who does not get it wrong, rather than someone who gets it right. A disproportionate focus of attention on accounting scandals reinforces this negative perspective both within and outside the profession. Accountants lack a positive and compelling shared discourse which might facilitate ethical engagement and debate rather than precluding it. In the absence of such a discourse they must muddle on, compromising between incompatible and one-dimensional performance imperatives, and holding each other to account as best they can. It is perhaps regrettable, but nonetheless understandable, that their motivation in this effort sometimes seems lacking.

8

Conclusion

This book began by outlining a problem of trust. In advanced economies, the quantity, geographical spread, complexity, and sheer scale of economic transactions require us to place an unprecedented level of trust in standardized forms of financial knowledge, and therefore in those who create that knowledge. Beginning from the discourse of individual accountants, I have explored how that trust is discharged in the early twenty-first century, and have revealed a complex and sophisticated ethical landscape that is not well understood even by many accountants themselves.

Those who hope to read here of a regulatory quick fix to the problems faced by the accounting profession will be disappointed. Indeed, perhaps the most important lesson of the preceding chapters is that such a hope is misplaced. Trust in accounting is ultimately trust in accountants. It does not matter how sophisticated the rules are if accountants approach them as an irrelevant nuisance to be worked around. The ethical and interpretative approach accountants take towards rules is important, and a regulatory response to the issues raised in this book is of value only insofar as it helps to change that approach. To believe that we have or ever could have the regulatory resources, predictive capacity, swiftness of response, and analytical precision necessary to fully control a social practice as complex as accountancy from the top down, without the ethical involvement of individual accountants, is fundamentally misguided.

All this is not to say that there is nothing to be done, and indeed some concrete policy implications do arise out of the preceding chapters. However my focus, which I argue should also be the focus of reformers, has been on understanding accounting practice as it is, and only then extrapolating its implications with respect to what is possible in the future. Insofar as this conclusion makes policy suggestions, therefore, they will consist of general directions for change rather than desirable endpoints to be reached. More detailed work than is possible here would be needed to evaluate specific proposals, and in any case they would need to develop over time and in collaboration between the relevant stakeholders in ways which cannot be predicted in advance.

Overview

Accountants' Truth has offered a rich description of accounting discourse and practice, with the aim of opening up important debates in the field. I have approached the development of a vocabulary in which such debates can be conducted as an end in itself, irrespective of the subsequent directions the debates might take. For non-accountants, the book has offered an insight into what too often remains a rather hidden world; and for accountants, it has articulated the relation between accounting and wider political and epistemological issues in ways that should enhance accountants' sensitivity to the social significance and impact of what they do. Many of my findings are not specific to accountancy, but reflect broader developments with respect to the construction of specialist knowledge in an increasingly rationalized and globalized world.

The book began by suggesting that a deeper problem of knowledge underlies the problem of trust in the financial world. I have explored how facts are used as the building blocks of accounting knowledge, and have shown that the current method of simplifying and standardizing accounting knowledge for decision-making purposes, together with the corresponding professional socialization of accountants, engenders technocratism and consequently the abstraction of accounting from accountants. Accountants who feel little involvement in their work tend to conceive of their responsibilities narrowly. The example from the collapse of Enron in Chapter 1, as well as subsequent examples from my interviewees' own experiences, have illustrated how the lack of a language of broader responsibility accepted within the profession leaves individual accountants disinclined and disempowered to raise ethical questions.

Faced with these systemic difficulties, my interviewees were often tempted to adopt an overarching pragmatism with respect to the construction of accounting knowledge, and to bracket the question of truth out of everyday consideration. In this context an excessive interest in explicitly ethical matters, as we saw in Chapter 7, was often taken as a marker of naivety. We saw, for instance, how my interviewees avoided disputes and tried simply to think as their colleagues did. Although it is difficult to imagine my interviewees actually telling lies in a technically clear-cut situation, we have seen both that they can be vulnerable to unethical persuasion in debatable cases, and that at the higher levels of accounting a great deal is debatable. However, it has also become clear that my interviewees find a highly pragmatic approach to their work counter-intuitive and difficult. They experience disillusionment, and struggle to suspend their disbelief and to manage their emotions. They want to believe in a concept of truthfulness more substantial than obedience to accounting rules, and to maintain a standard of professionalism in its pursuit, despite not being able to articulate that standard. Many of them make strenuous attempts to do so despite the obstacles they face.

The conclusions that follow from these findings can be grouped into the four interrelated spheres of knowledge, truthfulness, work, and ethics. I will discuss the book's implications for each of these spheres, before reflecting upon the future possibilities open to the accounting profession. I will conclude that trust can best be secured in accounting through a reinvigorated conception of professionalism, and will propose some areas in which policy interventions might focus.

Knowledge

Accountants construct the standardized knowledge on which modern commerce relies. We have seen that they seek to construct that knowledge in the form of accounting facts, even when accounting rules do not predetermine the form those facts must take. The discussion of Champion Chicken in Chapter 3 explored the argumentative strategies accountants use to crystallize facts out of ambiguous situations, and subsequent chapters went on to reveal that many real-life accounting decisions are similarly judgemental. Accountants' strategies for making such decisions, moreover, often appeal to shared assumptions that are not well articulated, for instance regarding protagonists' agendas, common sense, operational reality, justice, and the plausibility of particular kinds of commercial narratives. There is therefore a gap between accountants' explicit discourse of rules-based factuality and their more tacit practices of fact construction. As a result, we have seen that accountants frequently find themselves disillusioned with their own technically oriented representations of commercial life.

Accountants often respond to this situation by approaching the process of fact construction technocratically, adhering to technical accounting practices as the best means of crystallizing legitimate accounting facts. Technocratism makes accounting seem simple and authoritative. In order to maintain a technocratic perspective, however, accountants find themselves obliged to employ a range of rhetorical strategies, such as limiting the scope of what falls within their purview, and avoiding dispute. By excluding matters from the accounting sphere, these strategies then exacerbate accountants' disillusionment with accounting knowledge. Yet their disillusionment generally does not displace, but coexists with, their technocratism when faced with specific accounting dilemmas. Disillusionment, therefore, only undermines my interviewees' technocratic approach to constructing accounting knowledge in extreme cases, even though it routinely undermines the value they see in that knowledge itself. In other words, the threat to accounting knowledge is not of the kind that gradually erodes the technical façade, which remains largely intact. Instead, the more calculatively refined accounting knowledge becomes, the less compelling it seems in overall terms to those who create and use it, and the less likely it is to form the ultimate basis for their decisions.

Chapter 4 situated this phenomenon in the larger historical context of the rationalization of accounting and many other forms of modern knowledge. The conclusions that follow with respect to accountants, therefore, also resonate beyond the accounting profession. In particular, the disillusionment experienced by accountants implies an important limit to economic rationalization. As I have argued in more detail elsewhere, economic rationalization defeats itself insofar as accounting knowledge cannot be endlessly rationalized and remain compelling (Gill 2008). There are two related sets of consequences which follow from this. The first concerns accounting's loss of compulsion as a system of knowledge, and the second concerns the pragmatism with which accountants and others increasingly exploit it.

Like any other form of knowledge, accounting influences the ways in which its users understand their interactions and the ends they pursue. A natural limit to rationalization might therefore seem fortunate from the perspective of those who worry about the unassailability of dominant perspectives, such as that of accounting (e.g. Hoskin and Macve 1994; Marcuse 1968; Weber 1992). Insofar as it persists as an uncompelling rational façade, however, accounting continues to fill the conceptual space in which alternative forms of knowledge might otherwise develop. Accountants are therefore left without the resources to articulate clearly what is wrong with accounting knowledge, or what substantive issues it excludes from the frame. Even if alternative forms of knowledge did develop, moreover, embracing them would entail accepting the loss, for instance, of the benefits to world trade promised by international accounting standards. The ideal solution, therefore, seems not to be diversity in our forms of knowledge, but rather a commitment to keeping the form of knowledge we allow to dominate open to revision and criticism. Yet such a commitment might easily be lost sight of as the obvious benefits of standardization are pursued. Standardization inevitably makes some valid perspectives more difficult to articulate in the process of making others easier to articulate, and if this is forgotten at the international level, standardization could come to function as a kind of discursive imperialism. Such an outcome is made more likely both insofar as technocratism tends to make accountants blind to alternative perspectives, and insofar as disillusionment leaves them without a reason to engage with those perspectives.

Accountants' disillusionment undermines the quality of accounting knowledge even when the form of that knowledge remains unchanged. Insofar as they are employed to construct knowledge that they do not find compelling, accountants find their work unimportant, and therefore lose the motivation to do it well. Knowledge constructed by disillusioned accountants will still look as it always did, but less care will have been put into preparing it. Furthermore, disillusioned accountants are likely to have less compunction about the ways in which they use accounting knowledge once it has been constructed. Disillusionment thus gives rise to the pragmatism discussed in Chapter 5. In the long term, moreover, accountants who rise through the ranks of their firms as disillusioned pragmatists may find themselves ill-equipped to fulfil or even to apprehend the ethical demands of senior positions. Recent accounting scandals suggest that this may be cause for serious concern.

Accountants can shore up accounting's compulsion through strategies of framing which exclude contentious questions, but beyond a certain point these defensive strategies begin to exclude too much of what matters to those who use accounting information. When accounting fails to capture what matters to its users, it can slide from being a system of knowledge they find compelling to being an abstract construct that accountants and others exploit pragmatically for reasons couched in other terms. It also becomes questionable whether accountants who focus closely on technical matters are able to understand the most important aspects of their clients' affairs, with inevitable consequences for the quality of their work.

Chapter 5 showed that even when acting outside of a technical frame, accountants are not merely pragmatists, but act according to various motivational metaphors. These metaphors include sport, strategy, and family, but also performance and professionalism. They are embedded in accountants' decision-making vocabulary, and are not reducible to mere expediency. For instance, accounting conceived as sport legitimates pushing legal boundaries, but also demands adherence to an ethos of fair play. The disillusioned pragmatism that prioritizes expediency is, however, the default when such metaphors are not applied, or when accountants are unable to adjudicate between the various competing metaphors in terms of which they might frame a given situation.

The disparity remains, therefore, between the apparent clarity of an accounting decision once made, and the opacity of the decision-making process itself. Much of this book has been devoted to making that process less opaque, so that accountants' practice can be more rigorously and consequentially debated. It may be in accountants' short-term interests to maintain the disparity: as long as facts can be abstracted from value statements in accountants' public discourse, those facts can seem to possess a technocratic authority that would be belied by a greater public understanding of accounting practice. Yet since this form of authority is increasingly fragile, it seems increasingly possible that a debate around how accountants actually construct knowledge might catalyse a reappraisal of the epistemological and ethical status of the accounting fact.

Truthfulness

Accounting facts, as we have discovered, are not as straightforward as they might seem. Various interrelated histories – of statistics, of bookkeeping, of professional expertise, and of the idea of fact itself – have structured their current form. What counts as fact in a given situation is often debatable in ways that are not resolvable in technical terms. Broader considerations with respect to the construction of knowledge, which I have called ethical considerations, must be imported to resolve such debates. I have therefore argued that accountants are wrong to use factuality as their most basic unit of analysis. Instead, I proposed the notion of truthfulness, which articulates a connection between knowledge and ethics as I have used those terms.

Knowledge and ethics in accounting are inseparable, because accountants with particular ethical perspectives more readily understand and construct particular types of knowledge. Examples such as Champion Chicken demonstrate that the facts of the matter do vary according to the perspective accountants adopt. This is not to say that there is no single underlying state of the world, but that accountants cannot fully describe that state of the world, and so must adopt a perspective from which to determine which of its features are salient. The fact, being an object of precise limited agreement, comes after such perspective-taking, and is thus partial: a full and impartial representation of reality is unattainable. The picture is further complicated by the significant extent to which we have seen that accounting does not merely describe, but also constructs, the state of the world as experienced by those engaged in economic activity.

If accountants were only concerned to construct accounting facts technocratically, we would now have reached an impasse. Yet this is not the case. We have seen throughout the book, and particularly in Chapter 2, that they recognize a range of influences over the role they play in the process of constructing knowledge. Even formal considerations such as the limitation of scope and duty of care render the appropriate facts different, depending on their purpose. Less formally, considerations such as managing information, risk, and client service also involve tailoring knowledge to its intended recipients. Of course, these considerations can be strategically pragmatic, but I have argued that they are not always so, and that accountants do to some extent observe an ethos that can be characterized as one of truthfulness.

Truthfulness means not only that knowledge is factually verifiable, but also that it rests on accounting work well performed. Accounting knowledge is truthful when the accountant's task of simplifying and editing is responsibly discharged, and the most important or appropriate facts or perspectives have been selected. Truthfulness is not achieved, therefore, by simply passing large volumes of information on, even when that information is technically correct. Truthful work is not that in respect of which an accountant can answer negatively to the question 'did I get it wrong?' but rather that in respect of which he or she can answer positively to the question 'did I do what I could to get it as right as possible?' Accountants motivated by truthfulness are concerned in each concrete instance not just about the factuality of the accounts they construct, but also about whether the facts they include give a fair impression of a company's affairs to those whose decisions depend upon them.[87]

Truthfulness, then, derives from accountants' responses to situations, and what counts as truthful does not depend solely on the properties of what is being described. The construction of accounting knowledge is therefore an ethical matter, as I will discuss further below, and also a performative one. Chapter 2 revealed the complex nature of accountants' performance, and demonstrated the close interrelation between performance's two meanings of quality of work and quality of self-presentation. I argued that these two meanings are not necessarily contradictory, and that accountants' role-play, emotional labour, management of expectations, and attempts to seem in control are often legitimate and necessary aspects of the construction of accounting knowledge. Yet truthfulness is not consistent with merely going through the motions. It relies more heavily on accountants' involvement in their work than does technocratism, and so is particularly vulnerable to erosion as a result of their disillusionment with accounting knowledge.

Work

Truthfulness is a way of working, which explains why this book, being primarily interested in accounting knowledge, has devoted so much attention to accounting work. I have presented a complex picture of accountants' working lives, which has shown that their performances at work are addressed to a variety of audiences including hierarchical superiors, clients, and peers, and that they are justified in terms of a variety of discourses including technocratism, pragmatism, commercialism, and professionalism. A common theme has been that these aspects of accountants' work are psychologically demanding. This reflects broader trends in the development of advanced economies towards the provision of services, and in the more flexible organization of the modern workplace, which increasingly require service workers to perform emotional labour of the sort described in Chapter 2. Although accountants are privileged relative to many other service workers, they share with them the increasing difficulty of opting out of these psychological demands in favour of a clearly demarcated, albeit alienated, sphere of working life (see Rose 1999; Sennett 1998). The modern service economy strongly encourages accountants, like other service workers, to define themselves through their work, and refusal is no longer an effective response to this. Although embracing the demands of truthfulness could be conceived as another onerous requirement, however,

I would suggest that it may be better conceived as a strategy by which accountants can re-appropriate the psychological investment demanded by their work.

Accountants already employ various other strategies for dealing with the demands of their work, one of which is commercialism. As we have seen, employee ethics in accounting demands not merely obedience to instruction but the adoption of one's employer's perspective. Embracing this by thinking solely in commercial terms, for instance of salesmanship, career, or client service, can enable accountants to demarcate their responsibilities at work. A myopic insistence on treating accounting as a solely technical activity can also be a coping strategy, when it is engaged in without the enthusiasm implied by technocratism. Even surface acting, as a means of performing emotional labour impersonally, may be another way of keeping the demands of work in their place. All these strategies are responses to the constraints under which accountants work that have direct consequences for the truthfulness of the accounts they give. Furthermore, they are all problematic because, by keeping their work contained, they fuel accountants' doubts as to whether their involvement in it is ultimately worthwhile. Many factors already conspire to raise these doubts, including deference to institutional superiors, to clients, and to the demands of employee ethics, as well as the apparent technical abstraction of accounting work and the need to manage risk by limiting its scope. On the one hand, we have seen that these factors combine to create a sense of relief – work is not too serious. On the other hand, however, we have seen that they also create deep-seated anxieties over self-worth.

An alienated response to work might simply seem realistic. If workers' minds have become the production lines of the knowledge economy, then the sphere of alienation has simply expanded, and knowledge workers must learn to live with that. Yet if the complexity and subtlety of modern knowledge work instead means that an ethic must replace an instruction manual, then this conclusion does not follow. Surpassing alienation, after all, entails becoming ethically motivated by one's work, so if that is what the modern workplace requires it is not inevitably to the worker's detriment. Nonetheless it raises the stakes. The alienation workers will suffer, if such ethical motivation is reduced to emotional labour, is becoming ever more severe as the demands of work mine their psychological resources ever more deeply. For this reason, accountants' ethical discourse and practice is not only important because of its influence over the truthfulness of the knowledge they construct, but also because it is increasingly central to their ability to lead fulfilled working lives.

Ethics and responsibility

The above discussions of knowledge, truthfulness, and work have been unable to avoid frequent mention of ethics. It has been a recurrent theme throughout the book that accountants have no option but to approach their everyday practice with an ethical sophistication that goes far beyond the system of rules and principles that they explicitly adhere to. That sophistication, nonetheless, is not clearly articulated, and is therefore vulnerable to erosion and distortion according to the pragmatic requirements of the specific situation at hand.

Chapter 7, by contrast to previous chapters, explored the impoverishment of accountants' ethical discourse, demonstrating that it leaves them without a vocabulary in which to discuss, evaluate, and reinforce the ethical aspects of their practice. The impoverishment of accountants' ethical discourse reflects the dominance of their technical discourse. As Chapter 7 showed, conceiving of knowledge construction as a technical process creates a peculiar and limited understanding of what is right and wrong with respect to that process, which tends towards employee ethics and legalism. Even the word ethics itself has developed a narrow technical meaning for accountants. Yet to some extent this reflects a gap between accountants' language and practice, rather than a deficiency in their practice itself. We saw in Chapter 7 that accountants currently perceive their explicitly ethical discourse as legalistic, dogmatic, and fussy, and develop their sense of group membership as much by flouting it as by adhering to it. However we also saw that such flouting was itself done largely according to an unarticulated shared ethic which defined appropriate action differently. Although the lack of a vocabulary in which to debate their ethical practice is bound to undermine it to some extent, it is also true that accountants' technical, professional, commercial, and even sporting discourses embody tacit ethical standards.

Of course, accountants could be portrayed as exploiting the weakness of ethical discourse in the financial world for their own and their firms' gain. Accountants do sometimes produce a kind of knowledge that wilfully obscures what is really being done, as in the example Adrian gave of tax advisers submitting deliberately confusing information to the tax authorities, discussed in Chapter 5. However, even such instances as these seem to be thought of as, or at least to have legitimating stories which cast them as, appropriate behaviour within a given context, rather than as deviance. The accountants I spoke to behaved in ways they considered deviant very rarely indeed. Consequently, this book has focused instead on the ways in which normality has become dysfunctional, and particularly on the ethos that has become normalized in accounting work.

The tendency for ethical debate amongst accountants to be oversimplified, and for difficult questions to be relegated to the tacit realm, is doubtless exacerbated by accountants' desire to conform to the norms of, and thus to secure their place within, a social and economic elite. Yet accountants cannot be understood as fully autonomous moral agents, because of the constraining effect not only of regulation, but also of superiors, clients, and peers. Even senior decision-makers rely to a very large extent on how the information on which they base their decisions is constructed for them by their subordinates. These factors suggest that although we might legitimately hold an accountant responsible for his or her behaviour relative to the profession's existing moral framework, we cannot expect a morality external to the profession to have much purchase within it. Insofar as the current moral limits are legalistic ones, for instance, in which lying is unacceptable, but persuasion of almost all types is not, those who hold themselves to different standards will simply lose money, status, and influence. Individuals acting alone rarely flourish or rise to powerful positions in environments with which they find themselves at odds.

Instead of making unrealistic demands of individual accountants, therefore, we must ask how it could become more generally possible, acceptable, and expected for accountants to hold themselves and their peers accountable in new ways. Achieving this is not as straightforward as redefining accountants' formal roles in some way. An ethic, such as employee ethics, that prioritizes fulfilling a role over acting virtuously justifies the exclusion of certain consequences of one's behaviour from consideration. Such exclusion would not be a problem in a perfect bureaucratic system, where everything fell within someone's explicit remit and everyone had powers commensurate with their responsibilities. Yet not only does such a system not exist empirically, but it is also a theoretical impossibility. Events in the world are too diverse and unpredictable to be anticipated to the extent that would be necessary to construct such a system.

Perhaps, therefore, we must hold individuals responsible when things go wrong, since there is no alternative locus of blame and punishment.[88] If we are to avoid things going wrong in the first place, however, what matters is the likelihood that responsibility will be appropriately understood and discharged, and this is a question of the interplay between individuals and institutions, and even of the development of particular kinds of individual selves through socialization into institutional life.[89] It seems only reasonable that accountants' responsibility should be determined relative to the norms and expectations of their working environments. Yet we have established that it would be better for accountants to take a higher level of individual responsibility than they do at present. This implies that the norms and expectations of accountants' working environments should change, and that accountants should receive the institutional support necessary to render demands for greater individual responsibility reasonable (see May 1996, especially 119–22).

Some squandering or misappropriation of resources will always happen, but it is most likely to be prevented by accountants whose involvement in the construction of knowledge, conceived of as a collective project, is nonetheless active and critical. Individual involvement in a collective project can only avoid being a contradictory aspiration insofar as accountants are concerned to develop a common ethos, and then to adhere to it in performing their specific and various work. Professionalism, sustained by an appropriate institutional framework, might offer accountancy's best means towards realizing such an aspiration, since it potentially articulates a shared ethical enterprise. Before evaluating the prospects of professionalism, however, we will need to review the ways in which it currently functions in accounting.

Professionalism

As we saw in Chapter 6, professionalism can be difficult for accountants to define. Why, then, do they continue to use the term at all? Does it convey anything important that cannot be expressed otherwise?

Of course, there are instrumental reasons why accountants might adhere to the idea of professionalism. In particular, it enables them to claim jurisdiction over an area of work deemed inaccessible to the layman, and therefore to claim authority, status, and fees. However, by exploring professionalism in relation to expertise, commercialism, and client relationships, Chapter 6 demonstrated that accountants do also invoke professionalism in order to articulate and to sustain an ethical relation between self and work. Since the discourse of professionalism has no obvious substitute in this regard, its lack of clarity in accounting remains a problem for accountants, rather than being a reason to dispense with the idea altogether. The sheer variety of my interviewees' attempts to narrate their shared professional ethos in a commercial context – adding value, client relationships, selling as helping, cog in the wheel, apprenticeship, employee ethics – is symptomatic of their difficulty. A vacuum is left because the meaning of professionalism is unclear to them, and there is no shared discourse through which that meaning can be refined, reinforced, or even replaced. Nonetheless, in the context of the discussion of work above, the concept of professionalism is potentially empowering. Service work or knowledge work relies on the ethical engagement of workers if it is to be performed well, and so if those workers can articulate their ethical perspectives they can exert at least some control over their working lives. Could professionalism form the basis of an articulation of a shared ethical perspective? Could it actually carry the meanings it would need to carry if it were to perform this function? The findings of previous chapters give us at least some reason to think so.

Professionalism, I have argued, potentially offers accountants an approach to their employment that can adapt to the commercialized workplace better than its alternatives. The instrumental approach to work, which entails embracing alienation in a limited sphere, cannot adapt, because the psychological demands of accountants' work erode the limits to that alienation. Narratives of career cannot adapt, because the more exceptional the defined career narratives offered by the large accounting firms become in relation to the rest of the flexible economy, the more power those firms consequently wield over employees who cling to such defined career narratives. Craftsmanship of the traditional kind cannot adapt, because it values good work for its own sake, on its own terms, and so is hostile to the flexibility and compromise accountants' work requires. Insofar as their conditions of work are intractable, the development of a shared ethos enabling accountants to respect themselves and each other for responding to those conditions in a virtuous way seems to have no viable substitute. Their commercialized environment makes a professional ethos harder to sustain, but at the same time it fuels accountants' need for it, because it is the most promising response to their work's demands for emotional labour and flexibility.

Professionalism is not, therefore, as is often thought, only ideological deceit, or a residue of a former age, or a project in the pursuit of profit or power. It may be all these things, but it also offers an alternative vision of good work, success, and identity to that proposed by commercialism. Accountants do, moreover, partially succeed in making that vision compatible with their commercial working environments. Appropriate professional relationships, for instance, enable accountants to exert greater influence over the information clients produce than they would otherwise have. Professionalism sustains an ethos of client service which translates at least to some extent into good work. However, we have seen that accountants' training, their early work experience, and the hierarchical structures of their firms can encourage deference rather than professional self-confidence. The dominance of a commercial measure of value leaves accountants needing to appeal to commercialism in order to demonstrate their own worth, whether through a discourse of adding value or through the construction of commercialized career narratives. Accountants' professionalism is real, therefore, but is not particularly strong. However, its weakness does not derive from its lack of persuasiveness to practitioners, but rather from the difficulty practitioners have in articulating and operationalizing it.

The fate of the professional ethos does not only matter to professionals themselves. Others also have reason to be concerned about the ethical relation between individual accountants and the commercial and regulatory contexts in which they work. Professionalism is relied upon to guarantee the quality of accountants' work not only by clients, but by other stakeholders and the general public as well. As we have seen, such work demands trust from its beneficiaries: the appropriate application of a specialized technique to a particular case is something that only the professional is qualified to judge. Professionals are relied on to make such judgements, and the ethos of professionalism justifies that reliance.

If professionalism of the kind described here is to flourish, a shift is needed in the discourse through which accountants are held responsible for their actions. A renewed discourse of professional ethics would be more open to debate and argument than is the discourse of employee ethics, and would

145

recognize and be informed by the practical complexity of a situation to a greater extent than bureaucratic or legalistic discourses. In terms of such a discourse, ethical maturity would be prized and respected rather than seen as onerous and deferred to the later stages of a career. It would be less easy to evade individual responsibility where a bureaucratic system failed or where superiors gave inappropriate instructions. The discourse would also, however, offer accountants terms in which to more rigorously debate what should be done in concrete situations and why, and in which to defend doing the right thing even when it went against the interests of their employers or clients. If such a discourse were more strongly established it might, in time, help to overcome the vulnerability to unethical persuasion that many interviewees displayed.

In order to achieve this kind of shift, it is neither enough to exhort accountants to think differently, nor to incentivize them to do so with incentives that presume the kind of self-interest or disinterest they seek to overcome. The former can only exacerbate accountants' frustration and alienation if the context in which they work remains unchanged. The latter predicates the management of accountants on the assumption that they have no deeper ethical sense, and so not only encourages them to behave as if they do not, but to believe that they do not. In this way, the micromanagement of employees to ensure ethical behaviour can in fact corrupt them. The task is not therefore to demand an unrealistic heroism from individuals, or to force them to act in consistent but clumsy and oversimplified ways. As I argued with respect to responsibility more generally in the previous section, both the engagement of individuals and change to the systems within which they work are needed; neither individual nor system can develop effectively whilst the other remains the same. Yet there is reason to be optimistic, nonetheless, because we have seen that many of the foundations necessary to a reinvigorated professional ethos do already exist in accounting.

Policy implications

What practical steps might be taken in order to bring about a professional ethos such as that described above? Although it cannot be legislated for directly, the conditions necessary for it can be established and institutional arrangements can be put in place to foster and sustain it. Firstly, we might look to reform some aspects of legal and professional regulation, reducing its technical detail and directing it less at the ultimate form accounting knowledge takes than at the way in which it is constructed. Secondly, changes might be made to the recruitment, training, and socialization of accountants. Thirdly, attention might be given to the relationships that develop between accountants, as influenced by the structure and continuity of client service teams, the hierarchical distance between junior and senior accountants, appraisal and mentoring arrangements, and other social and professional groupings. Fourthly, and most radically, the relation between employee, employer, and profession might be rebalanced, rendering employees more directly responsible for their actions, and relatively more answerable to the demands of their profession over those of their employer.

More broadly, the relationship between knowledge and ethics in the financial world as described in previous chapters gives rise to a variety of policy implications which, though they include those outlined above, are not limited to the nurturance of professionalism. The remainder of this section will therefore discuss those implications in general terms and from a long term perspective. I am concerned to identify areas in which attention should be focused, rather than to make detailed prescriptions, for reasons outlined at the beginning of this chapter. In brief, these areas of attention concern how rules are written and applied, and in particular their effect on accountants' shared ethos; the debate over rules versus principles; the development of accountants' day-to-day ethical discourse; accountants' training, socialization, mentoring, appraisal, and social networks; the level and type of responsibility assumed by individual accountants; the structure of the firms and their relationship to other professional institutions and to individual accountants; the presumed audience for financial information; the definition and scope of profit; the politics of translating matters into financial terms; and reputation as a basis for public trust.

Historically, we have seen that rules have been indispensable to developing trust in accounting. A regulatory response to accounting scandals and to developments in commercial and financial markets can still be effective, and not only in closing technical loopholes. Francois, for instance, attributed increased discussion of fraud and money laundering amongst his colleagues directly to new legislation. However I have emphasized in this study that such effectiveness comes at a price. In practice, accountants can only deal with so much prescriptive complexity, and the more of it there is the more pragmatically they must approach the rules in order to get anything done. It is important therefore to prioritize, and to decide when a rule needs to be a rule, and when accountants could be trusted to deduce it from some more general rule, principle, or perspective. Such a decision, moreover, should not be made simply according to whether trust would be well placed as things stand, but whether the placing of trust would encourage accountants to become worthy of that trust over time. Regulation is important, but should be approached as a necessary evil, the necessity of which can be reduced by discouraging dependence upon it.

More broadly, previous chapters have shown that a system of technical rules can never supersede the ethical aspects of accountants' work. It is just not possible for accountants to construct knowledge without being far more sophisticated than the system of rules that governs them. The uncomfortable consequence of this is that we must rely on the ethics of those who create knowledge to validate that knowledge – there is no viable technical alternative. However I have argued that we can place trust in a collective ethos into which accountants can be socialized. Regulation can reinforce this socialization, but if it is to do so it must focus on decision-making processes as well as outcomes, and it must be sufficiently limited to give accountants space to take responsibility for their own work.[90]

Ryan exemplified the approach accountants would ideally take towards rule-following when he commented that an auditor sometimes has to think beyond the details of the rules in order to apply them appropriately to a given situation. 'You have to think: "What is this rule or guidance driving at? What was in the mind of the person who wrote it and what were they trying to guard against? What evil were they trying to prevent?"' Ryan's concern to adhere to the spirit of the rules leads him to seek the narrative behind them, and to try to empathize with the intentions of their authors. Such a practice would be rejected by a technocrat, for whom that kind of context would be irrelevant. Ryan's approach is not, however, to set himself above the codified standards applicable to his work, but to try to cooperate with them to achieve a common objective that motivates both the rules' authors and himself.[91]

The extent to which it is realistic to expect accountants to approach regulation in this way is a key issue in the ongoing debate over how far accounting standards can productively be couched in terms of principles rather than rules.[92] The findings of this book clearly add fuel to the drive towards principles. A shift towards principles, however, is necessary, but not sufficient, to overcome a rules-bound mentality. In particular, practitioners often request guidance as to how principles are to be applied, and insofar as that guidance then takes on the status of rules, the distinction between rules and principles is lost. If a principles-based approach is to work, then pressure for guidance and interpretation needs to be resisted by standard-setters and regulators where possible.[93] Such pressure will be lower, of course, if accountants are familiar with, and engaged by, the issues underlying the rules versus principles debate. Those issues relate, in any case, as much to how practitioners should apply judgement in implementing standards, as to their design. The debate itself, therefore, could be just as important as its regulatory outcome. The same is true of other professional debates, which could be more widely engaged in as an integral aspect of accountants' ethical training and development.

In broader terms, we have seen that accountants need to get better at talking about accounting as well as doing it, particularly with respect to its ethical and political dimensions. Although this is best achieved through the efforts of practising accountants themselves, an example could helpfully be set by senior figures in the profession. The perspective adopted in this book is itself a proposal for a new way of talking about and evaluating accounting work, and the language of performance, professionalism, ethics, truthfulness, and fact construction offers a starting point, rooted in accountants' existing discourse and practice, from which a new vocabulary might grow. In particular, the tacit and metaphorical conceptions of appropriate behaviour that accountants already share could develop into more explicit terms in which they could evaluate and debate their own and each others' actions. In developing such critical tools, as well as accountants' capacities to use them, ethics training that genuinely surpasses the box-ticking mentality is essential.[94] The endgame must be to move from a situation in which raising ethical matters in commercial settings can all too often seem irrelevant, naïve, or rude, to a situation in which doing so is taken as a mark of insight and authority. This necessitates, after all, a credible ethical discourse in which good practice can be described and propagated.[95] Its credibility must ultimately be assessed against a very high benchmark: Could one accountant actually hold another to account in the discourse's terms, and expect to be backed up by his or her colleagues, even when no explicit rules were being broken? It is such practical intervention which needs to become possible on an everyday basis, rather than only through an exceptional discourse of whistle-blowing which is very often too simplistic or too late.

Accountants, we have seen, construct knowledge most truthfully when they find accounting knowledge in general compelling; care about constructing it well in specific instances; and are sufficiently engaged with, and critical of, their profession to contribute to its development over time. This has various implications for the training and socialization of accountants. The striking breadth of academic disciplines from which accountants are recruited in the United Kingdom undoubtedly does help to maintain critical perspectives within accounting. Yet the recruitment of very young graduates, whose unfocused ambition can leave them particularly vulnerable to commercial pressures, compromises this effect. In this context, mentoring arrangements, project team structures, and social networks within the firms are extremely important, and deserve serious attention. This is not simply an argument for more mentoring, since accountants must learn to think and act independently, nor for more stable working relationships, since accountants must learn to cooperate effectively with unfamiliar colleagues. Instead, it is an argument for careful adjudication between the competing organizational requirements of training, socialization, and professional independence. The basis on which accountants are formally appraised is also important in this regard, and is of legitimate interest to stakeholders other than their employers. These issues are developmental, but are not thereby restricted to accountants' early years or to the realm of 'professional development' programmes. The influence the social structure of their working lives has over accountants' ethics is very broad, and very significant, at all stages of their careers.

We have seen that the hierarchical structure of the firms and the competitive training and examination process are problematic, since they encourage accountants to approach their work instrumentally, to defer to authority, and to pass responsibility upwards. If responsibility were to be spread more broadly amongst accountants, rather than being concentrated at the top of the firms' hierarchies, however, all the structural aspects of accountants' working lives discussed above would need to adapt accordingly. Whether or not such a change in emphasis was characterized as a shift towards professionalism and accompanied by an expanded role for professional institutions, it would imply a shift in responsibility from accounting firms and systems of accounting rules to individual accountants. This shift would rely on a greater ethical accountability between peers, and the level of contact between accountants at different stages of their careers would need to increase. It would also imply corresponding changes in the relationship between employer and employee. We should at least be cautious, for instance, as to how far such changes are compatible with the extent to which the large accounting firms are now run as corporations rather than partnerships, despite remaining partnerships in legal form. All other things being equal, being partnered with one's colleagues seems more likely to sustain professional virtues than does being employed alongside them.[96] Nonetheless, to the extent that the firms are professional as well as commercial institutions, they have the potential to be part of the solution rather than part of the problem, and should be engaged with as such.

This study has implications for the kind of knowledge accountants should construct, as well as for how they should do so. I have emphasized, indeed, that these issues are interconnected, and that the construction of knowledge is inherently an ethical matter. I have argued, for instance, that in practice accountants have no option but to construct knowledge from a particular perspective.[97] It might seem to follow from this that different information should be prepared for different purposes, or for different stakeholders. Financial accounts, on such a view, are for the shareholders, and should present the information most relevant to them. However, tailoring information for an audience's use is not the same as tailoring it to that audience's economic interests. Perspective-taking by accountants remains an ethical matter, and its necessity should not obscure the moral question of whether particular audiences, such as shareholders, should be able to know about their investments in such a way that other concerns, for instance about the environment, become invisible to them. The interests of different stakeholders are interconnected, and to artificially separate them at the level of accounting knowledge is to facilitate, legitimize, and institutionalize the pursuit of interests defined more narrowly than a less directed form of knowledge might sanction.[98] Even if accounting knowledge is directed towards shareholders' interests, moreover, it still entails assumptions as to when it is appropriate to recognize a profit as such and when it is not. There remain important ethical debates as to what constitutes a legitimate profit, and what kinds of behaviours are appropriate in pursuit of profit. Such debates are not merely post-accounting matters, but are integral to determining what counts as profit or loss.

There have recently been moves to broaden the focus of companies' attention beyond short-term returns, with the duties of company directors to pursue what has become known as "enlightened shareholder value" being formalized in legislation (*Companies Act 2006* (c. 46), part 10, chapter 2, paragraph 172).[99] In the accounting field, voluntary initiatives such as 'triple bottom line' reporting have gone further, seeking to translate non-financial matters into financial terms (see Henriques and Richardson 2004). The bottom line refers to a company's profit or loss, and the triple bottom line requires that three figures be generated, one summarizing a company's financial performance, and the other two summarizing its social and environmental performance. Triple bottom line reporting entails the monetary quantification of what would ordinarily be seen as social and environmental externalities, and as a result brings them within the accounting frame. Its achievements have been considerable, not least in helping to create an expectation that a range of non-financial aspects of a company's activities be disclosed and therefore subject to scrutiny. However, there is a limit to what can be achieved by triple bottom line reporting both because it entails the quantification and comparison of often unquantifiable or incommensurable factors, and more broadly because the translation of social and environmental matters into financial terms still defers to the financial mindset with respect to subsequent decision-making around such matters. It may not be appropriate, for instance, to think of the destruction of a natural habitat in the same terms as the cost of a machine.[100] Translation, therefore, does not obviate the need to evaluate the perspective into which matters are translated.

Although the pursuit of 'enlightened shareholder value' still focuses on long-term returns to shareholders, companies can nonetheless find themselves obliged to consider their social and environmental impact for reputational reasons, because maintaining a good reputation is in shareholders' long-term interests. Reputation translates, for instance, into the goodwill of customers, staff, and the wider public. For accounting firms, maintaining reputation in this sense depends heavily on the display of professionalism. Accountants' professional reputation is closely associated with public trust, and so maintaining this is in accountants' interests even when it requires them to work beyond the scope of their economic engagements or legal responsibilities. Liam, for instance, distinguished his firm's 'professional reputation' from formal risk management considerations as a separate reason why 'it was inconceivable' that he would represent misleading information provided by a client as fact in a report. The importance of reputation means that public discussion of what should be considered ethical behaviour in the financial world can have a direct influence over accountants' practice, and we should therefore seek to maximize the quality of such discussion.

The suggestions I have made here are all at least indirectly related to the ethos accountants adhere to when constructing knowledge, and so cannot take effect without the commitment of accountants themselves. A change in ethos can be catalysed from outside the accounting profession, but not straightforwardly imposed, even from within. This makes resistance to change, amongst those who exploit ethical ambiguity for commercial gain, harder to overcome. Nonetheless, the latent desire for ethical engagement I have identified amongst most individual accountants, and the fact that rebuilding public trust in their profession must be in their long-term collective interests, are significant reasons to be optimistic.

Building trust

There is no perfect solution to the problem of trust in accounting. PricewaterhouseCoopers admitted as much after the Enron scandal, saying that what happened to Andersen could happen to them,[101] and that the risk of audit-related litigation was 'uninsurable, unquantifiable, unmanageable and could at any time destroy our firm, or any of our competitors' (Schlesinger 2004). No system the firm might impose could fully prevent unfocused ambition from becoming abstract competitiveness, the need for peer approval from becoming disregard for third parties, or, as a corollary to these and other factors, the objectification of knowledge from becoming abdication of responsibility.

As the case of Enron revealed, apparently extreme spectacles can easily arise out of everyday accounting practice. There are limiting cases in accounting, where the right answer and the wrong answer are in plain view. Yet because accountants must make judgements about how to translate their observations of economic life into accounting terms, such limiting cases are scarcer than one might think. Disputes occur often, and there can be a fine line between entrepreneurship and sharp practice. In some cases that line can be defined legally, and in such cases it is important to do so. Yet we have seen that much of accounting work takes place in inherently grey areas that cannot be made black and white, and moreover that the attempt to make them black and white can undermine accountants' capacities to apply appropriate judgement when dealing with them. In grey areas, the accounting profession can be worthy of public trust only insofar as its members go beyond compliance with the rules, and behave according to a shared ethos that is worthy of such trust. The challenge facing the profession, therefore, is to articulate, institutionalize, and reinforce such an ethos.

A shift in emphasis from rules to professional trustworthiness is far from being a soft option for accountants. It requires them to take greater personal responsibility for the implications of their decisions, and to more readily hold each other accountable not only when rules are broken, but also when power is abused or responsibilities are poorly discharged. Qualitative rigour is possible even in areas where quantification and regulation are not, and so what seem like grey areas from a legalistic perspective can often be more clearly defined from an ethical perspective. This book has shown that accountants can think with the sophistication necessary to such rigour, and has proposed that they be enabled and encouraged to do so. Given that accountants' work is to construct knowledge, their trustworthiness is most importantly manifested in their standards of truthfulness when working in judgemental areas. I have therefore argued that truthfulness should be conceived of as an integral part of accountants' work, not merely an optional virtue. I have also argued that we need to conceive of accounting knowledge commensurately, not merely as a collection of technically verifiable facts, but as the result of an ethically sophisticated practice in which we necessarily place trust.

The task at hand, then, is difficult but unavoidable, and we can now state it more clearly. The accounting profession needs to overcome the dichotomy between ethical engagement and technocratic calculation. A system of accounting needs to be developed which performs its functions of simplification and standardization more effectively, not in spite of its reliance on individuals, but precisely *because* it places sufficient trust in individual accountants for them to remain subjectively involved in their work. Progress must be made in this direction if accountants are to do their work well in the future, and if accounting is not to lose its compulsion as a means of framing economic life.

In these pages, I have sought to facilitate such progress by making aspects of accounting practice that were previously opaque more explicit. Explicitness of this kind is necessary if practitioners are to develop the discursive tools they need to hold themselves and each other to meaningful ethical standards. It is also necessary if practitioners and non-practitioners alike are to reflect critically on the practices through which we define economic value in modern society. Those practices affect all our lives, and as they become increasingly standardized, rationalized, and globalized, our capacity to debate and challenge them has never been more important.

Methodology

Accountants' Truth is based on in-depth interviews with employees of the largest account-ing firms in London. Interviewees were asked to explain how they would account for a fictional scenario, concerning which the accounting rules were indeterminate, and then to describe similarly contentious accounting problems from their own experience. The interviews focused on the ways in which interviewees constructed accounting knowledge, but also included broader discussion of professionalism and ethics. The interviews were recorded, fully transcribed, manually coded, and interpreted qualita-tively using techniques of discourse, narrative, and textual analysis.

This appendix is addressed primarily to fellow researchers who want to understand the methodological choices I made. It will discuss my selection of interviewees, the ques-tions I asked them, the manner in which I did so, my interpretation of the results, and the limitations of the research as well as the steps I took to overcome these. It will also discuss the opportunities and challenges posed by my having shared my interviewees' professional experience. The overall objective of the research was not to understand accountants' life experience, their behaviour, or their social environment, but rather to understand the workings of an increasingly rationalized, globalized, and powerful dis-course. All these are inextricably connected, but nonetheless my primary focus on accounting discourse affects all aspects of the methodology.

Interviewees

I conducted twenty interviews between June 2003 and October 2004. Interviewees were fully qualified chartered accountants,[102] aged 35 or below, male, and employed by one of the 'big four' firms in London (Deloitte, Ernst & Young, KPMG, and Pricewaterhouse-Coopers). Five interviewees were selected from each firm. I used the snowball technique to identify them, beginning with personal acquaintances and asking each interviewee for a maximum of two follow-on contacts.[103]

My sampling decisions regarding gender, age, employer, and location were always in favour of the majority.[104] In the United Kingdom, there are more male than female chartered accountants; the big four firms are the largest employers of them (and employ more people under 35 than over); London has a higher concentration of chartered accountants than any other city; and the Institute of Chartered Accountants in England and Wales (ICAEW) is the largest of the various institutes serving the profession.[105]

Accountants meeting all these criteria at once are, nonetheless, a minority group. Yet they remain of particular interest as an archetype of the profession, embodying in concentrated form the predominant characteristics of the profession's members. These selection criteria for interviewees, together with their relatively recent socialization through the profession's three-year examination and training period,[106] maximized the interviews' salience as information-rich examples of a standardized discourse.[107]

Relative to the field of accounting and finance taken as a whole, fully qualified chartered accountants working in the largest London firms occupy a somewhat elite position. None of my interviewees were employed to prepare accounts, or to record a company's transactions; they worked, for instance, as auditors, financial consultants, or insolvency practitioners, engaged in work that is inherently judgemental and high level. Although my interviewees were not partners overseeing teams doing the judgemental, high-level work I describe, neither were they the most junior members of those teams. Partners and other senior people, in any case, rely on other members of their teams to formulate the information on which they base their decisions. The more senior they are, the more decisions they have to make, and the greater the level of trust they must place in their subordinates. Consequential judgements are delegated to accountants like those I interviewed, in the form of dilemmas such as the following: Should I mention this to the partner? What information should I show him or her? How should I present that information, knowing that the way I present it will affect the decision he or she makes? Judgemental accounting decisions are therefore team efforts to which accountants like those I interviewed make important contributions.

More broadly, it is a sociological mistake to study only the senior people in large organizations. Senior partners, like chief executives of large companies, have limited control over their firms. This is firstly because absolute power does not pass through them but is instead diffused in complex ways through their organizations, secondly because they are themselves products of their institutional and professional environment to a large extent, and thirdly because they are constrained by social expectations of how they should perform their role (most specifically the expectations of clients and colleagues). Focusing on middle-ranking accountants (neither very junior nor very senior) enabled me to study the detail of how accounting work is done, rather than talking to people who are either too inexperienced and under-socialized to be representative, or so senior that their role is more to manage the work than to actually do it. I was therefore able to explore the accounting discourse in use, and it is the power of that discourse, not of particular individual accountants, that is significant here.

Interview questions

The questions I asked my interviewees were based on the interview schedule below, which I developed during my earliest interviews. However, it was no more than a prompt: I adapted my interview strategy to each encounter, using the schedule simply to ensure that I kept all the discussions relevant.

Interview schedule

1. Motivation (introductory)
   What do you do?
   Why?

2. Champion Chicken
   What would you do in this scenario?
   What are the facts? What are the value-judgements?
   Is the scenario familiar? Have you been in a similar situation?

3. Technical disputes
   Have you ever had to dispute a profit figure?
   More generally, what was the most intense dispute you've experienced professionally?

4. Professionalism and expertise
   What makes a good accountant? Who succeeds in your firm?
   Are you an expert? When have you acted expertly?
   Are you a professional? When have you acted professionally?

5. Performance and transparency
   When have you had to tread most carefully at work? Why?
   When have you not told the truth at work? Why?

6. Ethics
   When have you discussed ethical issues with colleagues?
   When have you experienced low ethical standards at work? Why were they accepted?
   When have you had to choose between personal ethics and those expected of you at work?
   How did you explain the conflict to colleagues or managers?
   How could you be corrupted?

The second section of the interview schedule refers to a broad-ranging discussion that I had with each interviewee about a fictional scenario I gave to them in advance. The scenario is discussed in detail in Chapter 3. It provided a common point of comparison between interviews, and a way of focusing interviewees on the types of situation I wanted to explore. After discussing the scenario, I asked for similar situations my interviewees had been in themselves, which we discussed by way of transition to their own experience.

I asked about technical disputes my interviewees had experienced in order to explore where the crystallization of accounting facts either failed or came under pressure. Asking about intense disputes brought out the emotive and argumentative aspects of knowledge construction, and broadened the discussion beyond areas that interviewees defined as accounting matters. I focused particularly on the difficulties of communication surrounding such disputes, in order to explore the limitations of the discourse with which my interviewees were working. In the final portion of the interviews I explored what communication and negotiation of ethical positions was possible between accountants in a professional context, and what kind of ethical vocabulary they used. Unless a specific opportunity arose to discuss them earlier on, I waited until late in the interviews, when interviewees were most comfortable, before broaching these increasingly taboo and hazardous topics.

Interview technique

Whilst interviewing, I did not try to elicit the attitudes of interviewees, but either to engage them in technical or professional disputes, or to explore practical situations they remembered. Variations in attitudes expressed in response to different lines of questioning in the same interview, as often occur, undermine attempts to identify what interviewees really think. I therefore elicited responses from interviewees that I could analyse in terms of practices and conditions of possibility rather than attitudes (Potter and Wetherell 1987).

Although I did not seek my interviewees' attitudes in the abstract, however, I did explore their motivational thinking with respect to specific actions, often by asking why. There was a danger in doing so of asking closed questions which drew out particular kinds of reasons and focused on particular actions as needing to be justified. Whilst being sensitive to this, I nonetheless chose to treat my interviewees as peers who might change my mind, rather than as specimens demanding impartial representation. 'The interpreter does not dispense with his prejudices. He puts them at risk' (Weinsheimer 1985, 208). I was therefore actively engaged throughout each interview, offering alternative perspectives, seeking contradictions, revisiting key questions, and challenging the positions taken by interviewees. This active approach enabled me to test the limits of my interviewees' discourse and the responses that they were able to make through it. My interview practice thus embraced, rather than resisted, the impossibility of impartiality in an interview setting. I could have made other choices, but not no choice at all. An interviewer, like an actor on stage, changes the scene simply by being there. Even standing on a stage in 'neutral' is very different to being offstage; it is not actually neutral, but rather a choice to interact with an audience in a particular conventional way.

Each interview lasted around ninety minutes. I interviewed my respondents on an anonymous basis at the London School of Economics (i.e. away from their places of work), in order to set them at ease about speaking to me openly. Our conversations confirmed that accountants are very sensitive about the slightest impression they create within their firms, so worries about being seen in the office with a researcher or about being overheard would have restricted their responses there. This is particularly the case given the difficulty of achieving privacy in offices that are largely open plan.

Interpretative strategies

Whilst I argued with interviewees in order to draw them out when we spoke, I did not use the same strategy when analysing the interview transcripts afterwards. At that stage, my priority was to understand rather than to challenge their discourse:

When we try to understand a text, we do not try to transpose ourselves into the author's mind but, if one wants to use this terminology, we try to transpose ourselves into the perspective within which he has formed his views. But this simply means that we try to understand how what he is saying could be right. If we want to understand, we will try to make his arguments even stronger. (Gadamer 1989, 292)

My analysis was, therefore, more sympathetic to my interviewees than were the interviews themselves. I interpreted the interviews qualitatively using techniques of discourse, narrative, and textual analysis, and in particular by asking such questions as the following: What stylistic choices has the speaker made? Is there a subtext that might alter the most obvious interpretation? How has a particular kind of utterance become possible or impossible in my interviewees' social context?[108] What story is being told about the speaker, as well as his subject? What role is the interviewee playing, and how? What does the interviewee want to persuade me of, and why? These questions are drawn from distinct critical traditions, including rhetoric, deconstruction, narrative analysis, and dramatic criticism. Cumulatively, asking them enabled me to gain a multidimensional perspective on what interviewees were doing in response to my interview questions. Of course, I was also sensitive to, and interested in, how my questions themselves provoked particular kinds of response.

The question about storytelling is more helpful in interpreting accounting discourse than one might think. Although accounting facts are couched in static terms, their construction is littered with competing narratives that are suppressed in the final product. More broadly, my interviewees appealed to a range of narratives in order to persuade both themselves and others of the legitimacy and coherence of their actions and beliefs. When I asked them what they did and why, I found that they understood their current work as part of a personal narrative, with a past and a future. The importance of such narratives leads me to adopt a different emphasis to that of many previous studies. The first full-scale ethnography of accountants' training in England, for instance, adopted a symbolic interactionist approach, focusing on the day-to-day aspects of accounting life. Insofar as accountants' personal narratives are considered under this approach, they are considered as processes of socialization, whereby accountants are gradually moulded by their day-to-day practice and by the institutions relevant to their work (Coffey 1993, 44–5). The only other full-scale study of accountants' training in England to date distanced itself from symbolic interactionism to some extent, although it retained a more general phenomenological focus on situational specifics (Anderson-Gough, Grey and Robson 1998a, 36–42, 126).[109] *Accountants' Truth* differs in its focus, taking a greater interest in questions of character, ethics, and identity, for instance. As Robert White puts it, describing the work of Henry Murray:

If small parts and short segments of human affairs have to be isolated for detailed scrutiny, they must still be understood as parts of a patterned organic system and as segments of a lifelong process. This has never meant [for Murray] that all research should take the form of collecting life histories. . . . It implies simply that isolating, fragmenting, and learning just a tiny bit about a lot of people tends to carry us away from what is most worth studying. (White 1963, xiii)

White, like several post-war contemporaries including Erich Fromm and David Riesman, used psychoanalytic techniques to gain insight into social trends (Fromm 1956; Riesman, Denney, and Glazer 1950). This research agenda suffered a setback, however, with the demise of psychoanalysis itself in mainstream psychology,[110] and was displaced by movements such as symbolic interactionism, ethnomethodology, and phenomenology, which were more interested in social practices and institutions (Blumer 1969; Garfinkel 1967; Schutz 1967). However a concern with the relation between character and culture did not only survive in the tradition of life history interviewing (on which see Plummer 2001). In economic sociology, it persisted in the interview technique of writers such as Sennett (1998), Sennett and Cobb (1977), Margolis (1979), Hochschild (1983), and Wajcman (1983; 1998).

My focus on accounting discourse rather than on accountants themselves, and on the accounting field rather than on society as a whole, does tend in a phenomenological direction. Although I knew some of my interviewees, most of the interviews were one-off encounters between strangers. My primary interest being in discourse rather than in individuals led me not to ask for my interviewees' overall life stories, or to seek details of their social backgrounds systematically. Nonetheless, I placed strong emphasis on White's observation that the part cannot be understood independently of the whole, exploring my interviewees' narratives and motivations as necessary to flesh out the contexts and back stories of the situations we discussed. My interest in character and ethics, and ultimately in the potential of professional identity in the accounting field, is commensurate with this difference in emphasis.

Advantages and limitations to the methodology

The general advantages and limitations of research based on in-depth interviews are well documented, and are relevant here (e.g. see Creswell 1998; King, Keohane, and Verba 1994; Lather 1991; Plummer 2001; Silverman 2001). However, there are particular reasons why in-depth interviewing suited this study. Firstly, my interest in accounting discourse made it appropriate to analyse a small number of interviews in detail, rather than using a larger sample or engaging in participant observation that would have necessitated a less detailed approach. Interviewing was better suited to studying accounting discourse than it would have been to studying how that discourse becomes established in particular institutional contexts, for instance, for which participant observation may have been preferable (e.g. see Born 2005, 97–128). Secondly, my prior experience of the field meant that I already had a lot of the background knowledge I might otherwise have gained through participant observation. Thirdly, the interviews to some extent replicated my interviewees' experience of debating accounting treatments with clients and colleagues. Therefore the artificiality of the interview context was not, in this case, as much of a drawback as it might at first seem, because the creation of accounting facts is itself an artificial process. Luke, for instance, even thanked me for my time after his interview, and was then embarrassed at having interacted with me as if I were a client.

Nonetheless, my choice of method assumes that accountants' discourse is highly standardized. If that were not the case, not only would a small sample be insufficient to draw worthwhile conclusions, but studying accounting discourse would itself not make sense. I have argued for this assumption in Chapters 1 and 4, but it was in any case supported by my experience of the field. Twenty interviews were sufficient to identify regularities in interviewees' verbal reasoning, and incremental interviews were becoming repetitive and yielding few fresh insights. Given that accountants are rigorously socialized, and that they must discursively represent commercial information in accordance with accounting standards that are scrupulous in establishing terminology, a lack of such regularities would have been surprising. Accounting language's continuity across organizations is, consequently, more interesting to me than its uniqueness in any particular firm, so I chose not to work within a case study organization. I did not restrict my sample to those engaged in a particular area of work within the big four firms, such as audit or tax, for similar reasons.[111]

I do not, then, seek to prove the existence of a standardized accounting discourse through my empirical research, but instead I establish that as a well-founded assumption at the outset. My research itself is directed towards achieving and communicating insights into that discourse. I justify some further generalizations by reference to the constraints my interviewees worked within, as with my discussion of what it was possible for them to say, and what roles they could adopt. Beyond this, however, it is only possible to make a persuasive but not conclusive argument for the broader relevance of research such as this. Patti Lather articulates some of the strategies that I have used to do so: I have sought to demonstrate 'triangulation validity' by reference to a range of relevant literatures and to written accounting standards and professional guidance, as well as to my interview material; 'construct validity' by looking for what counts as fact within accountancy rather than imposing external criteria; 'face validity' by making my interpretation of a specialist area as readily accessible to non-specialists as possible; and 'catalytic validity' by openly conveying my normative position with respect to the research and arguing for its importance on that basis (Lather 1991, 66–9). I am of course not solely describing accountancy but, inevitably, also participating in its ongoing social construction. The accounting discourse itself does not offer an impartial impression of social reality in any case, but is worthy of analysis precisely because it does not.

Readers familiar with work in other professional service environments, particularly consulting and law, will see many important parallels with accounting. Unfortunately, it is beyond the scope of this book to make detailed comparisons to other fields, although I do situate accounting within the broader social context it shares with them. My argument here relies neither on generalizability beyond nor uniqueness to accounting. It simply claims validity with respect to accounting, which matters as a specific case because of its central role in economic life.

Interview research as an insider

I conducted and interpreted the interviews as an insider, having spent four years training and working as a chartered accountant with PricewaterhouseCoopers in London between 1998 and 2002. The characteristics and experience according to which I selected my interviewees are characteristics and experience that I share. My interviewees were therefore not only my peers but, in some schematic respects, they were those of my peers who were most like me. I found that accountants were more at ease talking to me in the knowledge that I shared their professional background, so I made no attempt to hide that fact. Our shared experience was, in any case, our basis for discussion: it would have been difficult for a non-accountant to gain access to my interviewees, or to debate accounting matters with them in the detail necessary for this study.

I argued in the previous section that my personal experience of accountancy compensates in some ways for the absence of an ethnographic element to the research, but in reality it does both less and more than this. It does less in that I was not consciously researching during my time in the field, and so did not record my experiences or analyse them sociologically. I was not attempting to maintain objectivity, although I have argued above that this is a questionable ideal. Because most of my interviews were conducted with people who had not previously been my colleagues, I did not develop the trust and rapport with my interviewees that ethnographers gain. My experience gave me more insight than an ethnography could have done, however, in that I lived it for real, rather than as a temporary foray engaged in for research purposes. As both my own research and the other research I refer to during the book attest, the experience of young accountants in the large firms is an intense and demanding one. The discipline, competitiveness, insecurity, and camaraderie it breeds are difficult to access without having experienced the stakes involved when, for instance, your first job and career depend on passing a competitive exam, or your sense of self-worth becomes bound up with your colleagues' appraisal of your interpersonal impact. This is a visceral experience that cannot be readily observed from without. Having shared it with my interviewees gave me a heightened sense for which questions mattered most as our conversations developed, and for what their answers meant.

It might be asked why, having shared my interviewees' professional experience, I would want to ask them about it in interviews at all. Surely I already knew the answers to my questions? This objection is a challenge to anyone conducting research as an insider. Yet the kind of knowledge I shared with my interviewees was an inarticulate practical knowledge. The interviews created a kind of dialogue which does not ordinarily take place, and which made that knowledge explicit and debatable. The interviews were important not for what my interviewees could tell me that I did not already know, therefore, but for their witting or unwitting collaboration in an attempt, through dialogue and argument, to find ways to articulate, debate, and criticize our shared experience and practice.

Notes

Notes to Chapter 1

1. Well-known examples at the time of writing include Parmalat, WorldCom, Enron, Bank of Credit and Commerce International (BCCI), and Polly Peck.
2. On professionalism as an alternative logic to that of markets or organizations, rather than as an empirically observed phenomenon, see Freidson (2001). I discuss professionalism empirically in Chapter 6.
3. Christopher Stone expresses this problem more generally: '[E]ven if management *had* made an express promise to shareholders to "maximize your profits," ... I am not persuaded that the ordinary person would interpret it to mean "maximize *in every way you can possibly get away with,* even if that means polluting the environment, ignoring or breaking the law"' (1975, 82, emphasis in original).
4. For evidence of how far business regulation has come over the last century, see Robb (1992).
5. Enron appeared to be one of America's largest companies, having reported revenues over $100 billion in 2000 (Fusaro and Miller 2002, 173).
6. The fact that our society's large commercial and financial institutions are private businesses in legal form can make such narrow-mindedness seem not only acceptable but laudable. However, the recent interventions by various governments to bail out the global banking system demonstrate that its constituent institutions are, in practice, private concerns only when things go well. They are so interconnected with the rest of the economy that when things go badly, it is the public's problem.
7. Ninety-seven of the Financial Times Stock Exchange (FTSE) 100 companies had a chief financial officer early in 2008. Of these, sixty-six had previously worked for at least one of the big four, and fifty-six had qualified with the ICAEW (Fisher 2008).
8. Readers seeking a fuller description than is possible here should refer to these ethnographies (Anderson-Gough, Grey, and Robson 1998*a*; Coffey 1993; Power 1991). There are also several more general ethnographic and interview-based studies of the large firms in the United Kingdom and in the United States (e.g. Covaleski et al. 1998; Dirsmith, Heian, and Covaleski 1997; Empson 2004; Harper 1988; Montagna 1974).
9. 70 per cent of ICAEW trainees in 2002 were under 25, and only 1 per cent were over 35 (Financial Reporting Council 2003, 46). The average age of KPMG's UK workforce in 2004 was a mere 28 (KPMG 2004).
10. One of Amanda Coffey's interviewees was able to cope with his own lack of success as an auditor by reflecting that 'auditors are unexceptional people. If you are quiet,

diligent and have no real views of your own then you'll be a good auditor.... Auditors are solid and reliable but unexceptional.... Unexceptional people do exceptional audits' (Coffey 1993, 496).

11. The Institute markets its qualification, which is called the Associate Chartered Accountant (ACA), as follows: 'If you want a career with all the colours of the rainbow, choose Chartered Accountancy. If you want the gold, choose the ACA. It's not just the premier professional accounting qualification. For those looking to make it in business, the ACA is the most valuable financially based business qualification there is' (ICAEW [n.d.]). In the words of one of my interviewees, accountancy training seems to promise a very general opportunity to 'get a good business background'.

12. For critical discussion of this culture, see Heelas and Morris (1992).

13. I focus on the United Kingdom's largest institute, the ICAEW, for simplicity, although it does have several competitors.

14. When many of my interviewees and I trained, there were ten papers to be taken in total. The ICAEW average pass rates for individual papers in 2002 ranged between 76 per cent and 84 per cent of candidates (ICAEW 2003). Trainees at the large firms tend to do better than average, however. Deloitte, for instance, published overall pass rates of 89 per cent and 81 per cent for the June 2002 Professional and Advanced Stages of the exams, which each included several papers, compared to ICAEW averages of 67 per cent and 63 per cent respectively (Deloitte 2004). The current policies of the firms regarding exam failures were difficult to verify. I emailed all of their graduate recruitment departments in May 2004, but received only one response: Deloitte said that the policy was a confidential matter, and was disclosed only to those people who accepted its offer of a job, approximately six weeks before they started. PricewaterhouseCoopers' web site mentioned that only one resit of each exam was allowed in general (PricewaterhouseCoopers 2004). When I trained, although no resit was allowed for the first two exams, one resit was allowed thereafter.

15. The UK accounting standards I refer to throughout applied to all UK company accounts at the time this research was conducted (with exemption criteria for smaller companies), although at the time of writing UK listed companies are now required to use International Financial Reporting Standards (IFRSs). Some of the technical debates I discuss would be different in their specifics under the international standards, but these differences do not significantly affect my overall analysis.

16. Such an approach may seem shallow, but is also well adapted to the flexible modern labour market (see Sennett 1998).

17. I am grateful to Georgina Born for suggesting this point as a matter of class confidence, although I lack the data to confirm its class-based aspect.

18. In mediaeval universities, rhetoric remained a primary means of knowledge production (Poovey 1998, 37), although it was becoming an increasingly literate rather than oral process.

19. Of course, the history of accounting also needs to be set against the broader backdrop of Western economic history in general. The very idea of economic man as a rational chooser and systematic accumulator of wealth is itself relatively

recent, reflecting the transition from mediaeval feudalism to modern capitalism (Heilbroner 1991; Hirschman 1977; Weber 1992).

20. This is not a claim that statements can never be held to objective standards, although we shall see that with respect to accounting, apparently objective standards are very often debatable.

21. In formulating these definitions, I am indebted to Chaim Perelman and Lucie Obrechts-Tyteca (1969, 67–76).

22. In the pages that follow, I increasingly discuss individual accountants' experience of constituting (or struggling to constitute) themselves in this way in terms of the cultivation of character. In doing so I use an interpretive vocabulary which moral philosophers might identify as resembling that of virtue ethics (e.g. Aristotle 2000; Hursthouse 1999; Swanton 2003). I begin from Foucault, however, in order to maintain the empirical specificity of my analysis and to avoid defending a universal position in moral philosophy. Foucault's approach is, on my reading, largely compatible with virtue ethics, but it has the advantage of historicizing rather than black boxing what actually counts as virtue. In other words, his approach demonstrates how a collectively agreed desirable relation between self and action can be the foundation of ethics, at the same time as being historically relative and negotiable (Foucault 1983).

Notes to Chapter 2

23. Anderson-Gough, Grey, and Robson, for instance, seek to overcome this problem by connecting what they call conduct and context through the concept of professional socialization (2002). A vocabulary in which to discuss the psychological and emotional processes by which that socialization actually occurs would help to advance such efforts.

24. Studies of accounting which appeal to actor network theory tend to reject the latter view particularly strongly (e.g. Briers and Chua 2001).

25. I do not discuss accountants' physical self-presentation and grooming, although they do pay very close attention to this. For detailed description, see Coffey (1993, 184–219). Richard Harper's earlier ethnography also emphasizes appearance and professional image, commensurately with its dramaturgical paradigm (1988).

26. A bullshitter, for Adrian, is more of a salesman than a liar: 'Bullshitting in the sense of being good at thinking on their feet of what they're trying to do in a positive way.'

27. VAT is the most common UK sales tax.

28. The 'board pack' refers to the pack of financial information presented to the board at the meeting.

29. For more detailed discussion of the role of time management in the socialization of trainee accountants, see Coffey (1994) and Anderson-Gough, Grey, and Robson (2001).

30. Hochschild's insight here was anticipated by C. Wright Mills, who observed that 'white-collar people ... sell not only their time and energy but their personalities as well' (2002, xvii).

Notes to Chapter 3

31. The scenario is loosely based on a real-life example that arose during the first interview, and was used in the third and subsequent interviews.
32. FRSs can be found in the ICAEW's *Accounting Standards and Guidance for Members* (Accounting Standards Board 2001). See also *n.* 15.
33. SSAPs are UK accounting standards issued before the FRSs, and can be found in the same volume (see *n.* 32).
34. The phrase 'statutory accounts' refers to the accounts a company is legally required to publish on an annual basis. These are the accounts to which accounting standards apply. Management accounts, by contrast, are those used by the company's management for decision-making purposes, and are not publicly available.
35. Writing an amount off means treating it as an expense in the P&L.
36. Even Sir David Tweedie, Chairman of the International Accounting Standards Board (IASB), argues that readers of accounts should not focus too closely on profit. During a dialogue with Howard Davies at the London School of Economics on 6 February 2006, he compared 'the bottom line' to a haggis: 'If you knew what was in it, you wouldn't touch it with a bargepole.'
37. A bank covenant is a condition that a company must meet if its loan is not to fall into default. If Champion failed to meet a covenant concerning its profitability, the bank could demand immediate repayment of its loan, which might bankrupt the company.
38. On the rhetorical use of cliché to secure agreement in accounting, see Anderson-Gough, Grey, and Robson (1998*b*, 569).
39. These conclusions must be treated with caution because the wording of the scenario itself juxtaposes Champion employees' motives with their accounting proposals, perhaps suggesting the kind of approach Joe took. However, when we discussed examples of his own work later in his interview, Joe outlined a generic approach to determining accounting entries which was as much psychological as technical, and explicitly relied on protagonists' motivations.
40. Indeed, "creative accounting" has come to refer to fraudulent rather than routine accounting practices.

Notes to Chapter 4

41. Although I refer here to Bruno Latour and will later refer to Michel Callon, both of whose analyses of the economic derive from science and technology studies, what I refer to as technical is clearly not scientific or technological. My definition is instead consistent with my interviewees' use of the word to describe practices of knowledge construction that any accountant would feel obliged to publicly and explicitly accept.
42. This sketch of Weber's thought is necessarily simplified, particularly since he uses the terms rationality and rationalization in a variety of ways in different parts of his work. Helpful discussions of these concepts which go into more detail than is possible here can be found in Brubaker (1984, 35–45) and Espeland (1998, 34–7).

43. I therefore refer to disillusionment rather than to Weber's 'disenchantment' in order to avoid implying the stark division between knowledge and normative commitment that he assumes in, for example, *Science as a Vocation* (Weber 1946).

44. An overview of current regulation can be gained with reference to the Financial Reporting Council's web site, www.frc.org.uk. The International Accounting Standards Board (IASB) is developing an even more sophisticated system of accounting standards, which have already superseded standards issued by the Accounting Standards Board (part of the Financial Reporting Council) with respect to companies listed on the London Stock Exchange and the Alternative Investment Market. By contrast, David Myddelton comments: 'On the back of my office door I have the Companies Act rules from 1948. I've condensed it down to seven pages. We didn't have any accounting standards in those days' (Fielding 2004, 14).

45. The form accounting takes is, moreover, at least somewhat historically changeable (e.g. Burchell, Clubb and Hopwood 1985; Power 1992). However, such change is most likely to take place at what Peter Miller calls 'the margins of accounting' (1998), and the likelihood of what is marginal to accounting eventually becoming core to it is much greater than that of its core becoming marginal. Debates over accounting standards and practices, however politicized, are not evidence that rationalization is not possible or is not gradually happening over the long term.

46. At a very general level, this point of view is well established. Karl Marx, for instance, criticized nineteenth-century political economy for presenting the way the economy was as the way it had to be (Marx 1977). Callon is innovative, however, in his contribution to a long-standing debate in economic sociology concerning the embeddedness, or otherwise, of economic activity in social life. Many thinkers have debated whether or not the economy can be fruitfully analysed in abstraction from its social context (e.g. Granovetter 1985; Polanyi 1992; Simmel 1991; Zelizer 1997; for an overview see Slater and Tonkiss 2001). Callon appropriates the metaphor of framing to break new ground in these debates but, as we shall see, this focus leads him to be more concerned with individual market interactions than with longer-term developments in accounting.

47. My references to translation do not allude to Callon's use of the term to describe power struggles in actor networks (e.g. Callon 1986).

48. Readers familiar with these debates might think that my argument resembles James Carrier and Daniel Miller's theory of virtualism. Virtualism postulates, against Callon, that economics does not format market exchange by disentangling it in particular ways from its context, but rather by moulding the social world as a whole in its own image (Carrier and Miller 1998; D. Miller 2002). I depart from this view, with respect to accounting, in upholding the concept of framing. Although accounting clearly does influence aspects of social life already recognizable in accounting terms, unless public debates such as those highlighted by Callon force the issue mainstream accounting tends to exclude context from the accounting frame rather than seeking to mould it. As the next section will show, my interviewees, being keen to simplify, actively resisted colonizing what they considered to be non-accounting areas. If I am right that highly rationalized accounting knowledge is not compelling, moreover, then virtualism cannot succeed by means of such rationalization alone.

49. SASs can be found in the ICAEW's *Auditing Standards and Guidance for Members* (Auditing Standards Board 2001).
50. Intangible assets lack physical substance but have economic value (FRS 10, paragraph 2). The fair value of an asset (as distinct from its historical cost) is the price it would achieve in a current transaction between willing parties (FRS 7, paragraph 2).
51. Recall Weber's description of rationalization as an increase in 'the extent of quantitative calculation or accounting which is technically possible and which is actually applied' (1968, 85). This is possible within a given frame as a result of the same information being more finely worked over (an increase in intensity), or by the expansion of the frame to include more information (an increase in scope).
52. The reason this task was 'delegated' to Joe may well have been that no one at his firm expected there to be much argument over the number. Yet what matters here is not Joe's personal influence, but that of the accounting discourse he wields. The confidence of his superiors in the power of that discourse, even in the hands of middle-ranking members of staff, actually reinforces the point that the discourse is powerful enough to enable those who wield it to transcend potential disputes.
53. A provision is a liability recognized in an entity's accounts. It represents a present obligation which results from a past event and is of uncertain timing or amount (FRS 12, paragraphs 2 and 14).
54. The ritual aspects of auditing have been analysed more generally by Brian Pentland (1993).
55. Jason said this in the context of having qualified with CIPFA (uniquely amongst my interviewees).
56. All the interviews in which tax was discussed took place before the recent government initiatives requiring disclosure of tax avoidance schemes in advance of their implementation. At the time of writing it remains to be seen what long-term effect these initiatives will have.

Notes to Chapter 5

57. For an ethnographic description of how this distinction is experienced see Coffey (1993, 342–440).
58. It could be argued that accountants thus become pragmatists in the philosophical sense, defining truth as what it is useful to believe; however, it is beyond our scope here to map accountants' practice onto the debates surrounding philosophical pragmatism.
59. This does not imply that language limits cognitive capacity. Ways of thinking which are not readily facilitated by the language's structure, or are not made familiar through the conventions of its use, may be possible for speakers of that language, but they will be more difficult to express, to learn, or to think.
60. Whorf's argument does not, however, require the distinctions made in language to be conscious on the part of its users, as Max Black seems to assume when accusing him of 'the *linguist's fallacy* of imputing his own sophisticated attitudes to the speakers he is studying' (Black 1962*a*, 247). The demonstrable embodiment of

such distinctions in a language implies that its speakers have a practical rather than an intellectual capacity to make them.

61. Nonetheless, even insofar as language use merely reflects patterns of thought, it remains indicative of them and worthy of study on that basis.

62. I follow George Lakoff in this regard, who has studied metaphorical thought in various empirical domains (e.g. 1987; 2002; Lakoff and Johnson 1980). Little has been written about metaphor in accounting, but the exceptions include Walters-York (1996), Young (2001), and work in progress by Laura Spira and Michael Page. For discussion of metaphors in management more generally, see Morgan (2006).

63. Max Black calls this an *'interaction view* of metaphor' and has defended it against what he calls the substitution view (on which a metaphor substitutes for a literal expression with the same meaning) and the comparison view (on which a metaphor, like a condensed simile, compares one literal concept to another), and also against Donald Davidson's contention that a metaphor has no meaning beyond its literal one (Black 1962*b*, 38; 1979).

64. For a review of the broader empirical evidence that metaphorical language can constitute the actual framework through which people understand phenomena and respond to them, see Foley (1997, 179–91).

65. A more detailed discussion than is possible here would need to recognize that risk itself is understood through a variety of different metaphors. These metaphors have been explored by Joni Young (2001), who finds that they tend to reinforce the idea that risk can be contained and controlled, which is its salient characteristic here.

66. Of course accounts are prepared for users, some of whom might sue the auditors, so there is a link between the risk to the auditors and the appropriateness of the accounts to their intended audience. However, this approach defines auditors' responsibilities very narrowly in relation to the small subset of a company's stakeholders who might sue them.

67. The Inland Revenue was merged with Her Majesty's Customs and Excise in 2005, to form Her Majesty's Revenue and Customs.

68. In George Lakoff's terms, this would roughly constitute a strict father model of the family rather than a nurturant parent model, corresponding to conservative rather than liberal political and domestic sensibilities (2002).

69. Anderson-Gough, Grey, and Robson, having studied trainees in two of the large accountancy firms in northern England in 1997, argue that identification both with firm and profession are subordinate to identification with a career narrative, and that identification with a firm simply reflects the belief that a trainee may have a career there (1998*a*, 135; see also Grey 1994). Although their conclusion would be consistent with the strategic and sporting metaphors discussed above, the metaphor of firm as family nonetheless suggests that accountants do experience a particular kind of affinity with their firms (for further evidence of this see also Empson 2004). By contrast, we will see in the next chapter that accountants' affinity with their profession is much weaker, and Chapter 7 will explore the significance of this discrepancy for accountants' professional ethics.

70. It might be responded that Nietzsche is talking at a more general level than I am, and that the provisionality of accounting facts relates to an underlying, perhaps 'oper-

ational', or perhaps still more fundamental societal world view that my interviewees took for granted. Yet if they recognized such a bedrock, not only could they not articulate it in the uncritical way Nietzsche might lead us to expect, but they struggled to articulate it at all.

71. With respect to metaphors in management, Ramsay (2004) suggests ways of making the use of metaphor more rigorous, and Oswick, Keenoy, and Grant (2002) argue against an overemphasis on metaphor at the expense of other tropes.

Notes to Chapter 6

72. Even theories that find professional institutions to be of continuing importance may be consistent with the demise of a distinctively professional ethos. Walter Powell and Paul DiMaggio, for instance, explain the persistence of professionalism in large organizations by saying that 'the causes of bureaucratization and rationalization have changed', and that professions now function as drivers of these processes rather than as counterbalances to them, facilitating as they do the transfer of standardized knowledge across firms, and the common socialization of professionals (1991, 63–4, 71). Yet whether professionalism reinforces the type of homogenization embodied in existing bureaucracies, or conflicts with it, depends on the kind of knowledge transferred and the kind of socialization carried out. I will later argue that professionalism could advance homogeneity in accountants' approach to their work *without* advancing bureaucratization, rationalization, or commercialization in their current forms. It is not inevitable that professional know-how must be bureaucratic, rationalistic, or commercial.

73. Wilensky (1964) argues against this idea of what he calls 'the professionalization of everyone'. His arguments derive, however, more from his view of what the word professional should mean than from his analysis of what it is actually taken to mean in practice.

74. Cooper and Robson have more recently argued that the big four firms are gaining increasing importance with respect to regulatory processes (2006).

75. Preston et al. (1995) describe how this shift took place in relation to accounting in the United States. There is, nonetheless, some desire to make international accounting standards more principles-based (see Chapter 8).

76. Billing for value means billing according to the usefulness of advice to the client, rather than according to the cost of providing it.

Notes to Chapter 7

77. In Chapter 1, I provisionally adopted Michel Foucault's definition of ethics as 'the kind of relationship you ought to have with yourself... which determines how the individual is supposed to constitute himself as a moral subject of his own actions' (1983, 238). As explained in that chapter, my adoption of this definition demarcates a sphere of empirical interest, rather than asserting a preconceived position in moral philosophy.

78. My use of the term 'moral' again follows Foucault who, as discussed in Chapter 1, used it to refer to the prevalent behavioural code that individuals in a society are expected to observe.

79. At the extreme, of course, very senior people may be *liable* for their employees' actions, but it is hard to hold them *responsible* for those actions in any meaningful moral sense, so the concentration of responsibility at the top can actually create a moral vacuum (Thompson 2005, 14).

80. For arguments against this justification, see Bakan (2005) and Stone (1975).

81. As Hendry goes on to say, '[w]hat is perhaps most striking about Enron and World-Com is not the corruption but how so many people were too busy to notice that something was wrong' (2005).

82. There is reason to believe that this matters even within a narrow accounting frame. For instance, Ponemon and Gabhart, moral psychologists conducting empirical research in the United States and Canada, argue that the development of 'ethical reasoning' on the part of auditors directly affects the quality of their work. 'Auditors with more highly developed levels of ethical reasoning show greater sensitivity to potentially important signals of the client organization and its management when judging audit risk or the possibility of material accounting error' (1993, 82). For a critique of Ponemon and Gabhart's approach, however, see Power (1995).

83. The precise tax details of the scenario have been changed to preserve anonymity.

84. Generic audit software contains worksheets relating to several thousand tasks, known as 'steps', which might need to be carried out on an audit. Tom's colleague should have deleted those that were not relevant to the specific audit he was engaged in, rather than those he did not understand.

85. I do not mean to suggest that there are no opportunities for accountants to discuss ethical issues: both the ICAEW and the big four firms have been proactive in setting up helplines and counselling services, for instance. However these initiatives, though valuable, have not succeeded in making such discussions integral to accounting work: they are still seen as exceptional or as a way to deal with problems.

86. Richard Sennett criticizes Goffman, however, for failing to recognize the dynamic aspect to character. 'In Goffman's world, people behave, but they do not have experience' (Sennett 2002, 36). As a result, Sennett argues, Goffman cannot see how the roles people play might engender their commitment.

Notes to Chapter 8

87. The requirement to prepare accounts that are 'true and fair' has already been enshrined in successive Companies Acts (most recently *Companies Act 2006* (c. 46), part 15, chapter 4, paragraph 393). The challenge is to translate this requirement into practice in a more sophisticated way.

88. For development of this argument in a very different context, see Arendt (2006, 276–9, 296).

89. For further discussion see May (1996, 65–85). On the shaping of the self in various social and institutional contexts, see for example Goffman (1968) and Rose (1999). My argument does not imply that accountants' professional identities must become their only identities, but only that their professional identities must be conceived in ethical as well as functional terms.

90. For a more detailed argument as to why regulation should focus on processes as well as outcomes, see Stone (1975, especially 115–18).

91. Of course this approach presumes good regulation, and therefore that moral arguments for bypassing rules, or helping clients to do so, do not apply.

92. ICAS's report *Principles not Rules: A Question of Judgement*, defines a principle as 'a general statement, with widespread support, which is intended to support truth and fairness and acts as a guide to action' (ICAS 2006, 2). Principles are, therefore, less prescriptive and less detailed than rules (see also ICAEW 2006).

93. The Chairman of the International Accounting Standards Board, at least, is well aware of this (Tweedie 2006).

94. Recent changes to the ICAEW's ethics training and development programmes demonstrate sensitivity to this (details are available at www.icaew.co.uk at the time of writing). See also the ICAEW's recent report, *Reporting with Integrity* (Davis and Hodgkinson 2007).

95. Dennis Thompson rightly criticizes what he refers to as the John Wayne theory of ethics: '[S]tand up for what you think is right, but never say why' (2005, 8). Yet what is needed is not a technical discourse of professional ethics, which would, like other technical discourses, eventually displace rather than address questions of value. Collective ethical engagement requires discourse, but it will become superficial if it is reduced to the discursive level.

96. For a comparative study addressing this issue, see Empson and Chapman (2006).

97. Norman Macintosh proposes 'heteroglossic accounting' as a solution to this, whereby a company's accounts would present several different perspectives alongside each other (2002, 131–2). Whilst such accounting may be worthwhile in some specific cases, if taken too far it would defeat the objective of simplification, and would, effectively, delegate responsibility for interpreting financial information away from those best equipped to perform such interpretation.

98. A regulatory agenda that seeks exclusively to protect the interests of shareholders may not even maximize companies' economic success, because managing a business speculatively, in order to maximize share price and dividend payouts, can actually harm that business' operations in the long term (Krier 2005, 269).

99. Enlightened shareholder value refers to the long-term profitability of a company, which is affected by its development of cooperative relationships with various stakeholders, and by its reputation. The consultation preceding this legislation contains an interesting discussion of the more radical changes to directors' duties that were also considered (Company Law Review Steering Group 1999, 33–55; 2000, 9–16).

100. On the perils of translation more generally, see Marcuse (1968, 154–5).

101. Andersen, Enron's auditor and one of what were then the 'big five' accounting firms, collapsed due to lawsuits and loss of clients in the aftermath of the Enron scandal.

Notes to the Appendix

102. Most of my interviewees qualified with the ICAEW, so my discussion focuses on that institute. However Ernst & Young encouraged its trainees to become members of ICAS instead of the ICAEW in some years, so it was impractical to distinguish between ICAEW- and ICAS-trained employees of that firm. One interviewee (Jason) had trained with CIPFA but had since moved to the private sector.

103. Many of those I asked did not agree to be interviewed, so the sample was self-selecting to some extent. My emphasis on the common aspects of interviewees' shared discourse, however, minimizes this limitation.

104. I could have extended my sampling restrictions to cover race (English only) and class (middle class or aspiring middle class only). However, the dividing lines here are insufficiently clear to do so with any confidence, so I chose not to claim selection criteria which I could not uphold in practice.

105. Although 45 per cent of ICAEW trainees were female in 2002, only 20 per cent of qualified members were female (Financial Reporting Council 2003, 32, 43). The big four accounted for 46 per cent of all ICAEW trainees at 31 July 2003, and the figure would have been higher but for the fact that Ernst & Young had recently used ICAS as a substitute for the ICAEW in training many of their staff (ICAEW 2003). The fee income of the smallest of the big four in 2002/03, Ernst & Young (£755 million), was three-and-a-half times that of its nearest rival, Grant Thornton (£216 million) (Fisher 2003, 27). In 2002/03, 40 per cent of new UK students joined the London district society of the ICAEW, as compared to 5 per cent joining the Birmingham and West Midlands society (Birmingham being the United Kingdom's second largest city) (ICAEW 2003). The predominance of London remains but is less marked for ICAEW members as a whole, of whom 26 per cent were attached to the London district society on 1 April 2004, suggesting that London accountants are younger than average (ICAEW 2004). Evidence for the youth of ICAEW trainees in general, and big four trainees in particular, has already been cited in *n*. 9. In the United Kingdom and Ireland, the ICAEW had more than double the number of members of ACCA, its nearest rival, in 2002 (Financial Reporting Council 2003, 26).

106. For evidence of the striking effectiveness of this socialization, see the existing ethnographic studies of chartered accountancy training in the United Kingdom (Anderson-Gough, Grey, and Robson 1998*a*; Coffey 1993; Power 1997).

107. Of course this is not to endorse the age, gender, and regional biases in British accounting, but merely to recognize their potential salience with respect to the profession's dominant discourse. Further research would be needed to determine their actual salience.

108. The question of possibility in discourse is Michel Foucault's. He suggests that '[e]ach society has its regime of truth, its "general politics" of truth: that is, the types of discourse which it accepts and makes function as true;... the status of those who are charged with saying what counts as true' (1980*a*, 131). To ask about conditions of possibility, in this study, is to ask both how interviewees are enabled and how they are restricted by the politics of truth in accounting. What resources

are available to them to make themselves believed? What would not be believed if they said it? How have they become able, and unable, to think?

109. Although these studies of accountants' training are important examples, the picture is more complex when general ethnographies of accountancy practices, or interview-based studies, are considered. Harper (1988), for instance, adopts Goffman's interest in performance, and Empson (2004) focuses on the relation between organizational and professional identity.

110. For a recent discussion of the place of psychoanalysis in various disciplines, see Brooks and Woloch's *Whose Freud?* (2000). Psychoanalysis remains a popular paradigm in literary studies, where its emphasis on life histories can be translated onto the discussion of fictional lives and of narrative more generally (Brooks 1994; Mitchell 1981). The influence of the psychoanalytic tradition on my own interpretative practice, as described above, is clearly mediated through narrative analysis.

111. Most interviewees trained as auditors, but many had moved to different areas of their firms by the time I interviewed them. Anderson-Gough, Grey, and Robson found during their ethnography that although 'socialization processes vary between divisions', the claim that these processes 'give rise to differing conceptions of the role of the professional accountant' is 'largely false' (1998*a*, 5, 135–6).

References

Abbott, A. (1988). *The System of Professions: An Essay on the Division of Expert Labour.* Chicago, IL: University of Chicago Press.

Accounting Standards Board (2001). *Accounting Standards and Guidance for Members.* London: ICAEW.

Aho, J. A. (1985). Rhetoric and the Invention of Double Entry Bookkeeping. *Rhetorica* 3 (1), 21–43.

Anderson-Gough, F., Grey, C., and Robson, K. (1998a). *Making Up Accountants: The Organisational and Professional Socialization of Trainee Chartered Accountants.* Aldershot: Ashgate.

—— (1998b). Work Hard, Play Hard: An Analysis of Organizational Cliché in Two Accountancy Practices. *Organization* 5 (4), 565–92.

—— (2000). In the Name of the Client: The Service Ethic in Two Professional Services Firms. *Human Relations* 53 (9), 1151–74.

—— (2001). Tests of Time: Organizational Time-Reckoning and the Making of Accountants in Two Multi-national Accounting Firms. *Accounting, Organizations and Society* 26 (2), 99–122.

—— (2002). Accounting Professionals and the Accounting Profession: Linking Conduct and Context. *Accounting and Business Research* 32 (1), 41–56.

—— (2005). 'Helping Them to Forget...': The Organizational Embedding of Gender Relations in Public Audit Firms. *Accounting, Organizations and Society* 30 (5), 469–90.

Archer, W. (1957 [1888]). Masks or Faces? In: Strasberg, L. ed., '*The Paradox of Acting*' by *Denis Diderot and 'Masks or Faces?' by William Archer: Two Classics of the Art of Acting.* New York: Hill and Wang, 75–226.

Arendt, H. (1970). *On Violence.* London: Allen Lane.

—— (2006 [1963]). *Eichmann in Jerusalem: A Report on the Banality of Evil.* London: Penguin.

Aristotle (2000). *Nichomachean Ethics,* trans. Crisp, R. Cambridge: Cambridge University Press.

Auditing Standards Board (2001). *Auditing Standards and Guidance for Members.* London: ICAEW.

Bakan, J. (2005). *The Corporation: The Pathological Pursuit of Profit and Power.* Revised ed. London: Constable.

The Banks that Robbed the World (2003). The Money Programme. London, BBC2, 9 January [video: VHS].

Barry, A. and Slater, D. (2002). Technology, Politics and the Market: An Interview with Michel Callon. *Economy and Society* 31 (2), 285–306.

Beck, U. (1999). *World Risk Society.* Cambridge: Polity.

Benston, G., Bromwich, M., Litan, R. E., and Wagenhofer, A. (2003). *Following the Money: The Enron Failure and the State of Corporate Disclosure.* Washington, DC: Brookings Institution Press.

Black, M. (1962*a*). Linguistic Relativity: The Views of Benjamin Lee Whorf. In: Black, M. ed., *Models and Metaphors: Studies in Language and Philosophy.* Ithaca, NY: Cornell University Press, 244–57.

—— (1962*b*). Metaphor. In: Black, M. ed., *Models and Metaphors: Studies in Language and Philosophy.* Ithaca, NY: Cornell University Press, 25–47.

—— (1979). How Metaphors Work: A Reply to Donald Davidson. In: Sacks, S. ed., *On Metaphor.* Chicago, IL: University of Chicago Press, 181–92.

Blumer, H. (1969). *Symbolic Interactionism: Perspective and Method.* Englewood Cliffs, NJ: Prentice-Hall.

Booth, W. C. (1979). Metaphor as Rhetoric: The Problem of Evaluation. In: Sacks, S. ed., *On Metaphor.* Chicago, IL: University of Chicago Press, 47–70.

Born, G. (2005 [2004]). *Uncertain Vision: Birt, Dyke and the Reinvention of the BBC.* London: Vintage.

Boys, P. (2005). Evolution of the ICAEW. *Accountancy* 135 (1341), May, 40.

Briers, M. and Chua, W. F. (2001). The Role of Actor-Networks and Boundary Objects in Management Accounting Change: A Field Study of an Implementation of Activity-Based Costing. *Accounting, Organizations and Society* 26 (3), 237–69.

Brooks, P. (1994). *Psychoanalysis and Storytelling.* The Bucknell Lectures in Literary Theory 10. Oxford: Blackwell.

—— and Woloch, A. (2000). *Whose Freud? The Place of Psychoanalysis in Contemporary Culture.* New Haven, CT: Yale University Press.

Brubaker, R. (1984). *The Limits of Rationality: An Essay on the Social and Moral Thought of Max Weber.* London: George Allen and Unwin.

Burchell, S., Clubb, C., and Hopwood, A. G. (1985). Accounting in its Social Context: Towards a History of Value Added in the United Kingdom. *Accounting, Organizations and Society* 10 (4), 381–413.

Callon, M. (1986). Some Elements of a Sociology of Translation: Domestication of the Scallops and the Fishermen of St Brieuc Bay. In: Law, J. ed., *Power, Action and Belief: A New Sociology of Knowledge?* London: Routledge and Kegan Paul.

—— (1998*a*). An Essay on Framing and Overflowing: Economic Externalities Revisited by Sociology. In: Callon, M. ed., *The Laws of the Markets.* Oxford: Blackwell, 244–69.

—— (1998*b*). Introduction: The Embeddedness of Economic Markets in Economics. In: Callon, M. ed., *The Laws of the Markets.* Oxford: Blackwell, 1–57.

Carrier, J. G. and Miller, D. eds. (1998). *Virtualism: A New Political Economy.* Oxford: Berg.

Carr-Saunders, A. M. and Wilson, P. A. (1933). *The Professions.* Oxford: Clarendon Press.

Carruthers, B. G. and Espeland, W. N. (1991). Accounting for Rationality: Double-Entry Bookkeeping and the Rhetoric of Economic Rationality. *American Journal of Sociology* 97 (1), 31–69.

References

Certeau, M. de (1984 [1974] repr. 1988). *The Practice of Everyday Life*, trans. Rendall, S. Berkeley, CA: University of California Press.

Chomsky, N. (1988). *Language and Problems of Knowledge: The Managua Lectures*. Current Studies in Linguistics 16. Cambridge, MA: MIT Press.

Clark, H. H. (1996). Communities, Commonalities, and Communication. In: Gumperz, J. J. and Levinson, S. C. eds., *Rethinking Linguistic Relativity*. Studies in the Social and Cultural Foundations of Language 17. Cambridge: Cambridge University Press, 324–55.

Coffey, A. J. (1993). Double Entry: The Professional and Organizational Socialization of Graduate Accountants. PhD thesis in Sociology, University of Wales Cardiff.

—— (1994). 'Timing is Everything'; Graduate Accountants, Time and Organizational Commitment. *Sociology* 28 (4), 943–56.

Companies Act 2006 (c. 46). London: HMSO.

Company Law Review Steering Group (1999). *Modern Company Law for a Competitive Economy: The Strategic Framework*. London: Department of Trade and Industry.

—— (2000). *Modern Company Law for a Competitive Economy: Developing the Framework*. London: Department of Trade and Industry.

Cooper, D. J., Puxty, T., Robson, K., and Willmott, H. (1994). Regulating Accountancy in the UK: Episodes in a Changing Relationship Between the State and the Profession. In: Hopwood, A. G. and Miller, P. eds., *Accounting as Social and Institutional Practice*. Cambridge: Cambridge University Press, 270–98.

—— and Robson, K. (2006). Accounting, Professions and Regulation: Locating the Sites of Professionalization. *Accounting, Organizations and Society* 31 (4–5), 415–44.

Covaleski, M. A., Dirsmith, M. W., Heian, J. B., and Samuel, S. (1998). The Calculated and the Avowed: Techniques of Discipline and Struggles Over Identity in Big Six Public Accounting Firms. *Administrative Science Quarterly* 43 (2), 293–327.

Creswell, J. W. (1998). *Qualitative Inquiry and Research Design: Choosing Among Five Traditions*. London: Sage.

Davis, A. and Hodgkinson, R. (2007). *Reporting with Integrity*. Information for Better Markets 7. London: ICAEW.

Deloitte (2004). *Chartered Accountancy (ACA)* [Internet]. Available from: < http://graduates. deloitte.co.uk/index.cfm?p_id=29 > [Accessed 24 May 2004].

Deloitte Touche Tohmatsu (2007). *Use of IFRSs for Reporting by Domestic Listed and Unlisted Companies by Country and Region* [Internet]. Available from: <www.iasplus.com/country/useias.htm > [Accessed 7 May 2007].

Diderot, D. (1957 [1778]). The Paradox of Acting. In: Strasberg, L. ed., *'The Paradox of Acting' by Denis Diderot and 'Masks or Faces?' by William Archer: Two Classics of the Art of Acting*, trans. Herries Pollock, W. New York: Hill and Wang, 11–71.

Dirsmith, M. W., Heian, J. B., and Covaleski, M. A. (1997). Structure and Agency in an Institutionalized Setting: The Application and Social Transformation of Control in the Big Six. *Accounting, Organizations and Society* 22 (1), 1–27.

Elliott, P. (1972). *The Sociology of the Professions*. New York: Herder and Herder.

Empson, L. (2004). Organizational Identity Change: Managerial Regulation and Member Identification in an Accounting Firm Acquisition. *Accounting, Organizations and Society* 29 (8), 759–81.

—— and Chapman, C. (2006). Partnership Versus Corporation: Implications of Alternative Forms of Governance in Professional Service Firms. *Research in the Sociology of Organizations* 24, 139–70.

Espeland, W. N. (1998). *The Struggle for Water: Politics, Rationality and Identity in the American Southwest.* Chicago, IL: University of Chicago Press.

Fielding, R. (2004). The Refusenik: An Interview with David Myddelton. *Accountancy Age*, 8 July, 14–15.

Financial Reporting Council (2003). *Key Facts and Trends in the Accountancy Profession* [Internet]. Available from: < www.frc.org.uk/poba/publications/ > [Accessed 24 May 2004].

Fisher, L. (2003). Top 60 Firms: The Risers and Fallers. *Accountancy* 132 (1319), July, 26–7.

—— (2008). FD Factories. *Accountancy* 141 (1375), March, 24–6.

Foley, W. A. (1997). *Anthropological Linguistics: An Introduction.* Language in Society 24. Oxford: Blackwell.

Foucault, M. (1980*a* [n.d.]). Truth and Power (an interview with Alessandro Fontana and Pasquale Pasquino). In: Gordon, C. ed., *Power/Knowledge: Selected Interviews and Other Writings 1972–1977*, trans. Gordon, C., Marshall, L. et al. Harlow: Harvester, 109–33.

—— (1980*b* [1976]). Two Lectures. In: Gordon, C. ed., *Power/Knowledge: Selected Interviews and Other Writings 1972–1977*, trans. Gordon, C., Marshall, L. et al. Harlow: Harvester, 78–108.

—— (1983 [1982]). On the Genealogy of Ethics: An Overview of Work in Progress. In: Dreyfus, H. L. and Rabinow, P. eds., *Michel Foucault: Beyond Structuralism and Hermeneutics.* 2nd ed. Chicago, IL: University of Chicago Press, 229–52.

—— (1998 [1976]). *The Will to Knowledge*, trans. Hurley, R. The History of Sexuality 1. London: Penguin.

Freidson, E. (1986). *Professional Powers: A Study of the Institutionalization of Formal Knowledge.* Chicago, IL: University of Chicago Press.

—— (2001). *Professionalism, the Third Logic: On the Practice of Knowledge.* Chicago, IL: University of Chicago Press.

Fromm, E. (1956 repr. 1973). *The Sane Society.* London: Routledge and Kegan Paul.

Fusaro, P. C. and Miller, R. M. (2002). *What Went Wrong at Enron: Everyone's Guide to the Largest Bankruptcy in U.S. History.* Hoboken, NJ: Wiley.

Gadamer, H.-G. (1989 [1975]). *Truth and Method*, trans. Glen-Doepel, W., Weinsheimer, J. et al. 2nd ed. London: Sheed and Ward.

Garfinkel, H. (1967). *Studies in Ethnomethodology.* Englewood Cliffs, NJ: Prentice Hall.

Geis, G. (1987 [1978]). The Heavy Electrical Equipment Antitrust Cases of 1961. In: Ermann, M. D. and Lundman, R. J. eds., *Corporate and Governmental Deviance: Problems of Organizational Behaviour in Contemporary Society.* 3rd ed. New York: Oxford University Press, 124–44.

Gill, M. (2007). Facts in the City: How London Accountants Simplify Decisions. In: Calhoun, C. and Sennett, R. eds., *Practicing Culture.* Taking Culture Seriously 1. London: Routledge, 129–48.

—— (2008). Rationalization Defeats Itself: The Limits to Accounting's Framing of Economic Life. *Socio-Economic Review* 6 (4), 587–609.

Goffman, E. (1968 [1961] repr. 1970). *Asylums: Essays on the Social Situation of Mental Patients and Other Inmates.* Harmondsworth: Penguin.

References

—— (1969 [1959] repr. 1990). *The Presentation of Self in Everyday Life*. Harmondsworth: Penguin.

—— (1974). *Frame Analysis: An Essay on the Organisation of Experience*. Cambridge, MA: Harvard University Press.

Granovetter, M. (1985). Economic Action and Social Structure: The Problem of Embeddedness. *American Journal of Sociology* 91 (3), 481–510.

Grey, C. (1994). Career as a Project of the Self and Labour Process Discipline. *Sociology* 28 (2), 479–97.

—— (1998). On Being a Professional in a Big Six Firm. *Accounting, Organizations and Society* 23 (5–6), 569–87.

Gumperz, J. J. and Levinson, S. C. (1996). *Rethinking Linguistic Relativity*. Studies in the Social and Cultural Foundations of Language 17. Cambridge: Cambridge University Press.

Hanlon, G. (1994). *The Commercialisation of Accountancy: Flexible Accumulation and the Transformation of the Service Class*. London: Macmillan.

—— (1999). *Lawyers, the State and the Market: Professionalism Revisited*. London: Macmillan.

Harper, R. (1988). The Fate of Idealism in Accountancy. The Second Interdisciplinary Perspectives on Accounting Conference, 11–13 July, University of Manchester.

Haskell, T. ed. (1984). *The Authority of Experts: Studies in History and Theory*. Bloomington, IN: Indiana University Press.

Heelas, P. and Morris, P. eds. (1992). *The Values of the Enterprise Culture: The Moral Debate*. London: Routledge.

Heilbroner, R. L. (1991). *The Worldly Philosophers: The Lives, Times and Ideas of the Great Economic Thinkers*. 6th ed. London: Penguin.

Hendry, J. (2005). The Bimoral Society. *Accountancy Age*, 14 July, 13.

Henriques, A. and Richardson, J. eds. (2004). *The Triple Bottom Line: Does it All Add Up? Assessing the Sustainability of Business and CSR*. London: Earthscan.

Hirschman, A. O. (1977). *The Passions and the Interests: Political Arguments for Capitalism before its Triumph*. Princeton, NJ: Princeton University Press.

Hochschild, A. R. (1983 repr. 1985). *The Managed Heart: Commercialization of Human Feeling*. Berkeley, CA: University of California Press.

Hopwood, A. G. and Miller, P. eds. (1994). *Accounting as Social and Institutional Practice*. Cambridge: Cambridge University Press.

Hoskin, K. and Macve, R. (1994). Writing, Examining, Disciplining: The Genesis of Accounting's Modern Power. In: Hopwood, A. G. and Miller, P. eds., *Accounting as Social and Institutional Practice*. Cambridge: Cambridge University Press, 67–97.

Hursthouse, R. (1999). *On Virtue Ethics*. Oxford: Oxford University Press.

Hutter, B. and Power, M. eds. (2005). *Organizational Encounters with Risk*. Cambridge: Cambridge University Press.

IASC Foundation (2007*a*). *About IASB* [Internet]. Available from: <www.iasb.org/About+Us/About+IASB/About+IASB.htm > [Accessed 7 May 2007].

IASC Foundation (2007*b*). *IFRS around the World* [Internet]. Available from: <www.iasb.org/About+Us/About+IASB/IFRS+Around+the+World.htm > [Accessed 7 May 2007].

ICAEW (2003). *Education and Training Statistics* [Internet]. Available from: <www.icaew. co.uk/index.cfm?AUB=TB2I_31137,MNXI_31137> [Accessed 20 May 2004].

—— (2004). *Analysis of Membership by District Society as at 1 April 2004* [Internet]. Available from: <www.icaew.co.uk/index.cfm?AUB=TB2I_27010,MNXI_11399> [Accessed 20 May 2004].

—— (2006). *Fundamentals – Principles-based Auditing Standards.* London: ICAEW.

—— ([n.d.]). *The ACA Qualification* [Internet]. Available from: <www.icaew.co.uk/index. cfm?AUB=TB2I_35230,MNXI_34751> [Accessed 20 May 2004].

ICAS (2006). *Principles Not Rules: A Question of Judgement.* Edinburgh: ICAS.

Jackall, R. (1988). *Moral Mazes: The World of Corporate Managers.* New York: Oxford University Press.

Kanitkar, H. (1993). Real True Boys: Moulding the Cadets of Imperialism. In: Cornwall, A. and Lindisfarne, N. eds., *Dislocating Masculinity: Comparative Ethnographies.* London: Routledge, 184–96.

King, G., Keohane, R. O., and Verba, S. (1994). *Designing Social Inquiry: Scientific Inference in Qualitative Research.* Princeton, NJ: Princeton University Press.

KPMG (2004). *KPMG – Your Career at the Heart of Business* [Internet]. Available from: <www.kpmg.co.uk/careers/index.cfm> [Accessed 24 May 2004].

Krier, D. (2005). *Speculative Management: Stock Market Power and Corporate Change.* Albany, NY: State University of New York Press.

Kuhn, T. S. (1962). *The Structure of Scientific Revolutions.* Chicago, IL: University of Chicago Press.

Lakoff, G. (1987). *Women, Fire and Dangerous Things: What Categories Reveal About the Mind.* Chicago, IL: Chicago University Press.

—— (2002). *Moral Politics: How Liberals and Conservatives Think.* 2nd ed. Chicago, IL: University of Chicago Press.

—— and Johnson, M. (1980). *Metaphors We Live By.* Chicago, IL: Chicago University Press.

Larson, M. S. (1977). *The Rise of Professionalism: A Sociological Analysis.* Berkeley, CA: University of California Press.

Lather, P. (1991). *Getting Smart: Feminist Research and Pedagogy with/in the Postmodern.* London: Routledge.

Latour, B. (1987). *Science in Action: How to Follow Scientists and Engineers Through Society.* Cambridge, MA: Harvard University Press.

Luhmann, N. (1988). Familiarity, Confidence, Trust: Problems and Alternatives. In: Gambetta, D. ed., *Trust: Making and Breaking Cooperative Relations.* Oxford: Blackwell, 94–107.

MacDonald, K. M. (1995). *The Sociology of the Professions.* London: Sage.

Macintosh, N. B. (2002). *Accounting, Accountants and Accountability: Poststructuralist Positions.* Routledge Studies in Accounting 2. London: Routledge.

McKendrick, N. (1970). Josiah Wedgwood and Cost Accounting in the Industrial Revolution. *The Economic History Review* n.s. 23 (1), 45–67.

MacKenzie, D. (2003). Empty Cookie Jar. *London Review of Books* 25 (10), 22 May, 6–9.

McLean, B. and Elkind, P. (2003*a*). Enron Banks Dodge a Bullet. *Fortune* 148 (3), 1 September, 19.

References

—— (2003*b*). *The Smartest Guys in the Room: The Amazing Rise and Scandalous Fall of Enron*. London: Penguin (Viking imprint).

McSweeney, B. (1994). Management by Accounting. In: Hopwood, A. G. and Miller, P. eds., *Accounting as Social and Institutional Practice*. Cambridge: Cambridge University Press, 237–69.

Marcuse, H. (1968 [1964]). *One Dimensional Man: The Ideology of Industrial Society*. London: Sphere.

Margolis, D. R. (1979). *The Managers: Corporate Life in America*. New York: William Morrow.

Marx, K. (1977 [1844]). Economic and Philosophical Manuscripts. In: McLellan, D. ed., *Karl Marx: Selected Writings*. Oxford: Oxford University Press, 75–112.

Matthews, D., Anderson, M., and Edwards, J. R. (1998). *The Priesthood of Industry: The Rise of the Professional Accountant in British Management*. Oxford: Oxford University Press.

May, L. (1996). *The Socially Responsive Self: Social Theory and Professional Ethics*. Chicago, IL: Chicago University Press.

Miller, D. (2002). Turning Callon the Right Way Up. *Economy and Society* 31 (2), 218–33.

Miller, P. (1998). The Margins of Accounting. In: Callon, M. ed., *The Laws of the Markets*. Oxford: Blackwell, 174–93.

—— and O'Leary, T. (1994). Accounting, 'Economic Citizenship' and the Spatial Reordering of Manufacture. *Accounting, Organizations and Society* 19 (1), 15–43.

Millerson, G. (1964). *The Qualifying Associations: A Study in Professionalization*. London: Routledge and Kegan Paul.

Mills, C. W. (1940). Situated Actions and Vocabularies of Motive. *American Sociological Review* 5 (6), 904–13.

—— (2002 [1951]). *White Collar: The American Middle Classes*. New York: Oxford University Press.

Mitchell, W. J. T. ed. (1981). *On Narrative*. Chicago, IL: University of Chicago Press.

Montagna, P. D. (1974). *Certified Public Accounting: A Sociological View of a Profession in Change*. Houston, TX: Scholars Book Company.

Morgan, G. (2006). *Images of Organization*. Updated ed. Thousand Oaks, CA: Sage.

Nietzsche, F. (1911 [1873]). On Truth and Falsity in their Ultramoral Sense. In: Levy, O. ed., *Friedrich Nietzsche: Early Greek Philosophy and Other Essays*, trans. Mugge, M. A. The Complete Works of Friedrich Nietzsche 2. London: T. N. Foulis, 171–92.

Ortony, A. (1979 repr. 1986). Metaphor: A Multidimensional Problem. In: Ortony, A. ed., *Metaphor and Thought*. Cambridge: Cambridge University Press, 1–16.

Oswick, C., Keenoy, T., and Grant, D. (2002). Metaphor and Analogical Reasoning in Organization Theory: Beyond Orthodoxy. *The Academy of Management Review* 27 (2), 294–303.

Parsons, T. (1954 [1939] repr. 1958). The Professions and Social Structure. In: Parsons, T., *Essays in Sociological Theory*. Revised ed. Glencoe, IL: Free Press, 34–49.

Pavalko, R. M. (1971). *Sociology of Occupations and Professions*. Itasca, IL: Peacock.

Pentland, B. T. (1993). Getting Comfortable with the Numbers: Auditing and the Micro-Production of Macro-Order. *Accounting, Organizations and Society* 18 (7–8), 605–20.

Perelman, C. and Obrechts-Tyteca, L. (1969 [1958]). *The New Rhetoric: A Treatise on Argumentation*, trans. Wilkinson, J. and Weaver, P. Notre Dame, IN: University of Notre Dame Press.

Plummer, K. (2001). *Documents of Life 2: An Introduction to Critical Humanism.* London: Sage.

Polanyi, K. (1992). The Economy as Instituted Process. In: Granovetter, M. and Swedberg, R. eds., *The Sociology of Economic Life.* Boulder, CO: Westview, 29–51.

Ponemon, L. A. and Gabhart, D. R. L. (1993). *Ethical Reasoning in Accounting and Auditing.* Research Monograph 21. Vancouver, BC: CGA-Canada Research Foundation.

Poovey, M. (1998). *A History of the Modern Fact: Problems of Knowledge in the Sciences of Wealth and Society.* Chicago, IL: University of Chicago Press.

Porter, T. M. (1995). *Trust in Numbers: The Pursuit of Objectivity in Science and Public Life.* Princeton, NJ: Princeton University Press.

Potter, J. and Wetherell, M. (1987 repr. 1992). *Discourse and Social Psychology: Beyond Attitudes and Behaviour.* London: Sage.

Powell, W. W. and DiMaggio, P. J. (1991 [1983]). The Iron Cage Revisited: Institutional Isomorphism and Collective Rationality in Organizational Fields. In: DiMaggio, P. J. and Powell, W. W. eds., *The New Institutionalism in Organizational Analysis.* Chicago, IL: University of Chicago Press, 63–82.

Power, M. (1991). Educating Accountants: Towards a Critical Ethnography. *Accounting, Organizations and Society* 16 (4), 333–53.

—— (1992). The Politics of Brand Accounting in the United Kingdom. *European Accounting Review* 1 (1), 39–68.

—— (1995). Review of Ponemon, L. A. and Gabhart, D. R. L. (1993) 'Ethical Reasoning in Accounting and Auditing'. *Accounting and Business Research* 25 (98), 130–1.

—— (1996). Making Things Auditable. *Accounting, Organizations and Society* 21 (2–3), 289–315.

—— (1997 repr. 1999). *The Audit Society: Rituals of Verification.* Oxford: Oxford University Press.

—— (2007). *Organized Uncertainty: Designing a World of Risk Management.* Oxford: Oxford University Press.

Preston, A. M., Cooper, D. J., Scarbrough, D. P., and Chilton, R. C. (1995). Changes in the Code of Ethics of the U.S. Accounting Profession, 1917 and 1988: The Continual Quest for Legitimation. *Accounting, Organizations and Society* 20 (6), 507–46.

PricewaterhouseCoopers (2004). *Exams and Support* [Internet]. Available from: < www.pwc.com/uk/eng/car-inexp/university/exams.html > [Accessed 24 May 2004].

Quine, W. V. (1979). A Postscript on Metaphor. In: Sacks, S. ed., *On Metaphor.* Chicago, IL: University of Chicago Press, 159–60.

Ramsay, J. (2004). Trope Control: The Costs and Benefits of Metaphor Unreliability in the Description of Empirical Phenomena. *British Journal of Management* 15, 143–55.

Richards, I. A. (1936 repr. 1965). *The Philosophy of Rhetoric.* The Mary Flexner Lectures on the Humanities 3. Oxford: Oxford University Press.

Riesman, D., Denney, R., and Glazer, N. (1950 repr. 1967). *The Lonely Crowd: A Study of the Changing American Character.* New Haven, CT: Yale University Press.

Robb, G. (1992). *White-Collar Crime in Modern England: Financial Fraud and Business Morality, 1845–1929.* Cambridge: Cambridge University Press.

Rose, N. (1999 [1989]). *Governing the Soul: The Shaping of the Private Self.* 2nd ed. London: Free Association.

References

Schlesinger, L. (2004). *Big Four Teetering on 'Burning Platform'* [Internet]. Available from: <www.financialdirector.co.uk/News/1136818> [Accessed 21 April 2004].

Schutz, A. (1967 [1932]). *The Phenomenology of the Social World*, trans. Walsh, G. and Lehnert, F. Evanston, IL: Northwestern University Press.

Sennett, R. (1998 repr. 1999). *The Corrosion of Character: The Personal Consequences of Work in the New Capitalism.* New York: Norton.

—— (2002 [1977]). *The Fall of Public Man.* London: Penguin.

—— and Cobb, J. (1977 [1972]). *The Hidden Injuries of Class.* Cambridge: Cambridge University Press.

Silverman, D. (2001). *Interpreting Qualitative Data: Methods for Analysing Talk, Text and Interaction.* 2nd ed. London: Sage.

Simmel, G. (1991 [n.d.]). Money in Modern Culture, trans. Ritter, M. and Whimster, S. *Theory, Culture and Society* 8 (3), 17–31.

Slater, D. and Tonkiss, F. (2001). *Market Society: Markets and Modern Social Theory.* Cambridge: Polity.

Stanislavsky, C. (1980 [1936] repr. 1990). *An Actor Prepares*, trans. Reynolds Hapgood, E. London: Methuen.

Stone, C. D. (1975 repr. 1991). *Where the Law Ends: The Social Control of Corporate Behaviour.* Prospect Heights, IL: Waveland Press.

Sutherland, E. H. (1949). *White Collar Crime.* New York: Dryden Press.

Swanton, C. (2003). *Virtue Ethics: A Pluralistic View.* Oxford: Oxford University Press.

Swartz, M. and Watkins, S. (2003). *Power Failure: The Rise and Fall of Enron.* London: Aurum Press.

Tawney, R. H. (1920 repr. 1948). *The Acquisitive Society.* New York: Harcourt, Brace and World.

Thompson, D. F. (2005). *Restoring Responsibility: Ethics in Government, Business and Healthcare.* Cambridge: Cambridge University Press.

Thompson, G. (1994). Early Double-Entry Bookkeeping and the Rhetoric of Accounting Calculation. In: Hopwood, A. G. and Miller, P. eds., *Accounting as Social and Institutional Practice.* Cambridge: Cambridge University Press, 40–66.

Tweedie, D. (2006). The Role of Principles in the Current Convergence Process. In: ICAS ed., *Principles into Practice: Key Points from the 'Too Late for Principles?' Conference held in October 2006.* Edinburgh: ICAS, 9–11.

Vandivier, K. (1972). 'Why Should My Conscience Bother Me?' In: Heilbroner, R. L. ed., *In the Name of Profit.* Garden City, NY: Doubleday, 3–31.

Vaughan, D. (1997). *The Challenger Launch Decision: Risky Technology, Culture, and Deviance at NASA.* Chicago, IL: Chicago University Press.

Wajcman, J. (1983). *Women in Control: Dilemmas of a Workers' Co-operative.* Milton Keynes: Open University Press.

—— (1998). *Managing Like a Man: Women and Men in Corporate Management.* University Park, PA: Pennsylvania State University Press.

Walters-York, M. L. (1996). Metaphor in Accounting Discourse. *Accounting, Auditing and Accountability Journal* 9 (5), 45–70.

Weber, M. (1946 [1918] repr. 1977). Science as a Vocation. In: Gerth, H. H. and Mills, C. W. eds., *From Max Weber: Essays in Sociology*, trans. Gerth, H. H. and Mills, C. W. New York: Oxford University Press, 129–56.

—— (1968 [1922]). *Economy and Society: An Outline of Interpretive Sociology,* trans. Fischoff, E., Gerth, H. et al. Berkeley, CA: University of California Press.

—— (1992 [1905] repr. 2005). *The Protestant Ethic and the Spirit of Capitalism,* trans. Parsons, T. London: Routledge.

Weinsheimer, J. C. (1985). *Gadamer's Hermeneutics: A Reading of Truth and Method.* New Haven, CT: Yale University Press.

White, R. W. (1963). Preface. In: White, R. W. ed., *The Study of Lives: Essays on Personality in Honour of Henry A Murray.* London: Prentice Hall, xiii–xvii.

Whorf, B. L. (1956). *Language, Thought and Reality: Selected Writings of Benjamin Lee Whorf,* ed. Carroll, J. B. Cambridge, MA: MIT Press.

Wierzbicka, A. (1996). *Semantics: Primes and Universals.* Oxford: Oxford University Press.

Wilensky, H. L. (1964). The Professionalization of Everyone? *American Journal of Sociology* 70 (2), 137–58.

Williams, B. (2002). *Truth and Truthfulness: An Essay in Genealogy.* Princeton, NJ: Princeton University Press.

Young, J. J. (2001). Risk(ing) Metaphors. *Critical Perspectives on Accounting* 12 (5), 607–25.

Zelizer, V. (1997). *The Social Meaning of Money: Pin Money, Paychecks, Poor Relief, and Other Currencies.* Princeton, NJ: Princeton University Press.

Index

automatic dismissal 11
autonomy 37, 72, 102, 108

Bakan, J. 4, 170 *n.* 80
balance sheet 41–2, 48, 68
  full extent of debt kept off 5
bankruptcy 5, 6, 165 *n.* 37
banks 1, 6–7, 22, 30, 40–1, 64, 114,
  124, 165 *n.* 37
The Banks that Robbed the World 6
Barry (interviewee) 23, 30, 34–6, 80,
  81, 86, 106
Barry, A. 82
BCCI (Bank of Credit and Commerce
  International) 162 *n.* 1
Beck, U. 82
Benston, G. 5
billing for value 104
Black, Max 167–8 *n.* 60, 168 *n.* 63
blame 7, 47, 143
  difficult to attribute 5
Blumer, H. 158
bookkeeping, *see* double-entry
  bookkeeping
Booth, Wayne 79
Born, Georgina 159, 163 *n.* 17
box-ticking 120, 149
Boys, P. 96
Briers, M. 164 *n.* 24
Brooks, P. 173 *n.* 110
Brubaker, R. 56, 165 *n.* 42
Burchell, S. 166 *n.* 45
bureaucracy 112, 113, 125, 143, 146,
  169 *n.* 72
Bushnell, David 5–8

calculation 34, 49, 56, 67, 82, 137, 153,
  167 *n.* 51
Callon, Michel 59–61, 62, 82,
  165 *n.* 41, 166 *nn.* 46 47 & 48
camaraderie 119, 120, 161
capitalization 41–7, 48, 49, 51, 52, 65
career 12–14, 23, 82, 103, 144–5, 161,
  163 *n.* 11, 168 *n.* 69
Carr-Saunders, A. M. 93–4, 96, 100,
  107–8
Carrier, James 166 *n.* 48
Carruthers, B. G. 16
Certeau, Michel de 88, 131–2

Challenger space shuttle 4
Champion Chicken 40–54, 63, 64, 65,
  69, 70, 80, 87, 88, 139, 156
Chapman, C. 171 *n.* 96
character 19, 25, 71, 95, 130–1, 133,
  158–9, 164 *n.* 22
Chinese walls 121
Chinese whispers 89
Chomsky, Noam 77
Chua, W. F. 164 *n.* 24
circumstantial influences 52–4
Citigroup 5–7
city boys 6
Clark, H. H. 77
class 10, 80, 83, 163 *n.* 17, 172 *n.* 104
cleverness 5, 26, 85, 126, 128, 131–2
cliché 22, 27, 29, 48, 101, 113, 165 *n.* 38
client relationships 10, 85–6, 103–7,
  144
client service 10, 102, 103–4, 113, 114,
  139, 145
  discourse 8 *n.*, 104
Clubb, C. 166 *n.* 45
Cobb, Jonathan 33, 158
Coffey, A. J. 10, 11, 93, 158, 162 *n.* 8,
  162–3 *n.* 10, 164 *nn.* 25 & 29, 167 *n.*
  57, 172 *n.* 106
collusion 3, 91, 115
commercialism 10–11, 81, 122, 130,
  141
  professionalism and 99–103, 107,
  145, 169 *n.* 72
commercialization 95, 97, 113, 144–5
commitment 17, 57, 61, 63, 73, 92,
  107, 130, 152, 166 *n.* 43, 170 *n.* 86
  see also engagement; involvement
commodification 13, 97, 102
common sense 46, 51, 136
Companies Acts (UK) 151, 166 *n.* 44,
  170 *n.* 87
Company Law Review Steering
  Group 171 *n.* 99
competitiveness 5, 7, 10, 14, 101, 152
  encouraged 11
  prized 86
complexity 141, 146
  in accounting 57, 66
  in modern economy 2, 60, 96
  of regulation 75, 147